in the back alleys of aviation

ACE ABBOTT

Published by: Allen Morris
730 Greensward Ct, # J210, Delray Beach, FL 33445

www.therogueaviator.com | rogueaviator@gmail.com

Book cover design and formatting: Eli Blyden
www.CrunchTimeGraphics.net | crunchtimeg@msn.com

ISBN 13: 978-0-578-08508-1

Biography/Autobiography/Memoir/Aviation/Travel

Printed in the United States of America:
A&A Printing | www.printshopcentral.com

Dedication

This book is dedicated to Harold, the author's father, a maverick pilot who always had a good time playing with his airplane. Ace's father, a blue-collar farmer, got a pilot's license in 1937. He exposed Ace to the joys of aviation at age eight when the boy would ride as copilot for Pop in the old Taylorcraft, a plane similar to a Piper Cub.

The Taylorcraft would sit tied up in the "back forty" hay field, and every summer after the hay was in the barn the fun would begin as we would go buzz the other farmers while they rode their tractors in the fields. As we flew over their heads, often sneaking up from behind to startle them, it was fun to watch them cover their heads with their hands and duck for cover. When they stopped by at the old farmhouse around dusk to offer a friendly complaint, they were immediately escorted to the cellar, where they would socialize after a hard day in the fields—a welcomed glass of hard-cider, cloudy and golden, in their calloused hands. The playful fun-loving pilot who owned a small cider mill as a hobby was also a connoisseur of almost any alcoholic beverage that could be concocted. Along with the hard cider, the socializing guests were treated to various types of homemade wines and beers. They would soon become "high flying" revelers, who often needed a little extra "lift" to help them accomplish their climb back up the cellar stairs.

Harold's adventuresome flair for flying would be accented by an air-show-style takeoff over the old farmhouse, and as the locals heard the roar of the aircraft engine, they would run outside to watch the Taylorcraft doing a loop or a spin over the valley. During the winter months, snow skis were attached to the aircraft, and flights from the snow-covered fields provided a most unique aviation experience. Harold would often take his brother with him, and they would hunt fox from the airplane with their old single shot .22 rifle.

As the saying goes, "The apple doesn't fall very far from the tree." Ace's youthful fun in the Taylorcraft set the mold for thirty-six years of unmitigated joy in the cockpit—with the additional benefit of being paid to explore most of planet earth from the cockpit of a jet aircraft.

"BACK-FORTY" TAYLORCRAFT WITH ANGUS BULL

The dedication of this book will also go out to the most unsung, underpaid, overworked professionals of any industry. This large group of competent, professional pilots is comprised primarily of the following: the flight instructor, the commuter pilot, the freight pilot, the corporate/charter pilot, and the larger-aircraft, "non-sked" charter pilot. The number of pilots in this group is much larger than the lay public is aware of, and the majority of the lay public is not aware that these pilots are normally held to the same skill-level standards as those pilots who fly for the major airlines.

These pilots are frequently viewed disparagingly because their pay scales are significantly less than that of the major carriers, and they often work for obscure companies. These dedicated professionals may not have union protection to help them gain reasonable salaries and work conditions. In many instances, their duties are more demanding than the mainstream "legacy airline" pilots, since they do not have the advanced-level support system offered by the larger companies when confronting unusual and challenging circumstances that demand a high level of creativity and adaptability. We should view this group of dedicated aviators with great respect as they trudge forward in the face of adversity, while all too often they become trapped in an aviation career that leaves them overworked and underpaid.

The lay public and the more fortunate professional pilots who did not find themselves ensnared in these "back alleys of aviation" should salute these pilots.

Acknowledgements

Numerous wonderful people have assisted me through the trials and tribulations of this tumultuous aviation career, and they were all, in certain respects, contributors to the publication of this book. However, two of my aviator colleagues and lifelong, good friends provided most of the impetus for the author to finally put pen to paper. The ongoing support and enthusiasm of Jim Keeling and Marylee Bickford provided just enough lift to offset the author's self-induced drag of retirement lethargy and disdain for word processors.

Jim Keeling was an extraordinarily talented pilot and a good friend of thirty years until the big C (cancer) took him away a few years ago. Some pilots will strut and reek of arrogant pretension, but Jim was just the opposite. He engaged in his profession in a soft-spoken, mild-mannered fashion, even though he was a brilliant aviator. In the last few years before his death, his lifestyle became very restrained and reclusive, but we spent many hours on the telephone, reminiscing over the countless "airplane war stories" that we had accumulated. Often, our conversations would extend for hours, and Jim would frequently say, **"Ace, you've got to write a book!"**

My favorite aviatrix colleague, Marylee Bickford, provided me with wonderful support as a B-727 flight engineer and copilot with several airlines. Together, we searched for that aviation anomaly, a stable company. Her ongoing support during the many periods of unemployment and job seeking kept my aviation career alive. Marylee was a friend to all, frequently networking with unemployed pilots in order to help them find jobs. Our shared camaraderie and joy in aviation was regularly punctuated with the recommendation that I write a book about my aviation adventures. Eventually, I succumbed to her pleasant cajoling. **Her support was paramount.**

Too numerous to mention are the dedicated instructor pilots, copilots, and flight engineers who would often save the day when Captain Ace needed some able assistance on the flight deck. The high-quality flight attendants who were always gracious to both the passengers and the pilots were usually underpaid and overworked; however, their contribution to the success of so many flights cannot be overstated. The unsung heroes of aviation include mechanics, operations and scheduling people, gate agents, and the air traffic control specialists. The author would also like to recognize the many aviation entrepreneurs who entrusted him with their multimillion dollar air machines, and actually paid him for "taking a little airplane ride."

The chapter editing and formatting assistance from Bob Raddant proved invaluable. Ellen Kane, a long-time friend with a journalism background, provided the author with valuable mentoring.

David Wade, a high school classmate and man of letters, offered some excellent editing guidance for the second and the third editions. Dave corrected punctuation, spelling, and capitalization errors. He changed some of the clumsy verbiage into livelier, active sentences, helping instill a little humor along the way. To punctuate sentences, he also inserted transitions that created a smoother path for the reader. The frosting on the cake's first edition came from Rick Bogel, a Professor of English at Cornell University. His initial editing of the entire manuscript would smooth out some rough edges and untangle a host of dangling participles.

The brilliant creativity of Eli Blyden (CrunchTime Graphics) resulted in the eye-catching, quasi-surrealistic front cover design of the 3rd edition.

Table of Contents

Preface

The telling of one's story is hardwired into the primal nature of the Homo sapiens critter. Therefore, your author, Ace Abbott, will, with great pleasure, tell you his story of an aviation career that is almost too bizarre to seem plausible. Ace, for instance, once flew the famous singer-songwriter Jimmy Buffett and remembers well what the lyrics of one of his many poignant ballads states about the story-telling impulse: "If it all blows up and goes to hell, we could sit upon a bed in some motel, and listen to the stories we could tell." This story, like most, emanates from a bit of ego, but the story's primary source of motivation stems from a desire to share a unique adventure with pilots of all backgrounds and to inform aspiring pilots as well as the non-aviator layman of the unique and often challenging nuances of an aviation career.

The layman is going to receive an insider's perspective of the trials and tribulations of the pilot profession. On the other hand, the reader will learn of the subtle rewards of the pilot profession—those intangibles that keep pilots hooked on flying. This book will certainly dispel a number of popular myths amongst layman—including the belief that pilots are underworked, overpaid prima donnas. The reader will discover that the "four-striper" strutting down the concourse to his Boeing 777 represents a small minority of the pilot community. The aviation community is heavily populated with overworked but very skilled professional pilots who make one-fourth the salary of the veteran airline pilot. The reader will be both informed and entertained as he or she gets exposed to interesting, anecdotal "war stories," along with the chronological adventure of a thirty-six year aviation career that included twenty-five aviation employers until government-enforced mandatory retirement occurred at age sixty. Also included in this docudrama is a brief exposé of the smaller commercial airlines and the FAA.

It is the author's premise that an adventurous aviation career of this nature will remain historically unique as a result of the modernization and the sophistication of today's aviation environment. While flying airplanes is inherently dangerous, the process often does prove itself rewarding and exhilarating, and this book intends to elaborate on that premise.

Most of the unique aviation anecdotes are from Ace's personal experiences, but a few are third-party stories from fellow aviators. A few of the names have been shortened or edited, but in most cases the author has used the actual names of the many participants in this improbable saga.

Ace Abbott, author and ex-aviator, thanks you for climbing aboard.

Introducing Ace

Our protagonist, who will be referred to as Ace, or the author, grew up as a farm boy in the idyllic farm country of the Finger Lakes in upstate New York. His father, a rogue sportsman who hunted fox and deer from his airplane, spent a lifetime evading and avoiding the game wardens. His first-born son, himself an adventurous sort, not only tried to think outside the box but actually elected to get out of the box altogether by leaving the farm to pursue the life of a pilot. His maverick tendencies were genealogically structured, and he was convinced that the rules were made only for those fools who chose to follow them.

Just prior to college graduation, Ace hesitated briefly in front of the Air Force recruiter's office and was immediately grabbed by the recruiter, who started administering aptitude tests to see if this hung-over college kid could possibly figure out how to fly a jet airplane and drop bombs. This random encounter commenced the initial phase of Ace's transition from a slothful college student to a powerfully important participant of the United States nuclear-umbrella deterrent against Communism—**a critical cog in the cold war.**

While riding shotgun with his father in the old Taylorcraft, Ace had observed that if you pull back, the houses get smaller, and if you push forward, the houses get bigger. He also spent much of his youth playing in the forest, and his experience of tramping around in the woods helped him develop an internal compass that allowed him to know where he was, where he had been, and where he was going. This particular aptitude—commonly referred to as "situational awareness"—is very beneficial to a pilot and is constantly evaluated by instructor pilots in the aviation-training environment and check pilots during check rides. Despite Ace's borderline college GPA, the Air Force recruiter offered him the opportunity to become an Air Force pilot. With the Vietnam War intensifying, the Big Uncle badly needed warm bodies to fill the cockpits of all those airplanes that would eventually drop eleventine bazillion pounds of bombs on South Vietnam, North Vietnam, Cambodia, and Laos.

After four years of life in a near flat-line existence with the only goal being to get lucky and to score with a coed, Ace envisioned himself becoming a war hero and scoring at will. War and women would soon dominate this testosterone-crazed, twenty-two-year-old's primary agenda. The great myth, of course, is that young men go off to war in a patriotic fervor to fight for their country. This is a well-meaning idealization, but not always the case. Young men go to war for many and varied reasons, but more often than not, it is to enhance the macho factor and to attract women with their uniform and warrior posturing. Male peacocks have their brilliant plumage, and the human male will, somewhat analogously, often capitalize on some type of uniform or other stunning wardrobe to make a statement of power in order to attract the opposite sex. If you pay close attention at the airline terminal, you will often see young women ogling many a G.I. who is clearly not a candidate for the cover of *Gentleman's Quarterly* or *Men's Health*.

CHAPTER ONE

Lackland Air Force Base or Bust
(Training an Air Force Pilot)

With the misguided, underachiever-college-kid gig complete, Ace was now ready to get on with the next phase of his life. This began with an eighteen-hundred-mile road trip to San Antonio, Texas, where Ace checked in at Lackland Air Force Base for step one in pursuit of his new goal—to become an Air Force pilot. After a week of casual cruising with the convertible top down, Southern belles calling him "sugar," and not a care in the world, Ace arrived at Lackland, ready to cruise through the nuisance training of OTS (Officer Training School). In order to become a pilot in the Air Force, it was required that the aspiring aviator must first endure the rigors of OTS. Some of the fellows accomplished this through their ROTC training at college, and others received their commission by attending the Air Force Academy for four years. But the quickest and easiest path was OTS. After three months of intensive military indoctrination, those who could deal with this alien lifestyle became officers. This shortcut method to the elevated status of a fully commissioned officer earned them the moniker of "ninety-day-wonders." When they received their second lieutenant gold bars upon completion of training, they would then move on to UPT (undergraduate pilot training).

The three-month grooming of the new officer recruit started with a buzz cut. Some of the recruits (or "rainbows," as they were known), went from an Elvis-Presley-style pompadour to an unrecognizable skinhead in about forty-five seconds. Just before the barbers made several scalp-hugging swipes with their haircutting devices, they would take great joy in asking the recruit, "How would you like it?" The recruit would then stare at the mirror in disbelief, wondering what had become of his coveted coiffure. It was a very spontaneous transition, and the advancement from the lowly status of "rainbow" to OT (Officer Trainee) occurred so rapidly and subtly that it was barely noticed. "Rainbow" is the derisive term used to describe the new recruit, as he or she arrives on base with blue jean cutoffs, tie-dye tank tops, sandals, and great disdain for authority.

In a state of shock from the haircut, the new recruits were herded over to the supply building to get their new outfits. Wardrobe style was now an ancient concept from a previous life, and the new recruit was adorned with the mandatory military attire while being harshly addressed by a "DI" (drill instructor) who was shouting orders at the rainbow. The previous twenty-two years of *being just who you wanted to be* would soon be a forgotten concept. This transition from being a carefree college kid to saluting, marching, and responding incessantly with "Yes sir! Yes sir! Yes sir!" was a profoundly sobering experience.

After the first three days of belittlement and degradation, Ace considered going "over the hill." There were no locked gates, and the old Chevy sat there in the parking lot. Ace and the old Chevy were raring to go and to return to all of those creature comforts of the uncommitted civilian world. Luckily, one of Ace's squadron mates, Officer Trainee O'Connor, had some great insight into the situation, informing Ace that this lunacy they were both engaged in was just a stupid game they had to play in order to become jet pilots. Ace's desire to fly the jets more than offset his disdain for the regimentation, so he then settled in to the program. He started marching in step, making his bed, and shining his shoes. He had elected to "straighten up and fly right" in order that he might progress to the actual flying of airplanes.

Before he knew it, Ace had been ordained as an officer and a gentleman or as the slang term often used, a "second louie." Back in the Chevy with the top down on a sunny Texas day, he headed—with rampaging enthusiasm—for pilot training at Williams Air Force Base, Arizona. Once again, good fortune had shined upon Ace, for Williams Air Force Base, or "Willy," as it was called, was considered the "country club of ATC" (Air Training Command). Willy was located only about thirty miles from Phoenix and less than twenty miles from the Arizona State University campus (ASU). The base was sheer Shangri-La compared to most of the other pilot training bases, many of which were in dauntingly unpleasant, remote locations.

After the intensively regimented OTS training class, Ace's pilot training class (67F) was gifted with an additional bonus: the start of their training did not commence until two weeks after their arrival at Willy! This left Ace and his classmates in what the military calls a casual status, which was well capitalized on by taking trips to Las Vegas and partying with ASU coeds. The rookie pilots barely knew lift from drag, but they certainly succeeded in wooing the young ladies with great tales of aviation heroism. Many of the young pilots were fresh out of the Air Force Academy and supplemented their newfound pilot-bravado mystique by driving a brand-new Corvette or other comparable muscle car. Since every pilot easily and convincingly adopted the persona of "World's Greatest Fighter Pilot," pursuing female companionship was like shooting ducks in a pond. Never had so many young women been given the opportunity to hang out in the BOQ (bachelor officer quarters)!

Ace's class had 74 aspiring pilots when it began. The variety of student pilots was remarkable: a mixture of fellow OTS recent grads, ROTC guys who had finished college and wanted to fly airplanes, and recent Air Force Academy graduates (Zoomies), most of whom had just finished off a Master's degree in aeronautical engineering at Purdue University. Along with this motley array of potential MIG (enemy aircraft) killers were about a dozen German-Luftwaffe-pilot wannabes who provided the American pilots with great comic relief while demonstrating world-class prowess with their beer steins. Every Friday night the Rathskeller in downtown Phoenix became the favorite watering hole for these young German pilots who could consume mass quantities of beer.

One of the more colorful Luftwaffe pilots, Hans, was returning to the base after a big night at the Rathskeller when the Arizona Highway Patrol Officer caught him cruising down Baseline Highway at 120 mph. Hans went to traffic court to plead his case. He explained to the judge that there were no other cars in sight, and he thought he was on the *Autobahn* back in Germany. The judge responded, "But what if a cow had been in the road?" Hans said he then came through with a brilliant retort, "So too bad for the cow!" Hans then paid his fine and in the future, restrained his long-range, road-machine cruise speed to slightly less than 100 mph.

The first month was anything but the glamorous and exhilarating jet pilot experience that everyone had anticipated. The Air Force wanted to examine basic aviator aptitude and this was accomplished with forty hours of training in a T-41A aircraft, commonly referred to in the civilian world as a Cessna 172. The training entailed a daily one-hundred-mile, round-trip ride in a non-air-conditioned school bus to Casa Grande Airport. Still, everyone was able to achieve the once-in-a-lifetime, exhilarating experience of the initial solo in an airplane. Every pilot's first solo experience is stamped indelibly in the forefront of his brain and remains crystal clear in the memory bank, even after the onset of advanced dementia and Alzheimer's disease. Ace has a clear recollection of glancing over at the right seat shortly after liftoff and reconfirming that there was no longer an instructor pilot sitting there. This resulted in a nearly hysterical state of exhilaration and the spontaneous emission of a smug chuckle.

ALL BY MYSELF: THE EXHILARATING INITIAL SOLO

The six weeks of T-41A training was relatively easy, and the entire class successfully completed this phase. Lt. Phil, one of Ace's classmates, provided the class with the most interesting teaching moment when he tried to taxi his aircraft with the wing struts still chained to the tie-down attachment on the tarmac.

Regardless of how much power he applied, the darn bird just wouldn't move. Lt. Phil was only one of the many thousands of rookie pilots who have attempted to taxi their aircraft with the chocks still in position, while wondering why full power wouldn't get the aircraft to budge!

THE FOUR HORSEMEN OF THE APOCALYPSE

"TWEETIE BIRDS"/aka-
"THE FLYING DOG WHISTLE"

Phase II of Air Force UPT was learning to fly the slow, ugly, and noisy T-37 aircraft. It was referred to as "Tweetie Bird" or the "flying dog whistle," because of its piercingly loud, high-pitch engine noise. The T-37 was produced by Cessna, a company that later produced an even slower jet airplane, the Citation. As Ace progressed through training, he became adept at formation flying, instrument flying, and aerobatics, including spins. Shortly after a few VFR (visual flight rules) transition flights, he advanced directly to the far more challenging phase, instrument flying, or as it was referred to, "getting under the hood." The VFR transition flights involved putting the aircraft through a variety of challenging maneuvers that would result in high-G situations as the aircraft "transitioned" through a large variety of positions in relation to the ground. It was much more fun than instrument flying (IFR). Instrument flying required not only the stick-and-rudder skill of manipulating the controls, it also required situational awareness and the need to interpret flight instrument readings along with engine instrument readings while making smooth flight-control inputs. This phase resulted in a few "washouts," since several of the pilots were unable to achieve the required proficiency. Ace struggled but eventually smoothed out and progressed nicely until fateful spin mission number one.

Spin mission number one occurred on a very warm and sunny June Saturday morning. Unfortunately, it was preceded by a Friday night of partying, during which Ace engaged in a mission to drink dry the Valley of the Sun. Every Saturday morning all of the troops were required to report to the flight line at 0530. After a short briefing by the instructor pilots, followed by a few salutes and "yes sirs," those pilots who were not scheduled to fly were allowed to return to their barracks to recover from the previous night's carousing. Lt. Ace had not been scheduled to fly Saturday morning, so he showed up at the flight line with about two hours of sleep and a blood-alcohol level almost certainly off the charts. As he entered the squadron briefing room, he observed through his blurry, bloodshot eyes that the scheduling officer was erasing Lt. Brown's name for spin mission number one and replacing it with that of Lt. Ace. Lt. Ace then made a serious tactical error by trying to act sober rather than going to the latrine and throwing up. Instructor pilot Lt. Joe most likely knew that Lt. Ace was severely hung over, but he may have thought it would be a good idea to teach the young lieutenant a lesson. So off they went for spin mission number one.

The trolley ride to the aircraft in the desert heat brought Ace to the brink of nausea, but he made yet another severe tactical error and saved it for later. Taxi, take off, and climb took place surprisingly uneventfully. At 22,000 feet, Lt. Ace initiated his first-ever spin in the T-37. After several turns of the very uncomfortable and dreaded spin maneuver, Ace initiated recovery using the proper technique with the appropriate four-G pullout, accompanied by the inevitable purging of the polluted gut. Lt. Joe took control of the aircraft while Lt. Ace groped for the barf bag from the pocket of his G Suit. Ace, however, had never before used a barf bag, and his initial reaction was to rip the top open, not realizing that he now had it upside down. He then barfed into the bottomless bag and thus emptied the contents of his stomach onto himself and his side of the cockpit. Another tactical error then followed. Feeling better now, Ace decided to show Lt. Joe that he was a real trooper by suggesting that he was fine to do some more spins. When spin number two resulted in barf number two, Lt. Joe said "enough." Upon the return to Willy, Lt. Joe informed the control tower that he wanted a straight-in precautionary landing since he had a sick student on board. The sick-student information was immediately relayed to the squadron briefing room, leading the other pilots to tab Ace as "the barf-bag boy." The humiliation was taken one step further when Lt. Ace was required to clean up the mess he had made in the cockpit.

T-37 "TWEETIE BIRD" UGLY AT ANY ANGLE

Ace recovered from this ignominious flight and continued his pursuit of the coveted Air Force wings. Luckily, he was gifted with excellent eye-hand coordination. The stick-and-rudder element of pilot skills, moreover, came to him almost second nature. However, in the academic phase, his background as a physical education major left him in the wake turbulence of the "Zoomies" (Air Force Academy grads) who had their Master's degrees in aeronautical engineering. A few of his classmates began to wash-out (their training terminated), and, since there was a need for Air Force Officers to man the many nuclear missile sites, most of which were located in very remote, barely habitable areas, the washouts went involuntarily to these undesirable assignments. Since Ace wanted no part of a Minot, North Dakota missile silo, he reluctantly decided to forego happy hour at the Officers' Club in favor of studying the manuals.

Each IP (instructor pilot) had a small stable of "studs" (students) who sat together at his table in the squadron briefing room. The NASA space program had recently trained a monkey to be an astronaut and actually launched the animal into space. On the outside of the vintage World War II tin shed that served as the squadron headquarters was a large mural depicting a monkey with an aviator's helmet and a stalk of bananas. Inscribed over the mural was the following motto: "with enough bananas," an obvious implication that Air Force pilot trainees are at least as trainable as a monkey. Although there was a message of light humor with this mural, it also served as a motivator. An additional motivator for Lt. Ace was his fellow tablemate, Lt. Chuck.

A contributing factor for the high level of camaraderie amongst the students was the notion that they were all striving for that same brass ring, Air Force Pilot Wings. If it appeared that a certain pilot was not doing well, the other pilots would try to help him along with tutoring or mentoring. The unspoken support from the classmates was somewhat like parents' unconditional love for their children. Despite the caring and sharing support, all of the pilots were also competing against each other, since class ranking at graduation determined the quality of one's aircraft and duty assignment upon completion of training. The competition was intense, not least because most of the instructors were already seasoned Vietnam War pilots and espoused the mantra that "If you ain't a fighter pilot, you ain't shit." This, of course, inspired the studs, most of whom were already intense type-A personalities, to work even harder in hopes of a choice assignment in a single-seat fighter jet, such as the F-100, the F-105, or the more sophisticated two-seater, the F-4 Phantom. Lt. Ace and Lt. Chuck became good friends, but they also welcomed intense competition between them. The wheat would eventually separate from the chaff by check-ride evaluations. Chuck was the first pilot to take the transition check ride. When he returned from the flight, all the other pilots waited anxiously to see how well he performed. When Chuck entered the briefing room, displaying his usual good-natured swagger, his colleagues immediately queried him as to how he performed. In his always confident but unassuming manner, he casually stated, "I was minimum magnificent." Chuck was not a shrinking violet!

Amongst Chuck's many talents was playing the piano. The base Officers' Club had a piano in a side room where Chuck was equally "minimum magnificent." On weekends the pilots, along with their wives and lady friends would often gather around the piano. Chuck would direct the group in a songfest, sometimes improvising ditties about his pilot colleagues or interesting happenings that had occurred during training. These gatherings helped create an even higher level of group cohesion. Chuck went on to be a fighter pilot in the F-4 Phantom, and after his Southeast Asia war tour, he became an F-15 operations officer for a fighter squadron based in Germany. He continued his piano playing and songwriting and later authored a poignant ballad about a down-and-out ex-fighter pilot. The words to Chuck's song appear in a later chapter.

For Ace, Chuck and the other trainees, four hours of each training day consisted of academics, which included meteorology, aircraft systems, and aerodynamic principles of flight, along with some unique training scenarios that might help save pilots' lives. One of these unique and educational ventures was experiencing a rapid decompression and hypoxia (inadequate oxygen) in the altitude chamber—a large room that accommodated approximately twenty people. The technicians operating the chamber would create an environment that simulated pressurized flight, but that also mimicked a pressurization problem resulting in diminished atmospheric pressure and an accompanying loss of oxygen. Through this exposure the pilots were able to discover what their personal symptoms and reactions might be in the event of a pressurization failure. Most of them came to realize that hypoxia is a life-threatening situation. Since one of its primary symptoms is euphoria; the affected pilot commonly wants to remain in his euphoric but perilous state when he should be attempting to solve the problem that created the hypoxia. Altitude chamber training can save the life of any pilot flying at an altitude of 12,000 feet or higher; unfortunately, very few civilian pilots receive such training, since it is readily available only to military pilots.

Most military jet-training aircraft, and all actual jet fighters, have ejection seats so that in the event of a catastrophic malfunction the pilots can abandon their aircraft and perform what was referred to as "the nylon letdown" (the parachutes were made of nylon). Training for this maneuver was twofold. The first phase involved strapping oneself into an ejection seat that was mounted on a rail approximately 100 feet high. The pilot would assume the proper ejection posture, squeeze the activation handle, and immediately black out from the ten-G force created by the ejection seat propellant. He would be sitting comfortably in his seat at ground level, and approximately one second later he would find himself seventy-five or eighty feet in the air with a panoramic view of the air base! Prior to that stunning view from the simulated ejection seat, the pilot experienced the unique physiological phenomenon of a high G-force blackout situation. High G-force blackout does not, as many people think, result in unconsciousness, only in a lack of vision. Military fighter pilots, while engaged in high G-force maneuvers, often experience tunnel vision comparable to the closing of the lens of a camera; it can be modulated by his elevator or back-stick input. If a civilian pilot were to attempt to pull to many Gs, it is possible that major structural damage to the aircraft would occur prior to tunnel vision or blackout. Aerobatic pilots, flying their advanced, structural-design airplanes, will often experience the edge of tunnel vision or vision blackout while entertaining crowds at air shows.

Another interesting training scenario involved parasailing behind a pickup truck. The trainee would be strapped to a parachute pack with the actual chute disengaged from the chute pack, the lanyards and canopy extending behind him. The parachute was equipped with a metal hook attached to the chest strap. A five-hundred-foot length of rope attached to a pickup truck was attached to the metal hook on the chest strap. As the pickup truck accelerated slowly, the trainee started running, and the parachute would fill with air. As the truck continued to accelerate, the inflated canopy of the parachute would lift him into the air. Several hundred feet above ground, he disconnected the hook from his parachute and drifted gently back to earth, performing the previously practiced PLF (parachute landing fall). The pilot's parachute and ejection seat are wonderful security blankets. The ability to exit an incapacitated aircraft has saved thousands of lives. The horrific terror of being in a burning aircraft and unable to escape it is a nightmare that untold numbers of civilian pilots and passengers have experienced.

THE T-38 TALON—
THE ASTROUNAUT CLASS OF AIR TRAVEL

After approximately one hundred hours of flight time in the T-37, Ace climbed into the sleek supersonic T-38 and experienced the next challenge: a profoundly exhilarating flight called the "dollar ride." This was an experience nearly as significant as the initial solo in the T-41A. It entailed a one-hour flight that resulted in high-flow adrenaline and wide-eyed awe as the instructor pilot, sitting in the backseat, put the aircraft through its paces. The T-37 had been fun, but the transition to the T-38 was like going from a dump truck to a Ferrari. The pilot trainee sat in the front seat as he did throughout his T-38 training, while the IP in the back seat engaged in high-performance aerobatic maneuvers.

As the pilot trainee looked out of his forward window, he could see the large pitot tube extending from the nose of the aircraft, creating a bizarre perspective, particularly when the IP had the aircraft pointed directly at the ground. The pitot tube in the T-38 was a long, cylindrical device (to measure

ACE DISPLAYING HIS CASUAL SWAGGER POSE

airspeed). It was visible from the front seat simply because it was mounted on the front of the nose of the aircraft. Its paint scheme resembled a candy cane, with its alternating white and red stripes. When the nose of the T-38 was pointed towards the ground, the tube created an illusionary sight picture that resulted in a sensation of being much closer to the ground than the actual altitude. The instructor pilots enjoyed this flight as much as the students since most of their flight time was riding in the back, "sitting on their hands," while the pilot trainee engaged in flying the aircraft. Also included in the dollar ride was an excursion through the sound barrier that qualified the stud for a "Mach One pin" to wear on his lapel. Ace later upgraded to a "Mach Two pin" when he flew the F-4 Phantom.

The T-38 aircraft has been part of the Air Force inventory since 1963. It is still being used as the advanced-training aircraft at pilot-training bases. The NASA astronauts have also used it from 1963 to the present as they travel about the country for both business and pleasure. The F-5 fighter aircraft is a replica of the T-38, remaining the mainstay of the air forces of many nations throughout the world for the last forty years. It is a true classic and most likely will be flying as long as there is fossil fuel remaining.

Now that the new studs were in the fast lane with their sleek, phallic-like T-38s, they also went on to seek fast-lane women to go with their recently enhanced status. In fact, the quest for fast-lane women became surprisingly easy since the class flight leader, Captain Bob, was a member of the Phoenix Playboy Club and was dating a Playboy bunny. He helpfully organized a little outing at the base, and the bunnies showed up in their normal Playboy Club work clothes for a photo shoot. The presence of the bunnies on the flight line created a most exclusive scenario. The pilots and the bunnies rapidly established a rapport and many pilots were now complementing their high-speed aircraft with high-speed, high maintenance women.

This Playboy-Bunny affiliation soon became common knowledge on the base; consequently, the instructor pilots, most of whom were bachelors, now treated the studs with a distinctly elevated level of respect. At the Officers Club happy hour the IPs would buy the beer and patronize the studs with the not-very-ulterior motive of getting to meet some bunnies. They even went so far as to reveal the secret behind the spread-finger gestures often utilized by these Vietnam War seasoned pilots as they elaborated on their own war stories. They explained that as they moved their hands in large circles while describing aerial combat maneuvers, they had to keep their fingers spread widely apart to allow the large quantities of bullshit to flow through. In reality, the instructor pilots were dedicated mentors and were all committed to making each and every student a better pilot. Nearly as much instruction took place over the numerous pitchers of beer at the O club as at the training squadron's briefing room. Since it was pretty much assured that most of the pilots would be going to war in Southeast Asia, the IPs were dedicated to providing the trainees with the highest level of training possible.

T-38 TALON TANTALIZING TALES

As the pilots progressed, the confidence increased and the swagger intensified. The sleeves on the flight suits were rolled up a little higher, and it appeared that there would indeed be "enough bananas" to propel the studs to the completion of training and to their coveted Air Force wings. But the continued training was no piece of cake. Many of the maneuvers they performed in formation flying were as difficult as the maneuvers of the elite Thunderbird aerobatic team. Many of the flights were in four-ship formation and involved close-trail formation as well as over-the-top (loop) maneuvers that were both challenging and exhilarating. The visual perception of being number four in the formation (last in line), while looking straight ahead at three other aircraft that are headed 90° nose low —straight for the ground—is such an intense experience that any attempt to describe it would be futile. This intense visual experience is further heightened by the demanding maximum-performance flying skills that are required to maintain the close formation. IMAX Theater aviation scenarios and flight simulators can provide a faint sense of the experience, which could be compared to seeing pictures of the Grand Canyon rather than the exhilarating experience of actually being there.

HIGH-SPEED AND HIGH-MAINTENANCE

Since the Grand Canyon was, in fact, located adjacent to the transition flying-practice area, Ace, on his initial solo in the T-38, decided that it might be fun to get a closer look. Standing on the edge of the south rim of the Grand Canyon is certainly a breath-taking encounter, but it doesn't compare to flying a high-performance jet through the Canyon itself! The undeniable thrill of flying the T-38 solo was significantly intensified by this unauthorized joyride by the blossoming rogue aviator.

THIS BABY IS REALLY FAST

Over the next few flights after the Grand Canyon caper, Ace was encumbered with an IP for the far less exhilarating, perhaps even punishing, instrument training "under the hood." Rather than awe-inspiring panoramic vistas, his only view was that of the cockpit and the flight instruments. Although most of the instrument training was quite boring, it was extremely challenging in that it required the pilot's total concentration. When the student gained a higher level of proficiency, he was then allowed to have a little fun by doing acrobatic maneuvers under the hood (no outside visual references). Engaging in acrobatic flying with reference only to one's instruments is a unique experience that non-military pilots are rarely able to enjoy. Its training value was that it allowed the pilot to recover the aircraft from an unusual attitude or from an out-of-control situation and to return to a wings-level, normal-flight attitude without outside visual references.

It was another crystal clear blue sky and a perfect day to fly at Willy, and Ace was now finished with instrument training. He was thus rewarded with a solo transition flight without an IP. The main menu of the pilot-training program involved intensely regimented training with an IP. The student pilot's dessert would result in the occasional solo transition flight that consisted of barrel rolls, loops, steep turns, and Immelmans without an IP looking over his shoulder. The Immelman, a unique dog-fighting maneuver named after Max Immelman, a notorious German fighter pilot, begins in the T-38 from level flight at 450 knots. The pilot then points the nose straight up and after an increase of altitude of several thousand feet, he pulls back on the control stick to take the aircraft to a level-inverted (upside down) position. He then rolls the aircraft 180 degrees to a wings-level position. However, on this particular day there were no Immelmans since the Big Kahuna that controls the fate of the flyboy had other ideas.

Shortly after lift-off and landing-gear retraction, Ace detected an unusual engine sound and slight airframe vibration. As he retarded the throttles out of the afterburner range, the noise and the vibration rapidly intensified, and the engine instruments for the left engine became very erratic. The increased adrenaline flow that Ace experienced was punctuated by a very loud "Bang!" accompanied by a significant aircraft yaw along with several red warning lights illuminating in the cockpit. Ace immediately radioed the control tower to make it known that he had lost an engine and was declaring an emergency. He then proceeded with the appropriate checklist items for engine failure and engine shutdown while turning to a downwind leg with the intention to land on the same runway from which he had just departed. Sometimes, however, as the old cliché goes, "The best intentions are filled with folly." Although gear and flap extension were normal, the right base turn to final was fraught with the aforementioned folly. A combination of asymmetric thrust from the right engine and a relatively strong crosswind from the right resulted in a runway overshoot into a position from which a safe landing could not be made. A single-engine, heavy weight go-around (missed approach) is not the favorite maneuver of most pilots, but in this case it was the only option.

On the next approach, Ace properly set himself up for a much wider pattern, resulting in a shallower turn to final approach and a successful landing. Despite the use of the drag chute, which initially produces a rapid decrease of airspeed, it became necessary, as a result of the increased kinetic energy of the heavy aircraft, to use relatively heavy braking in order to stop the aircraft on the runway. This would create a hot-brake situation—really hot. Within seconds after the aircraft came to a stop, the Fire and Rescue specialists sped up a ladder to the cockpit in order to expedite Ace's departure from the cockpit. The catastrophic engine failure had resulted in engine turbine blades penetrating the fuselage. Fuel lines were severed, and jet fuel gushed from the aircraft, just waiting for a catastrophic ignition by the hot brakes, an action that could easily have ignited the entire aircraft. Fortunately, the fire did not occur, and Ace was very grateful for the efforts of the Fire and Rescue team that helped remove him to a safe distance from the aircraft as soon as possible. After a debriefing with the flight safety team, the squadron training Colonels gave Ace their kudos and thanked him for bringing back their aircraft reasonably intact.

A few days later, Ace climbed back into the saddle again for another solo transition ride. He and his pilot trainee buddy, Lt. Pat, were scheduled to go to the same solo practice area at the same time. Getting wind of this, they clandestinely conspired to meet at a given place "in space" in order to engage in some simulated dog-fighting maneuvers. The join-up in the practice area was effectuated quite smoothly, and after they identified each other with a rock of the wings and a discussion on their preselected, discreet radio frequency, they commenced to play fighter-pilot games. After about ten minutes of dives, zooms, and high-speed, high-G turns, Ace lost sight of Lt. Pat's aircraft while Lt. Pat appeared to be engaging in a maneuver that involved hiding behind a ridgeline. Ace then attempted several radio calls to Lt. Pat and received no response. His last view of Lt. Pat's aircraft showed Lt. Pat in a steep dive quite close to the ground. Ace then engaged in some rudimentary but faulty logic that was cluttered with intense paranoia. Did Lt. Pat crash? Ace then flew around the area looking for the possible crash site until his low level of remaining fuel dictated a return to the base to land. As he taxied his aircraft to the parking area, he let out a great sigh of relief when he observed Lt. Pat's aircraft parked and chocked. As Ace entered the squadron briefing, he found Lt. Pat pouring down a post-flight cup of coffee while discussing his very first airborne radio failure, thus explaining the lost communication problem which piqued Ace's concern. Another disaster averted!

As Ace moved smoothly through the more advanced phases of training, the coveted wings were not far away. Night-formation take-offs and rejoins proved to be particularly exhilarating, and four-ship formation flying kept the aviator on the very edge of his seat.

"TUCK IT IN, NUMBER 4!"

After the normal 1.3-hour training flight, the fluorescent-orange flight suit would be saturated with sweat, and the adrenaline supply would be nearly depleted. The pilot trainees engaged in ongoing competition since the aircraft assignment that one received after completion of training was based on class standing. Therefore, the pilots, most of whom matched the classic success-oriented personality profile to a tee, worked very hard to impress the instructor pilots with their superior aviator prowess. Many of the instructor pilots had already served a combat tour in Viet Nam, and their experience fueled the trainees' fervent need to eventually become fighter pilots themselves. Everyone worked very hard to win one of those few but coveted single-seat, fighter-jet assignments, such as the F-100 or the F-105. Even those pilots who actually preferred to fly "many motors" cargo airplanes were reluctant to admit it for fear that they might be tagged as less-than-patriotic wimps. To admit that one would rather fly a B-52, also referred to as a BUFF (big ugly F?????), would be blasphemous. The B-52 is a vastly large, unwieldy eight-engine airplane designed primarily to drop nuclear weapons and was assigned to the branch of the Air Force called SAC (Strategic Air Command). Because of the extreme regimentation and discipline that defined SAC, it was said that SAC pilots had to be "SACumcised."

SACumcised B-52 pilots would have to sit alert for extended, seemingly endless periods of time in mostly remote locations. The BUFF pilot flew very infrequently; however, if he were to accomplish the mission for which he had been trained, he would have cut loose a nuclear bomb with the likelihood of killing a few million people. Ace, like most of his colleagues, had a different and more individually heroic vision: shooting down Russian MIGs over North Vietnam in order to become a bona fide aviation ace. The anticipated glory of being a war-hero fighter pilot superseded all else, and an assignment to SAC would be avoided at all costs.

Sleep tight America - your Air Force is awake.

THE EFFECTS OF NUCLEAR ALERT ON A YOUNG SAC PILOT

WINGS ARE ON THE HORIZON

When UPT training commenced for the "Willy" class 67F, seventy-four pilots made up the class. The washout rate was slightly less than 50%, as thirty-eight pilots successfully completed the program. Ace finished in the top one-third of his class, allowing him to gain a back-seat F-4 Phantom GIB (guy in back) assignment. As a second-in-command, back-seat fighter pilot, Ace would have the chance to go to war in order to avoid the humiliating plight of the SACumcised BUFF pilot. Ace relished the opportunity.

On March 25, 1967, Ace and his pilot-trainee colleagues of class 67F completed their 13-month training program and were ordained as true-blue

Air Force pilots. The graduation ceremony involved a sixteen-ship T-38 flyover, along with marching troops and the big brass band playing, "Off We Go into the Wild Blue Yonder." Ace felt a level of pride and a depth of accomplishment that far exceeded anything else that he had ever achieved. When the Air Force wings are pinned on the "dress blues" for the very first time, the brand-new pilot's chest size would seemingly increase by several inches. Ace had joined an extraordinarily elite fraternity. Only those who have "*been there and done that*" understand what is required to get there.

That wonderful moment of celebration with family, friends, and proud instructor pilots was followed by a day of somber separation as many of the 67F pilot classmates gathered at the O Club for a few beers and good-luck farewells. The thirteen months of eating, drinking, sleeping, flying, and carousing together ended abruptly. It was very likely that Ace would never again see many of his good friends, and there was a strong possibility that some would be killed in combat. After sharing so much, they had become genuine comrades. A melancholy mood prevailed because they all knew that the close-knit relationships that had been formed would cease to exist. Despite the somber tones, Ace enthusiastically anticipated leaping into the Phantom—even though he would have to serve as GIB (guy in back)—to become the right-hand man for the A/C (aircraft commander). As second in command, Ace would undeniably play the role of quasi-fighter pilot. Perhaps the GIB might even receive credit for at least half a kill if the A/C were to shoot down a MIG!

CHAPTER TWO
Flying the Fabulous Phantom

The first phase of F-4 Phantom training for the GIB was radar school at Davis Monthan AFB in Tucson, Arizona. The thrill of being upside down and accelerating through the Mach (speed of sound) in the T-38 was replaced by two boring months of sitting in a classroom and simulator training in order that Ace, the GIB, would be proficient in finding the enemy MIG on his aircraft's radar. The A/C (aircraft commander) could then fire a missile designed to destroy the enemy aircraft. The A/C would have another notch on his gun and be credited with a kill. Five destroyed enemy aircraft would allow him to claim the legitimate and exulted status of Air Force "Ace." The GIB, however, being second in command, would receive no official recognition. After thirteen months of pilot training, with instructor pilots schooling their studs to be "steely-eyed killers," the GIB would be regarded only as an accomplice, earning no credit for the kill.

The GIB training also taught recruits how to operate the inertial navigation system that was used for both navigation and nuclear weapons delivery. In addition, Ace and his GIB colleagues were forced to learn the intricacies of the nuclear weapons that the Phantom was capable of delivering. Since the F-4 carried sidewinders (heat-seeking missiles) and sparrows (radar-guided missiles) the curriculum included an in-depth understanding of these aircraft-killing devices. Despite the high combat stakes, the GIB training was boring and mundane, with lots of free time for golf and for the highlight of every week: Friday afternoon happy hour at the O Club, which served to function again as a magnet for attractive, young, single women. Each of these intrepid aviators was regarded as a prime catch, and as the attractive young lasses cavorted in their sundresses with their provocative, tanned bodies, the soon-to-be-steely-eyed killers could not defend themselves against the alluring ladies. Fortunately, there was no training during the weekend.

Davis Monthan AFB was an F-4 Phantom RTU (replacement training unit) base where the temporarily grounded GIB trainee would be relegated to hanging around the flight line, drooling in awe when the F-4s would take off and land. Observing a flight of four F-4 Phantoms approach the runway, pitch out and land, inevitably got the juices flowing for even the non-aviator. When the temporarily grounded GIB observed this phenomenon, he would froth at the mouth in anticipation of sitting in that Phantom cockpit.

A side note on military logic: just a few days prior to completion of this non-flying GIB training program, an F-4 Phantom departed on a formation takeoff when both engines failed. The pilots ejected safely. The aircraft crashed into a shopping-center parking lot. The response of the generals at training command headquarters was to immediately curtail formation takeoffs. This left Ace and his GIB colleagues scratching their heads in wonderment since the double-engine failure had absolutely nothing to do with the fact that the aircraft was involved in a formation take-off. This illogical reaction would reinforce George Carlin's premise that "military intelligence" should be regarded as an oxymoron.

Ace successfully navigated the first phase of Phantom training; however, before the Air Force administrators would let Ace go off to fly the fabulous Phantom, they had two additional hoops for him. The first hoop, namely the next phase of training, had him headed to survival school at Fairchild Air Force Base near Spokane, Washington. That would be followed by the second hoop: a sea survival training school at Homestead Air Force Base near Miami, Florida. As the air war in Southeast Asia intensified, there was a sharp increase in the number of aircraft being shot down, with pilots bailing out over enemy territory or the Gulf of Tonkin. The Air Force big-brass wanted their pilots to return intact, so they provided the pilots with a very realistic and effective survival-training program.

Ace and his survival-trainee colleagues were extremely fortunate because their training time frame took place in mid-June, which happened to be the nicest weather of the year in the Pacific Northwest. At the training location near Spokane, Washington, numerous unpleasant cold-weather anecdotes surfaced from pilots who had attended survival training in the middle of winter and suffered severe frostbite during a one-week trek through the snow-covered mountains in frigid temperatures.

The first few days of classroom instruction, which consisted of watching films and familiarizing oneself with the functionality of survival equipment, was a proverbial "walk in the park" compared to the upcoming walk in the wild known as "the trek." The serious, hands-on training began with a several-hundred-yard crawl on hands and knees underneath concertina wire with life and well being in danger as live rounds were being fired overhead. At what appeared to be the exit point at the end of the concertina wire, enemy captors greeted the escaping American warrior. Actually, the captors were Air Force enlisted personnel who nevertheless engaged in such effective role-playing that Ace actually felt as if he had just been captured.

The next few days were spent in a simulated prisoner of war (POW) camp. Most of the trainee captives were officers, and the captors were enlisted personnel. The lower-ranked troops took great joy in taking control of the officers, who now would have to endure the reduced stature of a prisoner. In actuality, the powerfully realistic role-playing of the enlisted training staff resulted in very realistic training. The prisoner/trainee had a very intense feeling of actually being a POW. Ace was told that he was such a pathetic piece of humanity that he would have to dig his own grave. As his supervisor/captor berated and belittled him with degrading obscenities while Ace was digging, the camp commander frequently intervened to demand that the hole be filled back up. This scenario continued for several hours until Ace was given a latrine pass. Ace found a hiding place in the latrine and was temporarily able to avoid the harassing prison guards.

The next phase of POW camp was the dreaded "black box" ordeal. This routine involved stuffing the POW into a box so small that almost no movement was possible. The guards walked by and loudly hit the outside of the box to prevent the sleep-deprived POW from getting a nap. After what seemed like days, but was probably just a few hours, Ace was removed for interrogation. He was promised release and a Caspian Sea vacation with Vodka, beautiful women, and fine Russian caviar if he would cooperate with the interrogators. Ace immediately spilled the beans. This angered the interrogators since they felt he was not playing the game seriously.

When the simulated POW camp came to completion, the survival-school trainees were confronted with the final exam that was required for course completion: the dreaded trek, a one-week journey through the forests and mountains of the Pacific Northwest while being pursued by potential enemy captors. The escaped POW was required to navigate to various checkpoints while travelling several miles each day through the rugged terrain. The simulated enemy had helicopters and airplanes flying overhead along with ground troops searching for the escaped POW. If the escapee was spotted and caught by the enemy, he was deemed to have failed the training and would be doomed to repeat the trek. Having grown up on a farm, Ace had spent a lot of time playing in the forests, which made this phase of the training like, well, a walk in the woods, if not the park.

For the trek, the trainee was issued a few pieces of beef jerky to help fight off hunger pangs. The beef jerky was consumed in the first two days, but on the fourth day Ace found an edible puffball, which slowed down the rumbling in his stomach. Ace and his colleagues were very fortunate to make the trek during perfect weather: clear skies and temperatures in the low seventies. Once again, Ace's Air Force career was blessed with good luck when, during the last day of the trek, he stumbled out of the woods into an open meadow filled with lusciously ripe wild strawberries. Gorging himself on wild strawberries, Ace also enjoyed a spectacularly beautiful view across the lush green meadow to a clear blue lake with snowcapped mountains in the background. Once again, Ace—and blind fate—would turn the proverbial pig's ear into a silk purse. The following day everyone returned to base camp, ate a steak dinner, put on their now baggy uniforms, and headed to the next assignment.

Immediately following this unique experience in the picturesque Rocky Mountains, Ace headed for a tropical vacation at Homestead Air Force Base near Miami, Florida. Air Force Sea Survival Training, the second and final hoop, saw Ace jumping from platforms into the ocean while attached to a parachute. The simple objective was to learn how to disconnect the parachute lanyards in order to prevent being dragged underwater by the soaking wet nylon of the chute. Another phase of this training was to spend a day in a raft while drifting randomly in Biscayne Bay. The trainee was given a plastic bag of survival enhancing goodies, one of which was a bag of shark repellent. A few months later, while watching a Jacques Cousteau TV special about sharks, Ace learned with surprise that the shark repellent actually attracted the sharks and that they would actually *attack* the bag of repellent as it floated in the water. This verified Ace's long-held premise that survival information required constant updating. Hopefully, the Air Force sea-survival experts have long since gone back to the drawing board to reconsider the formula for their shark repellent.

"ONE A DAY IN TAMPA BAY"

After a short drive across the Florida peninsula, Ace arrived at MacDill Air Force, where he would take his first step in a six-month training program, resulting in the exalted status of a combat-ready GIB and an assignment to Southeast Asia, where the air war over North Vietnam grew intensely. Every evening, Walter Cronkite and his journalist colleagues informed the American people of the number of "sorties" flown that day over North Vietnam. It was only much later in his F-4 Phantom career that Ace would become informed of the meaninglessness and folly of many these missions (the pilots called them "monkey missions" or "toothpick missions"). But meanwhile, back at MacDill Air Force Base, Ace and his F-4 pilot colleagues sat attentively in a classroom addressed by the squadron commander, Colonel Casper.

Colonel Casper, a larger-than-life, already seasoned Vietnam veteran, devoted himself intently to providing the highest level of training possible for these soon-to-be-steely-eyed killers. Colonel Casper stood 6'3" tall, weighed 230 pounds, walked with a well-deserved swagger, and spoke with such commanding authority that pilots in the training class would sit on the edge of their chairs attempting to absorb every scrap of knowledge and wisdom they could glean from their commander. Since it was assumed that Ace and his classmates would soon be off to war, they also understood that their survival was, to a degree, predicated on how well they paid attention. Unlike philosophy 101 back in the undergrad days, no one slept in this class. There had been a recent rash of F-4 Phantom crashes, prompting the local media folks to recreate the catchphrase, "One a day in Tampa Bay." The F-4 training staff members at MacDill Air Force Base did not particularly care for this bit of journalistic libel, and they worked very hard to reduce the possibility of any more F-4 Phantoms crashing in Tampa Bay.

The aircraft commander with whom Ace was assigned to fly was Lieutenant Colonel Lee. The Colonel had reached his late forties, and most of his flying experience took place in large, multi-engine aircraft. He was not used to the high G-flight conditions that occurred when flying the Phantom. During one of his first gunnery range training missions, he experienced a relatively bizarre phenomenon while pulling off the target on a dive bomb run. The normal high G-force pull-out recovery caused the Lieutenant Colonel's advanced hemorrhoid condition to deteriorate, resulting in the bursting of blood vessels in the anal sphincter area. The heavy loss of blood resulted in a serious emergency. The instructor pilot in the back seat then flew the aircraft back to MacDill since Colonel Lee was nearly incapacitated from loss of blood.

Ace was then assigned to a new aircraft commander, but in the first few training flights Ace got very little stick time. The RTU program (Replacement Training Unit) was oriented towards achieving a high level of flying skill for the A/C, often at the expense of stick time for the GIB. The F-4 Phantom was initially utilized by the Navy and Marines. The "back seater" was not a trained pilot, but rather he served the function of RO (radar operator) or RIO (radar intercept operator). Not only did the back-seat-guy not fly, he did not have a control stick back there. The Air Force eventually did install control sticks in the backseat of the Phantom, but actually flying the aircraft was well down on the list of skills needed to perform as a good GIB. The GIB's priority duties included operating the radar and providing a second set of eyes for the "front seater," providing as much helpful information as possible during flight operations.

The GIB would certainly rather be manipulating the controls, but his situation was still greatly preferred to that of the BUFF pilot flying ten-hour

"Chrome Dome" missions. Chrome Dome was the term for B-52 missions that originated at Thule Air Force Base in Greenland. The term Chrome Dome was apparently derived from the location of these missions situated at the very top of the world, often well within the Arctic Circle. The B-52s functioned as a quick strike retaliation in the event the Russians launched nuclear weapons. Since they orbited a very short distance from Russia, they would be able to respond rapidly. The letters sent back to Mom might read like this: "We had a great mission today: we flew in big circles for ten hours, but we didn't have to drop our nukes!"

Ace, the GIB, was, quite by coincidence, scheduled with one of the veteran instructor pilots for his initial airborne-refueling training flight. As the flight of four Phantoms approached the KC-135 tanker plane, the veteran IP, not knowing that back seater Ace had actually experienced very little stick time in the Phantom, suggested that he, the actual pilot, would sit back and relax while Ace hooked up to the tanker to engage the refueling process. Ace very reluctantly took control of the aircraft and maneuvered it into the refueling "envelope." Eventually, he was able to stabilize the aircraft within the small confines of the allotted space, at which time the boom operator inserted his big "dork" refueling boom into the "receiver aircraft" receptacle just behind the aft cockpit. Ace struggled hard to stay in the relatively small airspace required to continue the refueling procedure. As the aircraft weight and center of gravity changed, the stick forces changed, too, and Ace over-controlled the aircraft into a PIO (pilot induced oscillation).

The tanker boom operator promptly initiated an emergency disconnect. Unfortunately, it was too late. The PIO resulted in a "torque of the dork," which rendered the refueling boom inoperable. To make matters worse, there were several other Phantoms waiting in line at the big, flying Exxon station to refuel. Since Ace and his flying friends could not refuel from the broken boom, their mission was scrubbed. The tanker had about 200,000 pounds of fuel that would effectively become waste because the fuel had to be either burned off or dumped in order to reduce the craft to the maximum landing weight. Ace's ham-handedness had wreaked havoc on the morning refueling training. The aircraft commander remained calm and gracious and salvaged Ace's ego by politely saying something like, "Oh well, shit happens!" This was just another of the numerous and inevitable mistakes that had to be whisked away with the old cliché, "That's just part of doing business."

As the training program progressed, the fun began. ACM (aerial combat maneuvering), or as it was once called, "dog-fighting," prepared the new Phantom pilots for the high G-extreme maneuvering that would etch out the critical element in determining whether one would return back to the good life stateside or endure an indefinite stay in the Hanoi Hilton (North Vietnamese prison camp). Ace was lucky enough to have several back-seat ACM missions with Colonel Casper, a veteran combat pilot, who exposed Ace to some very advanced ACM skills. Turning and maneuvering the F-4 at high angles of attack required some highly specialized aviator skills, and Ace was able to learn from the master. During these ACM missions, the aircraft G meter would rapidly oscillate from an occasional negative one G all the way to eight or nine positive Gs. After one particular ACM mission, while taxiing to the ramp after landing, Ace observed that the G meter was pegged at an incredible ten. Incidentally, while Colonel Casper always excelled in the aircraft as well as in all of his training duties, he also performed at a very high level during happy hours and squadron parties. He drank his Tanqueray martinis from milkshake glasses. Regardless of how advanced the party might be, or how many milkshake glasses of martinis he had consumed, he would never abandon his persona of total control of self and situation.

ACM represented a scintillating, adrenaline-pumping phase of training, but the gunnery range/bomb-dropping game was equally challenging. The GIB provided the A/C with a bit of help by giving him altitude and airspeed callouts while the A/C had his "head out of the cockpit" looking at the target. The GIB also functioned as a cheerleader and occasionally provided tactful advice or constructive criticism. The effective GIB was not unlike the effective caddie for a PGA Tour golf pro in that he had a plethora of supportive duties and responsibilities, including both psychologist and cheerleader. During the gunnery training, the bomb-dropping phase made use of dummy, inert bombs; however, the strafing and rocket firing was done with live ammunition. The range officer on the ground provided very timely feedback regarding the accuracy of the bombs, rockets, and bullets. The A/C had to attain a certain level of proficiency before he would be certified as combat ready.

The GIB *did* have the opportunity to participate in a bomb-dropping game since nuclear weapons deliveries were also practiced. Most of the nuclear weapon delivery modes were controlled by the GIB using his radar and inertial navigation system. One of the more interesting modes of nuclear delivery involved the "loft" maneuver, which entailed releasing the bomb at a high rate of speed in a 45° climb, thus lofting the bomb a considerable distance forward, while the bomb droppers reversed course as fast as possible to distance themselves from the impending explosion.

Avon Park gunnery range was a very large parcel of land inhabited by wild deer. Since many of the A/C instructor pilots had recently returned from their combat tours and just wanted to kill something, there were numerous reports of deer being killed by 20mm. caliber bullets from F-4 Phantoms.

Since stateside training could become relatively boring compared to the actual combat that these instructors had just left, it was not uncommon for them to spice up their life a bit during training missions. This was epitomized, when, after a shortened range mission, the flight lead decided to treat his fellow Phantom pilots to a little joyride. This scenic jaunt involved a close-formation flight at treetop level at 450 knots across the Florida peninsula to Miami Beach— followed by an unsolicited fly-by for the sunbathers along Miami Beach. It is possible, given the predominately elderly population, that the four screaming Phantoms proceeding southbound a few hundred yards offshore, a mere fifty feet above the water's surface and at a speed of 450 knots, caused more than one cardiac arrest that morning on Miami Beach! Since the flight was already at treetop level, the flight lead determined that treetop level would also serve as a good altitude at which to return to MacDill Air Force Base. Among the many lasting memories of Ace's aviation career, the return flight and the sight of horses and cows running helter-skelter will remain especially vivid. The low-level buzz job flight-profile had now become so normal that the daring flight lead then led his marauding aviators along St. Petersburg Beach as elderly retirees grabbed their beach umbrellas and towels and headed for safety, perhaps fearing that enemy aircraft had penetrated the country's defenses!

The chutzpah that our adventuresome flight lead had exhibited came from the understanding that, during times of war, warriors can become unaccountable free spirits, since they are, in theory, responsible for maintaining the freedom and the security of the populace. This wonderful exhibit of carefree exuberance inspired Ace and his colleagues to rent Cherokee 140 aircraft in order to buzz the beach and to engage in low-speed, low-altitude, totally unrealistic dogfight activity. Despite the lack of power and maneuverability of these Cherokee 140 aircraft, their attempted formation flying was miraculously unaccompanied by a midair collision. Only a novice pilot injected with bad-judgment serum would attempt to fly formation in a Cherokee 140. Situations involving jet pilots disgracing and embarrassing themselves in small, propeller-driven airplanes will be elaborated on in a later chapter.

As Ace and his colleagues approached the completion of their training, they were soon promoted to the status of "combat ready." The common topic of discussion was base assignment in Southeast Asia, since the entire class was regarded to be "pipeline SEA" (Southeast Asia), which, of course, meant everyone was headed off to war. There were several F-4 bases in Vietnam, but the more desirable assignment was one of the many bases in Thailand. The missions flown out of Thailand were far more varied and interesting, and, amongst the Asian women in the Far East, the Thais were the most highly regarded. As all of this anticipation and enthusiasm began to reach a crescendo, Ace and several of his F-4 pilot trainee colleagues were stunned when they received their orders for their next assignment.

CHAPTER THREE

Finally, Off To War?

Ace and several of his colleagues had their war tour and tropical vacation to Southeast Asia derailed when they received orders to report to Misawa AFB in northern Japan. Oh well, what the hell, all will be well, because Ace will still be flying the F-4 Phantom. Some of his F-4 colleagues were given the dubious duty of ferrying Phantoms from a stateside air base across the Pacific Ocean to Southeast Asia, a buttocks-numbing task that would involve a pod of several Phantoms, along with several KC-135 tanker aircraft, and numerous refueling hook-ups. Although the F-4s were equipped with external fuel tanks, they still had a maximum range of about three hours, and this venture across the Pacific could be a twelve-to-fourteen-hour journey.

After a brief stop in Hawaii, Ace's commercial flight in the "soft-cushion" Boeing 707 proceeded to Tokyo's Haneda International Airport. Ace was met there by an Air Force bus that took him to Tachikawa AFB, where he would eventually catch a military flight to Misawa Air Force Base, his new duty station, located 300 miles north of Tokyo. He then checked into the bachelor officer quarters (BOQ) and slept for about twelve hours in order to purge the jet lag. Upon awakening, he noticed it was dinner hour, so he reported immediately to the Officers' Club where happy hour was gaining momentum. Interestingly enough, the Tachikawa AFB Officers' Club served as the social hub of the Far East. On this particular Friday night happy hour it was swarming with young American women, anxious to intermingle with the many single, very eligible, and very receptive pilots who dominated this Club Med-like environment. Ace had anticipated an extended period of stoic celibacy in his Far East assignment, but the celibacy was immediately shot down when he welcomed an unexpected introduction to a nice young lady who worked at the American Embassy in Tokyo. Since he was not required to be at his new duty station at Misawa AFB for several days, he stayed in Tokyo for a long weekend, honing his diplomatic skills.

When he finally arrived at Misawa AFB, Ace was greeted by a bleak, midwinter landscape. After years of fun in the sun, he did not relish the frozen tundra of northern Japan. This problem was soon solved when he received immediate orders for South Korea, where the local landscape, on the other hand, was even more forbidding.

Ace arrived at Kunsan AFB, also known as K8, just in time for what appeared to be another war with North Korea. The North Korean Navy had just captured a U.S. naval boat called the USS Pueblo, in reality a Naval Security Group ship on a mission to spy on North Korean communications networks. The North Korean captors held the ship's intelligence-gathering crew of eighty-two men and the ship's captain, Commander Lloyd Bucher, hostage for about eleven months, releasing the men, but not the ship, on December 23, 1968. This highly publicized, international incident had the generals in the Pentagon and the high-ranking NSA (National Security Agency) civilians on the edge of their chairs because the American intelligence-gatherers, according to several sources, only had the time to destroy a small percentage of long-established intelligence documentation required to identify and to keep continuity on "enemy" targets at the time, including, of course, the USSR. Along with highly sensitive intelligence information, the North Koreans took home encryption machines and radio equipment. The Pueblo continues today as a tourist attraction lying in the harbor at Pyongyang in North Korea.

Since the Air Force had a few F-4 Phantoms stationed in Korea, Ace and his fellow Phantom pilots would now find themselves in the right place at the right time to help stifle the evil forces of Communism. Armed with some rudimentary conventional weapons, Ace and his colleagues sat alert at Kunsan AFB until the Pueblo incident reached a conclusion through diplomatic channels.

After this little brush fire was extinguished, Ace returned to Misawa, where he participated in the rebirth of the 67th Tactical Fighter Squadron (TFS). This birthing process involved molding a motley crew of mostly brand-new F-4 pilots and F-4 aircraft that were being taken out of service in Vietnam and thrown together into a functional fighter squadron. These aircraft had been removed from service because of a "potting compound" problem that resulted in deterioration of electrical connections, creating some very troublesome electrical problems. For example, when the pilot extended the flaps, the airborne refueling door might open. The spurious electrical signals would result in some very unique malfunctions. Ace was assigned to be the GIB for Captain Buck, who aspired to be a test pilot on his fast-track path to becoming a general. This was one more stroke of good luck for Ace since he and Captain Buck flew many test flights together. Then, too, this particular experience would assist Ace's career advancement. These test flights, referred to as FCF (functional check flights) were required after certain maintenance functions were performed on an aircraft and involved taking the aircraft to the edge of its many performance "envelopes." The FCF mission was flown with a "clean aircraft"—no external fuel tanks, rockets, or guns.

The takeoff profile mandated an afterburner climb that would result in an altitude of several thousand feet after the aircraft had reached the end of the runway. The most remarkable element of the FCF profile was a climb to approximately 45,000 feet, followed by activation of the afterburners in order to accelerate to the maximum speed possible. The manufacturer, McDonnell-Douglas, advertised the aircraft as a Mach 2.5 machine. The speed of sound (Mach 1) at sea level is 761 miles per hour. The normal maximum speed achieved on these FCF flights was about 2.2 Mach. However, since this speed was achieved at a very high altitude above the terrain, the primary confirmation of the speed would necessitate a glance at the INS (inertial navigation system) ground-speed indicator, which would show in the vicinity of 1,400 miles per hour. With the aircraft at maximum speed, a pull-up to a forty-five degree climb angle would launch this immeasurable quantity of kinetic energy towards space. The ensuing steep climb would be maintained until the aircraft ran out of airspeed somewhere in the vicinity of 65,000 feet above sea level. At the top of the zoom climb, a stunning view would suddenly present itself by means of the noticeable curvature of the Earth. As the aircraft scraped the edge of space, the foreboding darkness of space became evident.

As exhilarating as this maneuver was, it was not nearly as exciting as the high speed Mach 2 run, when the variable ramp that controls the volume of intake air into the engines rapidly slammed open. This resulted in a compressor stall and an extremely loud bang as the aircraft yawed violently.

The suddenness and the severity of the situation had Ace, for the first and only time ever, briefly considering the possibility of having to eject from the aircraft. However, Captain Buck, the real ace of the base, handled the situation with great skill, resolving the problem promptly.

A few weeks later, a maintenance FCF resulted in a truly bizarre scenario. Luck was again with Ace and his front-seat leader, Captain Buck, as both of them were in Korea sitting nuclear alert. Two other FCF pilots at Misawa flew an unforgettable FCF. This particular mission was flown by the sister squadron, with the Squadron Commander in the front seat and a very experienced captain as the GIB. After completing the many maneuvers and system checks required by the FCF, a complete hydraulic failure occurred on their way back to base over the rough seas of the bitter cold, wintry Pacific Ocean. The aircraft flew in a slow descent, but without hydraulic pressure the pilots were unable to maneuver and were therefore left with no choice but to eject into the frigid 40° F temperature water of the North Pacific. The GIB ejected first. His parachute opened normally, but the first of many Murphy's Law incidents reared up its ugly head, when his survival raft, attached to him by a long lanyard, did not automatically inflate.

The aircraft commander then attempted to eject. The canopy jettisoned normally, but a malfunction occurred, and the usually reliable and highly regarded Martin-Baker ejection seat did not leave the aircraft. The A/C had no choice other than to un-strap himself from the ejection seat and to attempt to disembark using the World War I bailout method of climbing out over the side of the aircraft. Unfortunately, with the aircraft's speed creating a three-hundred-knot wind, this last-ditch effort to climb out of the aircraft was futile.

An incredible aberration then occurred, happily negating Murphy's Law with some highly improbable good fortune. As the A/C, Colonel Brown, settled back into his seat, he observed that through some magic of renewed liquid flow, his hydraulic pressure had returned to normal. Since he now had functional flight controls, the colonel returned to land his recently modified open-air convertible F-4 Phantom! His arrival at Misawa AFB left the ground crew in jaw-dropping astonishment as he taxied to the ramp with no canopies and no back seater!

Where *was* that back-seater? He now bobbed like a fisherman's cork in the frigid, four-to-six-foot seas of the Pacific Ocean. He wore a "poopie suit," which is an insulated, rubberized flight suit. The poopie suit was required during the winter months because it would extend an airman's longevity in 40° F water to nearly an hour. Without it, life expectancy would only last a few minutes. Since the raft did not automatically inflate, Captain Martin pulled it towards himself by the lanyard with the intention of manually inflating the raft. At this time, however, the downside of Murphy's Law reasserted itself. After the raft was nearly inflated by hand—or lungs—the CO_2 cartridge, which had previously malfunctioned, elected to activate. This additional volume of air *overinflated* the raft and it broke like a balloon, rendering it unusable—indeed, utterly destroyed.

There was, despite Captain Martin's tenuous situation, good news on the horizon. A rescue helicopter had been dispatched from Misawa AFB to search for Captain Martin. If he had been in his raft, he would be easy to spot. Unfortunately, trying to find a person in rough seas with only a head visible *is like trying to find a fly turd in a pepper shaker.* Captain Martin saw the helicopter approach him, and he attempted to activate his rescue flare. Because of now severely frostbitten fingers, he was unable to pull the activation clip, and the helicopter flew overhead without seeing him. A few minutes later the rescue helicopter returned to his area, and with his survival instinct at its peak, he put the flare in his mouth and bit off the end! This procedure activated the flare and someone in the helicopter saw him. Shortly thereafter he was pulled into the helicopter. The onboard flight surgeon (medical doctor) examined him and later stated that, if he had remained in the frigid ocean for another three to five minutes, he would most certainly have died.

Ace returned from Korea, and after hearing of this miraculous survival-rescue mission, he met up with the two fortunate FCF pilots at the Officers' Club bar. They eagerly exhibited a lot of cool regarding the incident—as if it had been just another day at the office—even though they both had cheated death by a very narrow margin. The Officers' Club was the hub of the social life at Misawa AFB. Ace could get a shot of Chivas Regal Scotch for twenty-five cents, while enjoying the companionship of the many fine young women who worked at the small base. Misawa AFB was the duty station for many nurses, Red Cross workers, civilian employees, and schoolteachers. The fact that they were located at the northern tip of Honshu Island in Japan more than indicated that these women were predisposed to boldness. They connected very well with the equally adventuresome single pilots. Once again, the anticipated Spartan austerity proved to be a seriously faulty prognostication. Not only were the parties nearly every weekend, but there was also excellent entertainment with top-quality musical groups. Moreover, since Misawa was only a two-hour train ride to excellent skiing areas, the single teachers and the single pilots would meet at the train station on Friday afternoons for weekend ski outings during the winter months.

There was, nevertheless, work to be done. The 67th Tactical Fighter Squadron was being resurrected, and its members were fortunate enough to have a world-class fighter pilot as their Squadron Commander. Colonel Gus was a low-profile amiable person—not big and imposing like Colonel Casper—and he always exhibited an affable demeanor along with a soft spoken casual cool.

On one occasion while leading a flight, he immediately disconnected his oxygen mask after take-off to smoke a cigarette on the way to the gunnery range. He then reconnected his oxygen mask and dropped bombs with extraordinary skill. He loved to make friendly bets during the pre-briefing for range missions. After the range mission scores were tabulated, he smugly collected his winnings and then spent ten times that amount buying drinks at the Officers' Club. Colonel Gus endeared himself to the GIBS by stating that the 67th was going to engage in a very progressive project to upgrade a few of the GIBS to the front seat.

Previously, the only route from the F-4 GIB position to the F-4 Aircraft Commander position was to serve a thirteen-month tour in Vietnam as a GIB. The GIB would then return stateside for a six-month training program, followed by a return to Vietnam for a mandatory second war tour. When Ace discovered this new possibility of upgrading within the squadron, he put his nose to the grindstone and chased this carrot with great enthusiasm. He immediately volunteered for additional duties while organizing and coaching squadron sports teams for the many base athletic activities. Misawa AFB had a large gymnasium with racquetball courts, swimming pool, and exercise rooms. Most military bases have excellent recreational facilities, and Misawa AFB was no exception. It also had an excellent golf course, and the fact that Ace frequently played golf with Colonel Gus may have been a contributing factor when selection for GIB upgrade occurred.

The mission of the 67th Tactical Fighter Squadron was multifaceted. It involved being current and proficient in both conventional and nuclear-weapons delivery. Occasionally, the 67th TFS provided escort for electronic surveillance missions of large unarmed aircraft. This mission required both airborne intercept skills and proficiency in refueling procedures. The primary design of the F-4 was that of a fighter/interceptor and its onboard radar could find an enemy aircraft at a distance of more than thirty miles. Combined with these skills, it was also necessary to be proficient in aerial-combat tactics in the unlikely event of an encounter with enemy aircraft. Unfortunately, this interesting and challenging flying was interrupted by frequent trips to Korea to engage in the dastardly duty of sitting nuclear alert.

The job satisfaction one derives from service time in the role of a nuclear-alert pilot is somewhere between negligible and nonexistent. Anyone who might get enthused about dropping a nuclear bomb would have to be seriously demented. Every few days the klaxon (loud horn) would sound, at which time the pilots expedited themselves to their assigned aircraft, started their engines, and waited patiently for the coded message. After the message was decoded, revealing that this was just another practice alert, everyone breathed a sigh of relief and returned to the barracks to continue the poker game. Despite this boring routine, everyone was aware that the assigned task of dropping a nuclear weapon into an area of dense population is very sobering. Miraculously, it has only happened twice—on Hiroshima and Nagasaki.

Likewise, most of the targets of nuclear-bomb flights were such a long distance away that after weapon release there might be only thirty or forty minutes of fuel remaining. Consequently, the flight crew would run out of fuel and have to bail out over enemy territory. Not exactly a nice day at the office. Amongst the few highlights during the boring days of alert, Ace heard a report of one young airman toking on a "joint" while towing an F-4

Phantom equipped with a nuclear weapon. In the late 1960s the popularity of marijuana extended from the Haight-Ashbury district in San Francisco all the way to South Korea, and "grass" was reported to have been readily available in Vietnam—an understatement, for sure.

Another interesting feature of the USA umbrella of nuclear deterrence was what appeared to be an inadvertent duplication of targets. Just before Ace left Korea, a group of high-ranking Navy intelligence officers visited Kunsan AFB with the purpose of comparing and evaluating assigned targets. The findings were somewhat startling, since they revealed that both the Navy, with its nuclear-missile-equipped Polaris submarines, and the Air Force were tasked to bomb the same targets! Perhaps this *was* an oversight—perhaps not. It was hard *not* to ask, especially in the late '60s, "What are these guys smoking?"

The drudgery and the seriousness of the nuclear-alert detail balanced itself with some very interesting flying in Korea. The 67th TFS also had a mission that involved aircraft stationed at another air base near Taegu, Korea. Taegu was in central Korea, located just a few miles from an Army base adjacent to a relatively large city. Although the Taegu Air Force Base had very antiquated facilities, there was not an alert commitment at Taegu as there was in Kunsan. This allowed Ace and his fellow pilots to leave the base to explore the local culture and to purchase many of the items of convenience and consumption typically available only in larger cities. Many of the GIs who served in Korea became so enthralled with the virtues of Korean women that they married them, and upon completion of their tour of duty, they brought their new wives back to the U.S. In fact, forty years later, a number of young women from Korea displayed exceptional character and a stoic work ethic by dominating the LPGA golf tour in the United States.

The 67th TFS pilots spent approximately half of their time in Japan at Misawa AFB and the other half in Korea at Taegu AFB and Kunsan AFB. After two weeks in Korea, the advanced creature comforts and the feminine companionship available at Misawa AFB was always a pleasant change. Friday afternoon happy hours at the Officers' Club were filled with good times, including some very simple—even childish—pleasures. The civilian game of "dead-bug" was renamed "SAM break." The concept was quite simple. When someone would shout out, "SAM break!" the last person to be on the floor in a prone position, would have to buy the next round of drinks. SAM is the acronym for surface-to-air missile. The schoolteachers, nurses, officers' wives, and other women in the bar were included in this game. Other fun-loving, youthful endeavors involved drinking "afterburners"—flame-covered shots of brandy ingested in such a fashion that excellent eye-hand coordination was required to avoid being burned. Only the highly skilled were capable of successfully performing this meaningless feat. Even the high-ranking officers would engage in this activity, and their non-participating colleagues would enjoy seeing them in the staff meeting on Monday with burns on their mouths and chins.

The first six months at Misawa were filled with interesting and unique experiences. Airplanes were ferried from various bases in Vietnam, and occasionally the 67th TFS pilots would go to Vietnam to pick up the older war-torn F-4C aircraft to bring them back to Misawa. The pilots in Vietnam were upgrading to the more advanced F-4D aircraft. Ace was lucky enough to have two of these assignments. His first venture involved catching military flights, or as they were called in the military vernacular, "hops." Hops could take as long as forty-eight hours to reach the massive joint forces base at Cam Ranh Bay, where pilots engaged in recreational activities that included waterskiing, fishing, and surfing in an environment that was truly Club Med-like—punctuated with live combat.

Numerous commercial flights shuttled the troops in and out of the war zone as well. The flight crews of the commercial carriers had extended layovers, and the young flight attendants, adventurous by nature, would seek the companionship of the war-hero fighter pilots. Each fighter squadron had its own area which included a "party hooch," where steak and lobster were served and live bands played rock 'n roll music—all accompanied with top shelf, ridiculously inexpensive, alcoholic beverages. The nurses and "doughnut dollies" (female Red Cross workers) assigned to Cam Ranh Bay were forced to compete with the transient flight attendants for the attention and affection of the large cadre of single pilots. While this sounds like an idyllic life for these warrior pilots, there was a small catch. These seemingly carefree pilot-party animals would engage in dangerous combat missions every day. Ace and his

Aircraft Commander would fly their war-torn, battered F-4Cs back to Japan, where Ace and his A/C, would not have to worry about being shot down. Of the 2,060 F-4 Phantoms made by McDonnell-Douglas for the United States military, more than 200 were destroyed in the Vietnam War. Based on the number of missions flown, the attrition rate was relatively low. Some of the helicopter missions resulted in attrition rates as high as fifty percent—fifty helicopters launched in the morning and twenty-five returned that afternoon! In most cases, even though the helicopter was shot down, their copter colleagues rescued the downed pilots since they usually flew in large groups, often referred to as "gaggles." There are numerous reports of the same helicopter pilots getting shot down on consecutive days!

There were occasional flights to Okinawa and to Clark Air Force Base in the Philippines, the latter considered one of the great oasis-garden spots in the world for military personnel. A refueling stop for many aircraft prior to their destination in Vietnam, Clark AFB hosted the dreaded jungle-survival school, also referred to as "snake school." Snake school was required before one could be a combat pilot in Vietnam. One of the most mind-boggling survival stories of all-time was that of Navy Lt. Dieter Dengler, who escaped from the North Vietnamese and traveled through the treacherous and pathless jungles for months until he finally reached friendly forces. He reported that he was so weak from malnourishment that he did not have the strength to walk. As he crawled on his stomach through the jungle, he came across a piece of rotted, maggot-infested meat that he immediately consumed. This tiny morsel of food, odd as it sounds, gave him the strength to continue. His escape and evasion adventure is testimony to the intense survival instinct of the human animal. A movie of his amazing escape from imprisonment was made in 2006. The name of the movie is *Rescue Dawn*, starring Christian Bale as Lt. Dengler.

Other interesting side trips involved flights to "IRAN." Ace sauntered over to the squadron scheduling board one morning, immediately entering into a state of shocked disbelief when he observed that he was scheduled to go with Major Houghton to "IRAN." Ace had never been to the Middle East, and he was quite disturbed by this pending venture, convinced, in fact, that he did not want to go there. Fortunately, a bit of research revealed that IRAN was not the country of destination but rather an acronym for Inspect and Repair as Necessary! The *actual* destination of this venture would take him to Tainan, Taiwan. The U.S. Air Force had contracted with the Taiwanese government to do an extensive maintenance procedure on its F-4 Phantoms. The aircraft had to be left there for several days, so Major Houghton and his obedient GIB, Ace, caught a flight to the opposite end of the island to visit the capital city of Taipei. Taipei was one of the most popular R&R (rest and recuperation) locations for the American GIs when they took their break from the murderous jungles of Viet Nam. The hospitality extended to the American GI was exceptional because the U.S. dollar, or the military currency (MPC), would go a long way. This hedonistic vacation at IRAN was just the opposite of what Ace had anticipated when he had first observed that he was scheduled to fly to IRAN. In the future, he would volunteer for all of the IRAN trips!

Meanwhile, back at Misawa AFB, *it was summertime and the living was easy.* Needless to say, Ace involved himself in many joyful, warm-weather endeavors, including pleasant interaction with the congenial schoolteachers and outdoor activities such as playing golf with the Colonel and his friends. Occasionally, Ace would be required to jump into the back seat of the F-4 to go for various joy rides around northern Japan. He continued to refine his GIB skills and worked hard to learn as much as possible about the F-4 Phantom in order to be prepared for any contingency—like getting upgraded to the front seat. Ace was still happy in the backseat, but most pilots want to be the captain (aircraft commander), and he was no exception.

Finally, in early September, the Squadron Commander, Colonel Gus, and the squadron instructor pilots announced they were ready to start upgrading GIBs to the front seat. Ace was selected to be the first GIB to begin upgrade training. This was the ultimate "brass ring" since Ace could become an aircraft commander in the F-4 without having to jump through the many hoops that were normally required. Upgrading within the squadron allowed Ace to become the youngest ranking F-4 Phantom aircraft commander in the U.S. Air Force. He became a skillful bomb dropper and attained squadron-level "top gun" status. He was then promoted to flight-lead status, occasionally assigned the responsibility of leading a flight of four

Phantoms to the gunnery range, and/or to rendezvous with the KC-135 tanker for refueling missions.

"FILL 'ER UP AND DO THE WINDOWS"

BACK TO THE BOOM FOR MORE BATTERING

A refueling mission may sound ordinary or routine; however, even in the best of circumstances, the mission could provoke a challenge. Occasionally, the refueling rendezvous with the KC-135 tanker took place in the clouds with the actual visibility being only a few hundred feet. The procedure involved getting a radar lock-on with the tanker and approaching the tanker from the rear and reducing the overtake speed until the receiver aircraft (the flight of four Phantoms) could gain a "visual" on the tanker. If the tanker aircraft was not visible when it reached 1/16 of a mile on the radar scope, a breakaway procedure would be implemented.

Once the rejoin procedure with the tanker had been completed, the lead F-4 moved into the refueling envelope, while the other three Phantoms would fly formation with reference to the wing tip of the KC-135. This was followed by a little airborne dance as the F-4s would move from tanker boom to wing tip formation. The tanker boom operator maneuvered his boom in order to "plug" the Phantom. The refueling receptacle in the F-4 was right behind the GIB cockpit, and the KC-135 boom operators frequently exhibited their skill by giving the F-4 pilots a playful bump on the canopy as the F-4 moved into the refueling envelope.

Ace had difficulty in erasing the memory of his initial, disastrous airborne refueling mission; accordingly, he experienced acute anxiety whenever he approached the tanker. The anxiety intensified ten-fold during a night refueling in the clouds, resulting in a severe case of vertigo for Ace. During the refueling operation, the tanker flies a racetrack pattern in which the KC-135 tanker goes from straight and level flight to a thirty-degree banked turn for a full 180 degrees of turn. This procedure would often induce vertigo because the pilot's inner-ear information to the brain and the actual flight attitude differed significantly. Another unfortunately unforgettable aviation moment occurred when, somewhere over the Sea of Japan, Ace's F-4 Phantom was connected to the boom while in IMC (instrument meteorological conditions), resulting in severe vertigo. Ace's inner-ear told him that he was in a forty-five degree, nose-low dive and *inverted*. He suffered severe emotional turmoil and significant dismay as a result. Then, a peripheral glance at the attitude indicator revealed that the aircraft was in level flight. Nonetheless, despite this updated and corrected information, the sensation of being inverted in a forty-five degree, nose-low attitude persisted. Ace applied the basic aviator discipline of trusting his instruments, but his personal angst meter was pegged off the scale. As the blood pressure skyrocketed and the pulse raced, Ace's body was in a state of near rigor mortis until this vertigo monster was finally slain!

Severe vertigo has resulted in hundreds, if not thousands, of aircraft accidents. When a pilot is afflicted with vertigo, the old aviator cliché, "Get on them gauges!" is the *only* solution. Unlike the pilot's erroneous bodily sensations, the instruments can be trusted. Ace had one other stressful encounter on the tanker, when, during a night refueling, the boom operator was either terribly inexperienced or engaging in OJT (on-the-job training). The tanker's boom operator took an inordinate amount of time to connect the boom to the receptacle, and Ace was approaching a very low fuel state. With not a moment to spare, the boomer finally plugged in and the refueling was accomplished.

Other than the always-exciting refueling missions, Ace had only a handful of serious stress situations. One of these involved an engine fire on a night-intercept mission. Fortunately, the usual procedure of shutting down the engine extinguished the fire, and Ace returned to base for an uneventful single-engine landing. The Phantom was designed for the Navy and was equipped with a tail hook. Ace never had the opportunity to land on an aircraft carrier, but he did get to use his tail hook for two "arrested" landings. Most military runways have what is referred to as the "wire" or "cable," allowing for an arrested landing utilized during certain aircraft malfunctions.

Ace's first arrested landing took place during a heavy snowstorm at Misawa AFB, resulting in a braking action called "nil." Nil is a military code word for "nothing" or perhaps "too slippery to even walk on." Decelerating from 180 miles an hour to a dead stop in two seconds within the range of only a few hundred feet proved to be quite an experience, as the inertial-reel shoulder harness demonstrated its life saving capabilities. Ace's second arrested landing occurred on Taegu Air Force Base in Korea. The U.S. had given the Korean Air Force a number of antiquated airplanes, and on this particular day a WWII vintage C-46 sat incapacitated halfway down the runway with its landing gear collapsed. Ace, returning to base with minimum fuel and with the old junk C-46 aircraft blocking the runway, had no other course of action but to complete an arrested landing.

These arrested landings on stable concrete were like a walk in the park relative to what might be the most challenging endeavor in aviation: the nighttime carrier landing. The skill and the intense focus required for this event is nearly incomparable, and the thrill of this unique and demanding endeavor is only available to Navy and Marine pilots who are "carrier qualified." The arrested landings increased Ace's respect for the Navy and Marine pilots and also gave him a hands-on demonstration of the effectiveness of the inertial-reel shoulder harness.

PHANTOM FLY-BY FOULS GENERALS' EGGS BENEDICT

Ace had one other opportunity to extend the tail hook of his F-4 Phantom. This occurred during an unsolicited and unwanted fly-by at the nearby Army base. On a slow Sunday morning at Taegu, Ace was given an F-4 Phantom to take for a joyride around the South Korean Peninsula. After he and his GIB got bored doing loops and rolls, they headed for the seacoast to terrorize the fishermen aboard their prehistoric, Chinese "junk-style" boats. It was impossible, unfortunately, to observe their reactions when this alien-monster airplane invaded their space, but the "shock and awe" most likely produced a plethora of Korean-language obscenities. At about ten feet above the water, the Phantom created a "rooster tail" in the water and this, along with the high pitched screaming of the Pratt and Whitney J-79 engines, very likely created a temporary sense of intense peril for the surprised fishermen. Ace never did kill anyone with his Phantom, but he may have scared a lot of people "nearly to death." After treating the Korean fishermen to a free air show, Ace and his GIB continued their low-level fun and games before they headed inland to do simulated strafing runs on trains and trucks.

During this devil-may-care rampage, Ace got zapped with a quick shot of adrenalin as a large antenna flashed by the left wing tip. In the event of an actual collision, it is quite likely that the antenna would have been credited with a kill, as the disabled Phantom plummeted to the ground where it would have created a large crater. This particular mass of steel, in actuality a TV-broadcast antenna, stood some one thousand feet tall. If Ace's aircraft had collided with this large structure, a massive, nationwide TV blackout across South Korea would have been the most probable side effect. After Ace recovered from this heart-stopping near miss, it was time to head home to Taegu AFB.

The route back to Taegu went directly over the Army base. Ace, ever the adventurous, rogue aviator, now had a sudden urge to provide the Army generals and their wives with a little variety to complement their Sunday brunch at the Officers' Club. His low-level fly-by was executed as a low approach down the 3,000-foot-long utility runway at the Army base. His intruding aircraft had its landing gear, flaps, and tail hook extended, and this imposing sight, accompanied by 120+ decibels of roaring jet engines, elicited—Ace learned shortly thereafter—an immediate call to Taegu Air Force Base. When Ace landed and returned to the squadron, the squadron operations officer, Colonel Don, who attempted to do his best imitation of an angry supervisor, greeted him. The colonel's expression varied between a scowl and a smirk—at the same time. As he faked his best tough-guy-stern-reprimand voice, he said, "Ace, you got caught red-handed! You were flying the only Phantom that was airborne." The tongue-in-cheek chastising continued as the colonel blandly expressed some mild anger, finishing the wet-noodle tongue lashing with an edict, "Don't do any more unsolicited air shows!" Ace is near certain that Colonel Don was envious because he had not mustered the gumption himself to give the "grunts" a little pizzazz in their boring Army regimentation.

A few days later, Ace, returning from the gunnery range with an entourage of four Phantoms, encountered a flight of F-106 aircraft engaging in a friendly dog-fight scenario with four F-100 National Guard aircraft. Ace's flight lead then engaged the four Phantoms in this playful "I'm on your six o'clock and could kill you" game of tag. This boondoggling, goat-roping escapade resulted in a dozen aircraft in a relatively small area of airspace engaged in unauthorized dog-fight pilot games without pre-briefing, providing nevertheless very good training and a lot of fun; on the flip side, had the generals back at PACAF Headquarters at Hickam AFB gotten wind of the adventure high in the sky, who knows how many would have lost their flying credentials. The reprimand certainly would have been significantly more severe than the one Ace received from Colonel Don.

This outrageous bit of playfulness was nearly trumped when Major Gene led a flight back to Taegu AFB after a gunnery-range mission. Major Gene decided to engage in some Thunderbird-training maneuvers when he put the flight of four Phantoms into close trail, initiating a vertical climb with the intent to perform a loop. However, the Phantoms had several drag-inducing, weapons-paraphernalia devices hanging from their wings. To make matters worse, the major initiated the maneuver about 100 knots *below* the necessary speed required for an "over the top" move. Ace flew in the number three position, and as the four floundering Phantoms became nearly vertical, he observed the airspeed disastrously decreasing below 100 knots. That ended the maneuver because all four Phantoms then became uncontrollable ballistic devices while doing the "tail slide" maneuver until the nose fell below the horizon and the pilots could regain control of their air machines. About twenty seconds later, after each airplane had recovered from its out-of-control, modified *Lomechavak,* tail-slide, free fall the flight lead announced his position and barked orders to "join up!"

PHANTOM PREDATORS SEARCHING FOR PREY

In yet another near disaster, a 67th TFS aircraft on a low-level training flight declared an emergency as a result of a bird-strike. After the aircraft was inspected by maintenance, it was revealed that both engines had been broken away from the engine mounts. In this incident, the pilot had elected to void the normal 500-foot AGL (above ground level) altitude restriction prescribed for low-level training missions in order to do some wave running over the Sea of Japan. At a stomach-churning altitude of only a few feet, a rapid control-stick input pushed the aft of the aircraft into the water. The aircraft, luckily, bounced off the water. The pilots immediately reported to air traffic control that they had experienced a bird strike—a bit of fast-thinking CYA (cover-your-ass). During a base-wide flight safety meeting a few days later, the wing commander discussed this incident and suggested that, based on his assessment of the severe damage to the aircraft, if the scenario actually involved a bird strike, "it must have been a flock of pterodactyls." In peacetime this incident might have cost the pilot his wings. Since there was a war going on, the issue resulted in only a mild and jocular scolding from the wing commander.

The 67th TFS was very transient with its multiple missions, and it was rare for pilots to remain any more than a few weeks at the permanent duty station at Misawa. There were occasional requirements to fly aircraft to Yokota AFB in the Tokyo area. On one particular trip to Yokota, Mt. Fuji was so close that Ace couldn't resist the temptation to descend to a very low altitude in order to ascend at treetop level from the base of the mountain to the always snow-covered peak in about five seconds at 450 knots and fifty feet AGL. The flight continued over the crater in the inverted position, which provided the pilots a better view of the awe-struck crater occupants, and facilitated the low-level run down the opposite side of the mountain. The many Japanese people camping in the crater at the top of Mt. Fuji might— even today—still harbor displeasure over this incident. All things considered, it had been only a little more than twenty years since American airplanes had devastated Japan, and the American flyboys seemingly did not show much sensitivity regarding this issue.

Occasionally, American pilots would experience an accidental, practice-bomb release that landed outside the confines of the gunnery range. Although it was a small, inert bomb, an off-range release would create great angst amongst the local inhabitants. While drinking hot sake with the very socially gracious Japanese skiers, someone would occasionally reveal his identity as an American *"sojushi"* (pilot). This would elicit an often-used Japanese expression of anguish that involves noisily sucking in air while inhaling deeply. This unmistakable body language would be followed by the words, "atom bomb" and *"taksan dame"* (Japanese for very bad). Eventually, the American pilots prudently decided to identify themselves as "businessmen" since it was evident that the image of horrific destruction by American airplanes was all too fresh in the memory of the Japanese people.

Life as a non-combat fighter pilot was getting better all the time. One of the many available schoolteachers determined that Ace qualified as good breeding stock and she selected him to become her husband. The honeymoon in Hong Kong later revealed that Ace had himself opted in favor of good breeding stock. He and his very fertile new bride returned to Japan with "one in the hangar." They purchased a new house quite close to the base for the paltry sum of $3500, and nine months later along came a fine young son. With the exception of the all-too-frequent TDY (temporary duty) assignments to Korea, Ace enjoyed his newfound family life and, with the U.S. dollar garnering 360 Japanese yen, he and his family lived large. But then came the realization that Ace had maintained his Viet Nam war volunteer status!

With a little over six months of his Air Force service commitment remaining, Ace received notification to report to the base personnel office to evaluate his career-progression possibilities. He learned that the Air Force would now allow him to be assigned to a combat tour in Southeast Asia. The Air Force also offered a career-promotion incentive: to change his status from reserve officer to regular officer. This would enhance his résumé, improving his chances for more rapid career progress. The personnel officer additionally informed Ace that, before he went to Vietnam, he would be required to serve a thirteen-month unaccompanied (without family) tour in Korea. Ace had gained great insight into the ugly reality of the Vietnam War as a result of many discussions with veteran Vietnam pilots. The consensus was that the war was micromanaged—micro-mismanaged, actually—from the Pentagon and the White House, resulting in the unnecessary deaths of many American aviators. This knowledge, along with a strong desire not to be separated from his wife and son, created a completely different perspective on war than what Ace had held a few years earlier. Ace's warrior instincts had waned. He politely requested the appropriate paperwork to formulate a date of separation (DOS).

As Ace rapidly approached his DOS, he became FIGMO (F_ it! I Got My Orders). The multitudes of military acronyms can become overwhelming, but the FIGMO term had a refreshing flair to it. Now back to FIGMO Captain Ace. He and his wife had accumulated just enough traffic violations to generate a written request from the captain in charge of the base driver education-training program to invite Ace to attend remedial driver's school. The letter to Captain Ace informed him that, according to AFM 54-33, he would be required to attend one week of remedial driver-education training. Ace felt that any disruption of his flying duties for one week would prove counterproductive for both him and for the U.S. Air Force.

Since a personal, severely biased evaluation of his own driving skills determined that he was an excellent driver, Ace elected to send a return letter to the driver-education captain, expressing Ace's perspective regarding the mandated driver-training course. However, his judgment warped by his rapidly approaching DOS, he went into a lengthy rant, explaining in detail the many reasons why he was such an excellent driver. He wrote that his only weakness as a driver was his failure properly to check his "six o'clock" position for the harassing Air Police. The final sentence of his letter of response stated, "Would you please take my spot for remedial driver-education in accordance with Air Force manual 54-33 and cram it?" Proud of his creative writing, Ace showed the letter to his pilot colleagues, including his squadron commander. Everyone got a good laugh out of it, but no one thought he would actually send it. Ace thought it might also get a good laugh at driver-education school. With no thoughts or concerns about possible repercussions, he sent the letter

Only a few days later, the repercussions of his words did elicit a response: Ace was called in to visit the squadron commander. The captain of the driver's education program did not find the letter in any way humorous. Ace was informed that a simple letter of apology would put this matter to an end. However, Ace had now fallen into a very advanced state of FIGMO, and, when he wrote the letter of apology, it was very clear that if one were to read between the lines, one could decipher that there was an additional message that said, "Screw you and your AFM 54-33!" Ace once again immersed himself egotistically and joyfully in his creative writing; nevertheless, the driver-training captain very astutely *did* read between the lines. The captain took the letter to the base commander, who dropped the "big hammer" on Ace. Ace's Air Force career was effectively finished. He would never again strap into that fabulous Phantom for another exhilarating flight. He would now sit grounded for the last month of his career, and he would be assigned to duty as a range officer in Korea. His extraordinary demonstration of hubris was the final straw.

PICK ONE—ALCATRAZ OR THE KIMSHI ROCK

The Koon-Ni gunnery-range lay in a remote location of Korea—a large rock surrounded by water. The range officer spent the day sitting in a small glass-enclosed building with his Korean helpers. The range-officer helpers would determine where a bomb had landed in relationship to the target. They then passed that information on to the range officer, who then relayed to the pilots the location of each bomb in relation to the target. Koon-Ni gunnery range, a cold, bleak environment, will always be remembered negatively since two of Ace's pilot colleagues were killed there during a night dive-bombing mission. Dropping bombs at night from a forty-five-degree dive angle requires intense awareness, particularly over water, because the pilot's depth perception is distorted. The use of visual references alone will often create a false sense of the actual distance to the surface.

Apparently, a split-second delay in initiating the recovery pull-up caused the aircraft to enter the water at a very high rate of speed. Ace and his flight of Phantoms checked in on the gunnery-range radio frequency just a few minutes after the accident occurred. The range officer announced that the range was closed since there had been a crash. The blunt, numbing knowledge that two of Ace's good friends, with whom he had laughed and joked with a couple of hours earlier at the squadron briefing room, just had their bodies splattered into oblivion, was a heart-wrenching, somber experience. The camaraderie that evolves in a fighter squadron is an inexpressible experience, and only a small percentage of people ever get even close to such a tight-knit work environment.

It was a bittersweet day in Mid-March of 1971 when Ace and his family bundled up their belongings and departed Misawa AFB. Despite the many wonderful relationships and exhilarating aviation experiences, it was time to move on. The normal career progression usually required the Air Force pilot eventually to transition into staff or office jobs. Ace, however, wanted no part of flying a desk for an extended period of time. It was difficult leaving after nearly four years at Misawa. Many wonderful people and close friends were left behind as Ace and his family headed for the "hard, cruel civilian world."

The quality of people with whom Ace had worked—measured in terms of accountability, responsibility, ethics, and integrity—stood solidly at an infinitely higher level than the norm in the civilian world. It is very clear to military personnel that they are an integral part of the whole, and this perspective will usually result in people who dedicate themselves to the highest possible level of job performance. The flight lead of the Thunderbirds or the Blue Angels, for instance, does not have the option of going half speed or being lackadaisical during his group's aerial demonstration. He *must* be totally prepared and committed. When hiring, most employers will wisely give the ex-military person the nod over those who have not served in the military. The unfortunate other side of the coin is that government bungling and Pentagon malfeasance have resulted, particularly in the last fifty years, in far too many dedicated military people dying unnecessarily.

THE LAST LOOK BEFORE DISCHARGE

THE "FIGHTER MAN" SONG

On a rainy, Sunday afternoon, while on TDY in the early 1970s to Aviano, Italy, a group of 91st TFS Fighter Jocks sat around the Officers Club bar commiserating (as was their habit). Among the topics discussed was the ignoble fate suffered by certain airmen returning from the Vietnam War. These unfortunate souls, whose only crime was to forget that they were no longer in a combat zone, often had a difficult time readjusting to the peacetime "rules" after being "wound up" for a combat tour. Those returning to Air Training Command had to make the greatest adjustment—and suffered the greatest punishments. The following story is about no one officer in particular but is a collage of the many stories swapped that afternoon.

One day while I was in pilot training…
and it was cold and raining,
We'd given up flying for the day, and headed for the bar.
We'd been there 'bout a half an hour…
when out of the cold, dark shower
Came a Fighter Man…You got to understand.

You'll always know it when you see one…'
cause not everyone can be one.
Though his flight suit he had torn it…
you could tell that he had worn it
Into combat, just like armor,
on innumerable occasions, cause…
He was a Fighter Man…You got to understand.

CHORUS:
You got to get your act together, Mr. Fighter Man…
Polish your teeth, get your tan,
Line up your "tickets," Mr. Fighter Man…
Better be "9s" or you won't make it on time!

His skin was wrinkled…
and his hair was slightly grayin'
As he picked up the dice cup and
he asked someone to play him.

It was then that his patch showed forth…
"200 Missions North"
In the 105…My God how'd you stay alive?

We'd played about an hour when
the Colonel kicked him out.
He said, "You're a disgrace to all those who wear the
BLUE…
From now on I'll be devoted to ensure you're not
promoted…
For starting that gamblin' game…tell me now,
what's your name?"

CHORUS:
You got to get your act together, Mr. Fighter Man…
Polish your teeth, get your tan,
Line up your "tickets," Mr. Fighter Man…
Better be "9s" or you won't make it on time!

It was not 'till some months later that I heard they'd
kicked him out.
His wife had gone and left him, after messin' him about.
He had the Air Force Cross, three Silver Stars…
and the DFCs hung to his knees,
But we didn't need him no more…we were out of the war!

The other day I saw him pumpin' gas in Philadelphia.
Stuck his head into my window,
and said, "Yes sir, may I help you?"
As I left that station cryin', I said there's no denyin'
There goes a Fighter Man…You got to understand.

FINAL CHORUS:

You got to get your act together, Mr. Fighter Man...
Polish your teeth, get your tan,
Line up your "tickets," Mr. Fighter Man...
Better be "9s" or you won't make it on time!

You didn't get your act together, Mr. Fighter Man,
Didn't polish your teeth...didn't get your tan.
You didn't line up your "tickets," Mr. Fighter Man.
They weren't all 9s...you didn't make it on time.

Thanks for your war...we don't need you no more.

CHAPTER FOUR

Cavorting About In the Learjet with the Rich and Famous

After three and one-half years of living in Japan and Korea in the relatively sterile, homogeneous environment of the military, Ace returned to the U.S., where he was greeted by a significantly changed and alien world. After a brief look at this profoundly different civilian culture, he attempted to return to the comfortable, structured life of the Air Force. He presented this proposal to an Air Force recruiter and was sharply informed that, "When you make your decision to leave the Air Force, there are no "do-overs." Ace then decided that playing golf might be a great way to make a living.

During his Air Force days, Ace had plenty of free time for golf and had developed a fairly good game. His extraordinary success as an Air Force pilot was primarily the result of being in the right place at the right time. But that success irrationally led Ace to harbor the delusion that he could climb any mountain. Therefore, his new plan was very simple: to work real hard on his golf game and then to go play on the PGA Tour! As the author Tom Robbins so aptly stated in his book *Even Cowgirls get the Blues,* "Fantasy is the deodorant in the shithouse of reality." Ace's PGA tour aspirations validated the truthfulness of this premise.

Phase one of preparations for the PGA Tour involved caddying in the 1971 PGA qualifying tournament. After six days of caddying and observing the level of play by aspiring rookies, Ace re-evaluated his golfing skills and abandoned his golf-pro pipe dream. On the first day after "Q" (qualifying) school, Ace got up real early and headed to the airport to seek employment doing something that he knew how to do: flying airplanes. He had settled in South Florida to pursue a golf career; as it turned out, he accidentally located himself in what proved to be a hotbed of aviation jobs.

While on a job-hunting search in Miami, Ace discovered the Burnside-Ott Aviation Training Center, a facility that provided Learjet training. This training could be paid for by the GI Bill, which Ace was eligible to receive. Ace enrolled in the training program and a few weeks later the instructor pilot arranged for an FAA examiner to administer a Learjet-type-rating-check ride for Ace. The program called for twelve hours of instruction, but Ace was only able to pay for eight hours of instruction, since he had previously used some of his GI-Bill funds. By now Ace had not flown in nearly a year, and his pilot skills were quite rusty. He did, however, manage to "ham-hand" this Learjet air machine well enough that the gracious FAA examiner, Mr. Chuck Smith, very benevolently credited Ace with a passed check ride. Ace now held a Learjet-type rating. Although the type-rating status qualified him to be a captain on a Learjet, Ace accumulated several hundred hours as copilot before he started flying the Learjet with the rank of captain.

With this new rating on his airman's certificate and a fresh résumé, Ace began his search for employment as a pilot. He was soon hired by World Aviation as a copilot for a Learjet charter operation with a salary at the paltry sum of $700 a month. World aviation had a time-share arrangement with the owner of the Learjet, Mr. George Weasel. World provided pilot services and maintenance for Mr. Weasel and then used the aircraft to fly charter trips when the owner was not using the aircraft. Mr. Weasel was also a pilot and he would often fly in the left seat, while the actual pilot-in-command (PIC) sat in the right seat. This was quite common in South Florida during this period of time since there were many wealthy people who owned Learjets. Many owners, in fact, had obtained a pilot's license and a few hundred hours of flight time to be able to impress their Palm Beach cronies by flying in the left seat of their own Learjet. Meanwhile, the experienced captain sitting in the right seat (who was technically and legally the pilot-in-command), would be fully engaged in a stringent oversight process: keeping the "boss" from crashing the aircraft while using "kid gloves" to avoid damaging his ego. The owner of the World Aviation Learjet was a relatively competent pilot and an extremely competent farmer and entrepreneur. A brilliant but eccentric millionaire, Mr. Weasel had made a small fortune as a radish farmer—the only radish farmer in the world who owned and flew his own private Learjet.

Unfortunately, he was unable to achieve his instrument rating, and an FAA rule change eventually prohibited him from flying his own aircraft.

CIVILIAN CAREER STARTS
WITH HARROWING WAR STORIES

Shortly after World Aviation hired him, Ace received a two a.m. phone call requesting that he report to the airport ASAP for an immediate departure to Atlanta. Mr. Weasel, the aircraft owner, had incurred someone's wrath regarding a $100-bill tip that he had left for the nice Waffle House waitress, and the ruckus resulted in intervention by the local police. Apparently, an alert and larcenous customer claimed the C-note for himself. Mr. Weasel's response was such that law enforcement intervention became necessary, and that precipitated a rescue mission flown by Captain Bob and his rookie copilot, Ace. Unfortunately, Ace had just gone to bed after a libation-assisted night of socialization. As a consequence, he was relegated to the simple task of talking to the air traffic controllers. Clearly hung over, Ace had never before flown in to the Atlanta airport. Although the flight itself went without incident, the ground trip, after landing, turned into an ordeal. Ace could only observe, through his blurred vision, a maze of what seemed like thousands of fuzzy-blue, taxiway lights that created a maze of confusion. Eventually, after numerous wrong turns and many miles of taxiing, Bob and Ace arrived at the appropriate FBO (fixed base operator/private terminal).

Unfamiliar airports at night can turn an uneventful flight into a very challenging situation. It is quite common for the controllers to issue a lengthy taxi clearance very rapidly, and, since the controller must maintain a steady flow of taxi instructions to other aircraft, it is imperative that the pilots hear and understand the clearance, since there is often no time for a repeat. The most-often-heard phrase in the cockpit is, "What did he say?" The JFK International Airport taxiing scenario, for instance, can be overwhelming, particularly for the foreign pilot whose English-speaking capability is largely confined to aviation terminology. It is not uncommon for a brief misunderstanding of taxi instructions to result in two aircraft reaching a nose-to-nose stalemate on a taxiway at JFK. Chicago's O'Hare Airport makes use of a "penalty box" that might be used in the event of aircrew confusion on the ground.

It was only a short time later when Captain Bob and Ace experienced yet *another* out-of-the-ordinary encounter with the nuances of runway and taxiway lighting. This situation involved a night landing on a relatively short runway (5,000 feet) at Newcastle, Pennsylvania. The challenges of landing on a short runway at night and at an unfamiliar airport require particular caution. The approach came from the south in VFR (visual flight rules) weather, permitting the execution of a straight-in approach. Captain Bob served as an ex-Marine aircraft carrier pilot; therefore, firm landings at the end of the runway were easy for him. He touched the aircraft down in the first 500 feet of the runway, performed relatively moderate braking, and increased to maximum braking. It appeared that the aircraft approached the end of the runway with so much speed that it would not be possible to stop the airplane on the hard surface. Going off the end of the runway is rarely fatal but always embarrassing for the pilots.

As the adrenaline flow and hyperventilation were reaching a crescendo, a split second later the aircraft arrived at the crest of a hill, and the remaining 2,500 feet of the runway came into view. The two pilots, with their "pucker meter" pegged, stared incredulously, at the bright lights of the remaining half mile of runway. The first half of the runway had a significant uphill slope and the second half was significantly downhill. The crowned runway had created an illusion, which had then created considerable concern in the cockpit regarding stopping the aircraft on the runway since the pilots could only view the first half of the runway. The positive side of this adrenaline pumping experience was learning that a Learjet can be landed on a 3,000 foot runway. Later in his career while flying as Captain, Ace had several opportunities to actually land the Learjet on 3,000 foot runways.

After only a few uneventful flights, Ace then returned to another adrenaline-pumping aviation experience when he encountered the first of many low-fuel-remaining episodes on a flight from Costa Rica to Grand Cayman. This frightful flight that nearly ended with a water landing just off the coast of Jamaica started in San Jose, Costa Rica. A few days earlier, a major earthquake had hit Nicaragua. Out of interest, the passengers of the chartered Learjet requested a low-level flight over Managua, Nicaragua's capital, to view the damage. The extra fuel burn resulting from the low-level diversion necessitated a fuel stop at Grand Cayman before proceeding on to Florida. Amongst the passengers was a private pilot, who wanted to experience the thrill of briefly playing the role of a jet pilot by sitting in the right seat of a Learjet. At Captain Bob's request Ace relinquished his copilot's chair and sat in the cabin while Captain Bob entertained the passenger in the cockpit. This exchange resulted in distracting Captain Bob to the point that he neglected to pay close attention to his navigation. In short time there was serious concern in the cockpit regarding the actual location of the aircraft.

The only navigation aid at Grand Cayman was the near-prehistoric ADF (automatic direction finder) radio beacon, which normally would not have been a problem since this area of the Caribbean is usually blessed with weather colloquially described as "severe clear." The island could usually be seen from nearly one hundred miles away. On this day, however, it was solid overcast. Captain Bob, busily entertaining his new copilot, didn't observe that the ADF signal was invalid. As the low-level fuel light illuminated, Ace returned to the cockpit. Since the location of Grand Cayman was now an unknown, the only course of action was to find another airport. Cuba lay reasonably close, but the Cubans possessed Russian-made MIG fighter jets. It had been only a decade since the Bay of Pigs incident, and anything American was not welcome by Fidel Castro. Thus, landing in Cuba was not a viable alternative.

A quick analysis of the Caribbean navigation charts revealed that it was only a little over 100 miles to Montego Bay in Jamaica. Luckily, a rare 120-knot westerly wind facilitated the diversion since Montego Bay lay straight east. The level of concern led to the removal of the onboard survival raft from the baggage area and placing it next to the cabin door since ditching the aircraft in the ocean was a distinct possibility. The pilot's stress-induced hyperventilation did not cease until the aircraft was safely on the ground at Montego Bay. It is likely that there was less than ten minutes of fuel remaining aboard the aircraft. In eight years and 5,000 flight-hours of Learjet experiences, Ace had numerous rapid-pulse-inducing low-fuel situations in his many Learjet excursions, but this was one of the most stressful.

A couple of weeks later, during what should have been a very uneventful flight from Miami to Pensacola; Captain Bob once again turned a routine flight into a nail-biter. Captain Bob and Ace picked up the charter passengers at the Miami International Airport terminal. While Ace sat in the cockpit completing the paperwork and getting the ATC clearance, Captain Bob retrieved the passengers from the terminal. However, before he left the aircraft and unbeknownst to Ace, Captain Bob installed the pitot tube and stall-warning covers. Captain Bob returned to the aircraft, and, now engrossed in conversation with the passengers, he hurriedly boarded the passengers, closed the cabin door, and got into his captain's seat. However, he failed to remove the pitot tube and stall-warning vane covers that he had just installed. During the takeoff roll, it was the copilot's duty to call "airspeed alive" as soon as the air speed needle started to move. The air-speed needle did not move, motivating Ace to declare, "No airspeed!" At this time Captain Bob had to make a split-second decision to abort the takeoff or to engage in flight with no airspeed indication and no stall-warning indication. Much to the dismay of Ace, Captain Bob continued the takeoff!

Ace's dismay intensified when Captain Bob elected to continue the flight to Pensacola rather than to return and land at Miami International, which had a 12,000 foot-long runway. It was a singularly odd experience to fly a jet airplane with no airspeed indication. By maintaining normal power settings and pitch attitude, along with paying attention to the noise level of the airstream, Bob and Ace proceeded to Pensacola. As they approached the destination airport, they also capitalized on frequent ground-speed updates from air traffic control. With assistance from ATC as well as sensory-perception guesses regarding their airspeed, they managed to complete a successful landing. When the aircraft came to a stop on the tarmac, Captain Bob usurped the copilot's normal duty of opening the cabin door to disembark the passengers. This was part of the ongoing CYA (cover your ass) episode, as he positioned himself directly in front of the red-flagged and still-installed pitot tube covers. Not even one disembarking passenger made a comment.

Captain Bob had once again demonstrated his uncanny ability to dig himself into a deep hole and to then climb out of it without even getting his fingernails dirty. He had elected not to declare an emergency. Therefore only Captain Bob and Ace knew of this major screw-up. As the passengers departed from view, the pitot tube and the stall-warning vane covers were removed, and the day concluded with an uneventful return flight to Florida. This once in a lifetime, seat-of-the-pants flight ended with no harm done. Captain Bob was a very pleasant cockpit companion, but his gregarious PR personality often distracted him from his piloting duties. An important element of corporate and charter aviation requires pilots to exhibit a high level of gracious hospitality towards their passengers. This distraction, brought about by the social needs of the passengers, can often jeopardize safety. There are many anecdotes illustrating this phenomenon, but one of the more interesting stories involved a takeoff from PBI (Palm Beach International).

After leaving the private-aircraft terminal, and while taxing for takeoff, the captain asked the copilot to leave his seat to serve drinks to the passengers. The control tower then informed the captain that he would be cleared to make an intersection take off which would serve to eliminate a long wait in line behind other departing aircraft. Since the tower requested an immediate take off, the captain responded—with no consideration for his copilot—by immediately pushing the power levers forward. The resulting rapid acceleration left the ex-copilot, now-bartender, pinned against the occupants in the back seats as he uncontrollably poured Jack Daniel's over them. Airline pilots and cargo pilots will close the cockpit door, pull out their newspapers, magazines, and other creature comforts, and settle into their own little world. The corporate or charter pilot, on the other hand, is quite often being watched and scrutinized by the passengers, since there is often no cockpit or cabin door.

One of the more profound examples of passenger intervention in the cockpit involved a famous golfer, who leaned over the pilot's shoulder to ask about various landmarks that he could see from the cockpit. This cockpit intrusion occurred during the approach phase into a very high-density traffic area, namely Los Angeles, and the cockpit workload was extremely heavy. The captain snapped at the golf pro, "Shut the F_ up and sit down!" What sounds like an overreaction in response to a stressful situation may well have been the best course of action, since the flight crewmembers could then channel all their attention to their cockpit duties. As the story goes, it was extremely quiet during passenger disembarkation, and one could cut the tension with a butter knife. As the captain addressed his boss, the iconic sports hero, he took the initiative to offer a creatively analogous situation that would play to the interests and experiences of this man who had won victories at the Master's in Augusta, Georgia. He described a golfer in the process of a back swing for the winning putt at the Masters when some fool running across the green tooting a trumpet rudely interrupts him. The famous golfer got the message, thus salvaging a successful relationship as a result of this fast-thinking PR maneuver by the captain.

SAVED BY THE "GOONEY BIRD" (DC-3)

Mr. Weasel, the aircraft owner, frequently engaged in extended cocktail hours, and his inebriated condition would result occasionally in a request to fly his Learjet to Paris for dinner. However, as the world turns, even the famous "city of lights" had been shut down by this time, and the early-rising Parisians were baking their croissants for breakfast. A brief discussion of time-zone change and required flight time to Paris would put an end to his ludicrous request. However, Mr. Weasel called the company very late one evening, declaring his intent to sell his Learjet at a price considerably less than the aircraft's actual market value. An executive with World Aviation, the company that provided pilot and maintenance service to Mr. Weasel, rejected his offer under the premise that he, Mr. Weasel, was experiencing an alcohol-induced, irrational mental state, reaching the conclusion, moreover, that Mr. Weasel would soon forget about selling his Learjet. He was wrong! Mr. Weasel *did* sell the aircraft to a more opportunistic, South Florida Learjet operator. Even though the sole Learjet in the World Aviation fleet had now flown off to another owner, the company kept Ace on the payroll by contracting him out to fly for other Learjet charter operators when they needed a copilot. World Aviation also put him to work as a copilot on the DC-3. World Aviation had a government contract for a Navy research project at Andros Island in the Bahamas. This involved a daily, one-hour-and-thirty-minute flight from PBI (Palm Beach International Airport) to Andros Island in the DC-3 aircraft.

THE AGELESS DC-3; C-47; "GOONEY BIRD" / "DOUGLAS RACER"

Although the DC-3 was a classic airplane that first flew in 1937, it continues to be flown today. This remarkable aircraft will probably boast its usefulness in the twenty-second century. But, Ace was a *jet* pilot. Now Ace would poke along in a fixed-wing, propeller-driven machine! Flying the DC-3, also sarcastically referred to as "The Douglas Racer" or the "Gooney Bird," was a drag: except for crosswind landings, co-piloting the DC-3 was a mundane process. When one's brain has been oriented to 500-mile-per-hour speed the transition to 150 miles an hour results in severe boredom. Droopy lids and neck-snapping head bobs always accompanied the daily afternoon return flight over Bimini. Ace would usually try to "straighten up and fly right" but whenever he glanced to his left, he would often observe the captain in a state of advanced drowsiness, too. Flying represents many hours of sheer boredom, interspersed with brief moments of stark terror. Ace became overwhelmed by the mind-numbing boredom. Some of the "AUTEC" (navy project) pilots, in fact, had flown this DC-3 routine to Andros Island daily for several years. Within one week Ace was bored silly.

After a couple of months, as fate would have it, one of the regular DC-3 pilots returned to the company, and Ace lost his job. His first civilian aviation job had lasted a little more than one year, representing, however, an omen that blinked an eye at future career orientation for Ace. From this point up until his government mandated retirement at age sixty, Ace's average length of employment would last just over one year. Ace started dispersing updated resumes while he familiarized himself with the wonderful government program called unemployment compensation. During this period of time, pilot hiring stood at a lull. Several months crept forward before Ace fortuitously stumbled into a new flying job.

MOTOWN MADNESS

Ace received a call from his Learjet training-instructor pilot, Mr. Dave Peale, who had a hot tip on a Learjet pilot job in Detroit, Michigan. Ace immediately called the company offering the position, talked briefly with the owner, and after a ten-minute telephone conversation he was hired. The next day Ace kissed his eight months' pregnant wife goodbye and headed for Detroit. When he arrived at the Zantop Airways office at Detroit Metro Airport (DTW), he took his first look at the classic mom-and-pop operation. Lloyd Zantop assumed several roles there at Zantop: a charismatic founder, CEO, president, and a jack-of-all-trades, hands-on, likeable, dynamic leader. He also stood tall as one of the few benevolent aviation entrepreneurs in the rich history of unique, maverick-aviation entrepreneurs. Lloyd's wife, his office and business manager, Glenna, assisted him, along with two of his daughters, who held part-time positions in the office. As Ace would soon find out, Lloyd's son, Rick, also functioned as Learjet pilot for the company.

Ace soon learned that this was more than just another fledgling mom-and-pop aviation operation. Lloyd Zantop had several brothers, and together they had created a company in 1946 called Zantop Flying Service. As growth occurred, the company expanded exponentially as a freight airline for the auto industry and became known as Zantop Air Transport. Lloyd Zantop founded his own company, Zantop Airways, and operated Learjets and Hansa jets used primarily to haul automotive parts. One of his brother's company, Zantop International Airlines, operated large freighter aircraft out of Willow Run Airport (YIP), situated ten miles directly west of Detroit Metro Airport. Zantop International Airlines evolved into one of the largest cargo airlines in the world. Though instrumental himself in its development and growth, Lloyd decided he wanted to do something different, a move that resulted in the creation of his own company, namely Zantop Airways.

It was now early June 1973, and back at Detroit Metro Airport, Ace reported for work and was given his company manuals. As the company indoctrination-familiarization program was about to begin, someone discovered that Ace might be needed over at the Willow Run Airport (YIP), where a company Learjet rested on the ramp waiting patiently for orders to zip away with a load of auto parts. Coincidentally, a Learjet prepared to leave DTW for a freight pick-up at YIP. The Zantop Learjets had the passenger seats removed in order to install a durable cargo liner. The cabin had one additional small seat, referred to as the jump seat or potty seat. Ace sat on the jump seat and rode the jet all the way to YIP (seven minutes of actual flight time), where the Learjet then parked on the gargantuan, grease-covered ramp with a motley array of large cargo aircraft. The YIP cargo ramp exemplified Ace's indoctrination into the hard, cold, nuts-and-bolts reality of his new life as a "freight dog." In his previous Learjet life, flying corporate moguls to their various playgrounds, Ace frequently "bunked down" in a five-star hotel at some world-famous vacation spot. After all, his flying "duties" at World Aviation had taken him to many of the garden spots that served the wealthy, including the Playboy Club at Lake Geneva, Wisconsin, and to the Waldorf Astoria Hotel in Manhattan.

As Ace walked across the ramp, big, ugly airplanes, large pallets stacked high with auto parts, and noisy lift trucks running frantically pell-mell to load the many freighters surrounded him. He knew right away that this particular "back alley" of aviation would not be pretty. Looking at the flip side though, he had mouths to feed and he would be paid a nickel for each mile flown. At a ground speed of eight miles a minute, the nickels would pile up fast. As requested, Ace reported to the dispatch area, where he was told that he should look for Rick, Lloyd Zantop's son, at the time attending Hansa ground school at the training academy. There was the likelihood of another Learjet trip soon, and Ace would be needed to "pull gear" for Captain Rick. Ace found Rick, but Ace's initial impression of Lloyd's son left him in a state of stunned disbelief: although Rick numbered twenty-two years in age, he looked no more than sixteen! Hair unfurling itself down to his shoulders and sporting funky platform shoes, bell bottom trousers, and a turtleneck sweater, he could have passed himself off as a rock star. Ace's aviation background had been primarily with clean cut (in appearance) military or ex-military pilots. He reacted with jaw-dropping amazement when he met his new captain.

A few hours later, Ace and Rick jumped into the cockpit on a six-leg "boondoggle." Within a matter of three flights, Ace's perception of Rick transcended from amazement to awe. Rick exhibited an extremely high level of expertise as a Learjet captain as well as the display of great patience with his raw-recruit copilot, the former U.S.A.F. "fighter-jock." The common myth that the pilot had to have gray hair and a Steve Canyon profile, or to be trained by the military, was now seriously debunked.

Rick was not just an exception. In fact, the Zantop Airways pilot group consisted of mostly young men in their twenties or early thirties. For many of them, Zantop offered them their first chance to fly jets. Competent, young pilots, they had an opportunity to make a decent salary while building flight time and experience that would prove valuable for their aviation careers. Ace flew with several of the young captains and quickly discovered, to his surprise, that the civilian-trained pilot could exhibit a very high level of skill. The company sponsored many parties, out of which, to a great degree, evolved a high level of pilot camaraderie. Of course, many aspects of the job demanded leather work gloves used for loading the sharp-edged, greasy metal stampings (auto parts) into the Learjet. Varying work schedules and ridiculously long duty periods complemented this blue-collar element of the pilot's duties. Understandably, the persona of the elite Learjet pilot fell to the side; however, because the pilots flew unencumbered by the credo of *passenger comfort* they capitalized on the speed and maneuverability of their Learjets, which allowed them to engage in some occasional airborne "hot-rodding."

As the pilots sat alert at the company office/hangar waiting for a flight to be assigned, they would seek an empty bunk in the "Tin Lizzy," the nickname for an old Airstream RV parked in the hangar. This would account for the first of many career situations, in which Ace would have to snooze in very cramped, confined areas with his pilot colleagues. When Ace first arrived in Detroit, he did not have an apartment. He could not afford a hotel room, so the Tin Lizzy served as his home for nearly a month until he went back to Florida to retrieve his family. In truth a flophouse, the old RV offered a place to rest or to catch a few winks prior to their next flight. Then, too, the Tin Lizzy often reached such a severely unsanitary state that it would have sickened even hard-core college males who are notorious for avoiding any semblance of cleanliness or orderliness.

Ace had made the transition from the fantasy world of a pampered corporate pilot to the far darker reality of the "freight dog." Ace derived consolation from the idea that his position had him flying a Learjet rather than actually working at a classic "9 to 5" job in order to make a living. He would soon enjoy the promotion to the status of co-captain. One of his copilot colleagues, Jim Worden, also had a Learjet type rating along with a few hundred hours of Learjet flight time. Lloyd assigned Ace and Jim to fly together as co-captains. Jim had been a student of Glenna Zantop when she was a schoolteacher in nearby Jackson, Michigan, and Jim's older brother, Al, had been an astronaut. Shortly after the co-captain liaison was formed, this self-proclaimed "dynamic duo" had the rare experience of a single-passenger charter flight, none other than the renowned astronaut and ex-Senator John Glenn, a former colleague of Jim's astronaut-brother, Al. Jim and Ace had a great time with ex-astronaut Glenn. Glenn, the first American to orbit the Earth and the third American in space, behaved himself in an extremely personable manner, but he did chide his pilots about their job being "so easy that they should have to back up to the pay table," since the weather was post-cold front "severe clear."

FREIGHT DOGS MORPH
INTO ROCK STAR CHAUFFERS

Flying freight comprised about ninety percent of the flights, but occasionally "people charters" would pop up. Rather than transporting another cabin full of "loose-loaded ball bearings," the freight dog pilots would have the opportunity to take "Mr. Big" on a business trip. In such cases, the flight crews would pull the cargo liner out and install the seats in less than an hour. This extra effort did not go without reward since it was quite common on the passenger flights to have leftover Danish pastries and sandwich-tray remnants. Zantop Airways, possibly through Rick's rock-star demeanor, gained the confidence of several rock groups, including the Doobie Brothers and the Allman Brothers. Needless to say, the senior pilots usurped these choice assignments. Ace had tuned out of the contemporary music scene, and, when informed he would be flying a rock group called Crosby, Stills, Nash, and Young, he repeatedly asked the scheduler, "Who are these guys?"

When Ace actually lifted off a few days later with this eclectic array of musicians aboard, he quickly discovered he would fly in companionship with a singular group of fabulous artists. The trip started with passenger pickup at the Butler Aviation terminal at La Guardia Airport in New York. It was very easy to find the group since they were the only people not encumbered with business suits, briefcases, and a corporately correct, blank stare on their faces. The forty-five minute flight to Buffalo, New York, represented an especially remarkable occasion for Ace: never before had he witnessed Learjet passengers having so much fun. This was his first assignment as captain for a passenger trip. When the musically gifted passengers requested an aileron roll, performed when the aircraft completes a full 360-degree revolution along its longitudinal axis, Ace did not even have to okay the maneuver with his co-captain. He responded immediately, negotiating a full 360-degree roll on the descent into Buffalo. Upon arrival, the group's manager gave Ace and his copilot backstage passes for their concert at Rich Stadium. Ace had seen Peter, Paul, and Mary perform in a live concert back in the '50s, but this was his first exposure to an outdoor concert in the '70s. As the concert gained momentum and the sweet smell of ganja intensified, Ace and his pilot colleague discovered themselves to be amongst a very tiny minority of concertgoers who were not smoking marijuana.

In the early '70s, flight crews did not have to subject themselves to the job-killing "pee test" that they must endure today. Amongst yesteryear's younger pilots, marijuana use was quite prevalent. It was not uncommon to attend a company party with joints freely floating from extended hand to another extended hand. Many young, male pilots, notorious for "partying hardy," would not hesitate to complement the alcohol consumption with a few tokes on the widely used popular herb. There have been very few aircraft-accident investigation reports that revealed the flight crew had been impaired as a result of marijuana use. On the other hand, the number of small-aircraft, alcohol-related crashes easily swells upwards into the thousands. Unfortunately, there are still pilots, even amongst well-trained, highly professional airline pilots, who will enter the cockpit with a blood-alcohol level that exceeds the maximum allowable.

Occasionally, the other Zantop aircraft (the Hansa Jet) would be used to transport company personnel to prime party locations. The Hansa Jet, a strange looking German aircraft, had wings that canted forward. Zantop operated these aircraft primarily as freighters, but as twelve-passenger aircraft they were quite desirable for passenger trips. Every few weeks, a Hansa Jet, stuffed with company personnel, including wives and girlfriends, took off for an all-expense-paid corporate vacation to Las Vegas. This serious partying represented a pleasant break from the serious flying and the unique situations that evolved from this unusual aviation environment. The interesting anecdotes from the Zantop experience could fill a small library, and the author is pleased to share a couple of stories with you.

REAL PILOTS CAN DO IT WITH ONE ENGINE

For starters, the Zantop brothers were notorious for engaging in three-martini lunches. Brother Howard had returned from lunch and, while walking across the cargo ramp, he observed a few pallets of cargo situated next to a C-46 aircraft. He also set eyes on a few cargo loaders (human "ramp rats") sitting idly next to the cargo, waiting for the lift truck to move the cargo to a different aircraft. Howard determined that the ramp rats should get to work immediately, barking, "Get that aircraft loaded." Since the loaders recognized the "big boss," they acquiesced and immediately began to load the C-46, a WW II vintage aircraft that flew in the famous Berlin Airlift and "The Hump" in Burma. Howard, viewing the aircraft only from its left side, did not realize that the aircraft was "down for maintenance," its right engine, in fact, completely removed. A big, fat, slow, and ugly aircraft, the C-46 had the nickname "Dumbo." Howard may have received a similar tag (Dumbo) after word got around about this "Get 'er done, boys!" faux pas. Surprisingly, there were no reports that he tried further to get a pilot to fly Dumbo with one engine.

Captain Ed, one of Zantop's Hansa jet pilots had flown the C-46 with a previous employer. He claimed that he hated flying Dumbo so much that he would find a small stone on the ramp and throw it against the side of the fuselage after every flight just to let it know that he was the boss. Captain Ed, the stone-throwing pilot, would not have even *considered* a takeoff with one engine inoperative in the C-46, but he *did* get to demonstrate this maneuver in the Hansa jet. He experienced a starter failure on one of the two engines, so he elected to engage in some test-pilot work since the aircraft was loaded with automotive freight badly needed at an auto-assembly line. The airplane was well below maximum takeoff weight with a light load of freight and a relatively light fuel load. The single-engine take-off succeeded, followed by the wind-milling air-start procedure on the second engine, resulting in an on-time delivery. This bold venture "outside the box" proved to be successful. Captain Ed received plaudits for his courageous airmanship, and once again, "All's well that ends well." Historically, cargo pilots have been prone to push the edge of the envelope. This last incident certainly embodies a glaring example of this tendency.

ONE MORE FOR THE ROAD

The Zantop pilots always worked hard to get the cargo to the destination, but they also played hard. All of the many company parties had the bar stocked with the very popular Coors beer. Because the product could not be purchased east of the Mississippi River, the Zantop pilots bootlegged it back to Detroit on west-coast cargo runs. This "Colorado Gold"—brewed in the foothills of the Rockies—could easily market for twelve to fifteen dollars a case to some of the local-area watering holes in Michigan. Purchased for five dollars a case at some of the western-state FBOs, the pilots had the beer delivered with great haste to the airplane during refueling. While Coors beer did have a unique flavor that most consumers enjoyed, its popularity was based on the consideration that one would need to have connections in order to have it available. Its availability inevitably increased as larger aircraft-cargo operators, capitalizing on the profit motive, returned to Detroit with hundreds of cases.

San Jose, California, the most popular trip destination, earned the pilots not only a healthy paycheck; they could also tote back a few cases of Coors. Detroit-area beer drinkers enjoyed the unique flavor of their own locally brewed Stroh's beer. A few of the San Jose ramp rats originated out of Detroit, so the delivery of auto parts was supplemented with the delivery of some Stroh's beer. A case-for-case swap was effectuated, and everyone got to enjoy his or her favorite brew. The refrigerator at the company hanger would usually contain a few six packs of Coors, allowing the pilots to get a head start on happy hour after a long day (or night) of flying.

After one particularly long duty day, Ace and his copilot watched the sunset over the Pacific during their approach into San Jose. About six hours, later Ace caught sight of the rising sun over the Midwest as they approached the Detroit area. Ace piloted the aircraft while fellow pilot Jim Worden took a nap in the cabin, stacked with cases of Coors. Thinking ahead of the aircraft, Ace envisioned a good hot breakfast, when he unexpectedly heard the sound of the all-so-familiar snap-cap removal. Ace looked over his shoulder. Did his ears betray him? Not at all! His cockpit colleague was consuming the "breakfast of champions," a lukewarm Coors. Ace was already in an altered state of sleep deprivation, and the sight of his fellow pilot perched on cases of Coors while drinking a beer created a dream-like, seemingly implausible situation. Ace thought that perhaps Jim's sleep-induced, cotton-mouth feeling needed a bit of moisture and that particular condition totally trumped the FAA regulation regarding alcohol consumption during flights.

The surreal scene described in the previous paragraph took a back seat to another Zantop radically bizarre scenario during a return from a West Coast trip. The cockpit crew had a new pilot occupying the jump seat while receiving company indoctrination training. After a long day and during the return flight in the early morning hours, the copilot chose to take a break from the cockpit to snuggle into a sleeping bag in the cargo-free cabin. It was a long, boring flight in the wee hours of the morning, so the newly hired pilot also lost interest. He sprawled out on the cabin floor for a nap next to the copilot. The flight crew engaged the aircraft's autopilot because there was very little airway activity over the Rockies at three a.m. The last responsible person awake, the captain, left the cockpit, went to the cabin, and stretched out on the floor next to the newly hired pilot, intentionally bumping the new guy and faking a deep-sleep posture. The fun-loving members of the prankster crew took great joy in observing the bewildered pilot trainee's state of disbelief as he looked forward to take note of an empty cockpit!

Long hours and backside-of-the-clock work schedule resulted in frequent but necessary "power naps" by the pilots. Proper coordination dictated that the pilot getting ready to nap would inform his cockpit colleague that he would be briefly "evaluating his inner eyelids." This was standard cockpit protocol in view of the fact that the non-napping pilot was then required to maintain a higher level of awareness. The recuperative effects of a twenty-minute power nap can be wonderfully refreshing. Ace was in the process of a power nap somewhere over the Catskill Mountains of upstate New York at about three a.m. while enroute to Westchester County Airport, just north of New York City. He awoke in a frenzied state of uncertainty as the New York Center controllers loudly issued instructions—which also served as a wake-up call! The aircraft was in a descending turn, and, when Ace looked over at his copilot, he observed that the man slept soundly! Ace then took a few microseconds to clear the cobwebs, and while regaining control of the aircraft, he reoriented himself with some situational awareness restructuring, and the instant wake-up panic state subsided. As the often-overused expression goes, "Flying is many hours of sheer boredom, interspersed with brief moments of stark terror." This incident of a terrifying awakening (in a strange place) *did* result in that rare but intense emotional state of stark terror.

WHETHER OR NOT TO WEATHER THE STORM

Later that summer Ace had the opportunity to experience the frightening exhilaration of flight into a severe thunderstorm at 37,000 feet. The entire Midwest as well as Northeastern United States was entrapped in an August heat wave accompanied by severely embedded thunderstorms. An inoperative airborne weather radar during night flight resulted in an inadvertent adventure into a very large mature thunderstorm. The severe turbulence was so violent that maintaining the aircraft in a controlled flight situation required Ace's maximum effort. The loud noise of the heavy hail pelting the aircraft windshield along with deafening thunder and eye-blinding lightning brought about a case of serious distraction for Captain Ace Abbott.

Upon entering a level-five (most intense) thunderstorm, the pilot's only recourse is to maintain aircraft control by disconnecting the autopilot to fly the airplane manually. Severe turbulence and erratic airflow can result in "jet upset," spontaneously turning the aircraft upside down. During this adrenalin-gushing flight, Ace made a silent vow that should he survive this experience, he would retire from aviation to sell insurance; a vow soon broken when the following day he very briefly considered the nature of "real" work.

With today's effective and reliable radar systems, an inadvertent entry into a mature thunderstorm is quite rare. Yet even today, a pilot's healthy fear of entering a mature thunderstorm is an extremely important perspective that will greatly enhance both pilot and passenger longevity. The severe turbulence in such a storm can also result in structural damage that might cause an aircraft to break apart in flight. This appears, unfortunately, to have been the demise of the Air France Airbus aircraft that recently crashed off the northeast coast of South America.

The pilots' salary during Ace's years of flying at Zantop was directly related to how often and how far they flew. This, of course, resulted in flight crews that would always go the extra mile. For example, during or after winter snowstorms, the pilots would hustle to the tarmac with snow shovels to clear away accumulated snow in order to launch the jet. They would also "man" the brooms to sweep snow and ice off the aircraft. Lloyd Zantop would often leave the warm comfort of his office to join the pilots on the tarmac for this detail. The effort and the dedication to get the cargo to its destination were necessary because there were competing Learjet charter operators in the area. Hence, rapid response was a critical element in the success of this small-aviation operation. The big-three auto companies had vendors that supplied parts for production that could barely keep up with fast-moving assembly lines. The Zantop jets had to deliver the cargo in a timely fashion, or the big auto-plant assembly line might shut down. The cost of shutting down an automobile assembly line for even a few minutes would result in the loss of tens-of-thousands of dollars of unproductive labor costs.

On a gloomy winter morning Ace was assigned to depart the Detroit Metro Airport (DTW) ASAP for a pickup at Detroit City Airport (DET). Unfortunately, DTW Airport lay enshrouded in pea-soup fog. In due course, a taxi clearance was received even though the visibility remained less than that required for takeoff for commercial operations. However, since there was no cargo or passengers aboard Ace's aircraft, this flight was not considered commercial but rather operated as a FAR Part-91 flight, which meant that a takeoff could be made regardless of how low the visibility might be. This premise allowed Ace and copilot John to take off in their Learjet (N1ZA) even though the large commercial jets could not take off. DTW had two parallel runways, 3R/21L and 3L/21R. The very efficient DTW ground controller assisted N1ZA for an expeditious takeoff by providing progressive taxi instructions to runway 3L. Since there were many large aircraft on the parallel taxiway waiting for the visibility to increase to their required takeoff minimums, the ground controller instructed N1ZA to taxi to an intersection on 3L/21R. This manipulation and maneuvering of the aircraft on the ground was done, of course, without the pilot's ability to see other aircraft as a result of the near-zero visibility fog.

As N1ZA entered the runaway to backtrack down the runway for the 3L runway departure, Ace advised John, his copilot, to monitor the tower frequency on the aircraft's secondary radio. This proved to be very timely because only a few seconds later the DTW tower cleared a Northwest 747 for take-off on runway 3L, the runway on which N1ZA taxied. The takeoff clearance elicited an immediate response from Ace, who grabbed the microphone and informed the tower that N1ZA was taxiing on that runway and that Northwest 747 should hold its position. Apparently, someone in the tower had transposed 3R/21L to 3L/21R, and this temporary "miss-communication" nearly resulted in a squashed Learjet. A few years later, on March 27, 1977, a similar low-visibility, taxi-takeoff situation occurred at Tenerife in the Canary Islands. The collision of the two 747 aircraft on the runway led to the deaths of 583 people. Shortly after this occurrence, the FAA adopted a policy that required an aircraft either entering a runway or crossing a runway to monitor the appropriate tower frequency for that runway. Flying jet aircraft is inherently safe but sometimes vulnerable to seemingly minor details.

The Zantop experience was enjoyed by all because an occasional "people trip" would punctuate the cargo flights for the automotive companies. Together with a few local area CEOs, Ace had the opportunity, for instance, to fly Howard Cosell, the renowned sportscaster known for his staccato voice, accent, syntax, and cadence. Suitably nicknamed "the mouth," Howard's outgoing personality and talkative nature became very evident during a flight from DTW to LGA (LaGuardia) in New York. On this flight he celebrated a reward that he said he had just received at a sportscaster's gathering in Detroit: a large "victory cigar" that he ignited and puffed during the trip. Despite the unpleasant stench polluting the planes cabin, "the mouth's" mouth busied itself with the cigar, intermittently relieving the crew of the incessant, disjointed ramblings of the famous sportscaster.

Since the auto air-cargo business now boomed, Ace averaged nearly one-hundred hours of flight time per month. This resulted in a very high level of proficiency, and, since the Learjet was originally designed to become a highly maneuverable Swiss fighter jet, Ace and his pilot colleagues frequently added a little zest to their flights by doing barrel rolls. On one particular occasion, just prior to the final-approach fix for landing on runway 21R at DTW, Ace rolled the aircraft. It is likely that anyone on the ground, including the air traffic controllers in the tower at the DTW Airport, might have thought they had just witnessed an illusion as they observed an aircraft on final approach that was very briefly, upside-down. On another occasion, just after climbing through an overcast layer and breaking out into the clear blue sky, Ace pulled the nose up and did a barrel roll. The right-seat pilot, who had not yet experienced the inverted state of affairs, responded with open-mouth, stunned disbelief, a sight smugly enjoyed by Ace.

The Learjets high-performance capability allows it to climb to high altitudes in a relatively short period of time. On a cold winter night in January 1974, Ace flew his Learjet to Louisville, Kentucky, to deliver some badly needed auto parts. After landing, the fuel remaining on the aircraft was just enough (approximately 3,000 pounds) to return safely to Detroit. Because Ace carried no cargo, the aircraft was very light. The outside air temperature at Louisville was minus 5° F. As all pilots know, jet engines love cold air. As the takeoff roll began, a stopwatch timer was initiated, and six minutes later the aircraft leveled off at 41,000 feet. For much of the first 20,000 feet of climb, the vertical speed indicator "pegged" at 6,000 feet per minute. It is quite possible that the six-minute climb from brake release to 41,000 feet was, and perhaps still remains, a record for civilian aircraft.

Ace approached another record: his longest period of steady gainful civilian employment. Then along came the OPEC oil embargo, which threw a "monkey wrench" into the automotive industry. The big slowdown in activity at the auto-production plants also resulted in a comparable slowdown for Zantop. A pilot-force reduction became necessary, and in late November of 1974, Ace found himself laid off and returned to Florida. Flying automotive air cargo had served him well, and shortly after his return to Florida, he was able to gain employment with a previous employer.

BACK TO CHAUFFERING THE TRUST-FUND BABIES

World aviation had been renamed Imperial Aviation, and Ace was hired as a Learjet Captain to fly the relatively new, more sophisticated Learjet 25 aircraft for corporate owners and charter flights. Ace eventually returned to the chaos and clutter of the greasy airfreight ramp, but for now his new employer brought him back to hobnobbing with the Palm Beach jetsetters. Imperial Aviation also operated a Learjet 24 for a Palm Beach socialite, Mr. Carr, another owner-pilot who had somehow managed to get a Learjet type rating. The Learjet business continued to flourish, and Learjet-rated pilots virtually fell like ripe oranges from the tree. Only a few of them, however, could serve even marginally safe as captains. Therefore, when Mr. Carr climbed aboard for a Learjet ride, he always made sure that an experienced Learjet captain sat in the right seat.

BOYS WILL BE BOYS

Most of Imperial Aviation's charter flights reached successfully out to wealthy Palm Beach socialites and South Florida business people; a few of the flights, however, transported clients referred to as "*the boys.*" From a historical perspective, the burgeoning drug business was focused in South Florida, and various illegal controlled substances were being smuggled into Florida. Most of the kingpin drug dealers had set up shop somewhere between Key West and West Palm Beach. Their products entered the U.S. on larger cargo aircraft or tucked inside high-speed boats. When the kingpins traveled for personal pleasure, they chartered Learjet services. Ace had no knowledge of the boys ever carrying illegal drugs on the flights that he piloted. The *boys* were so prolific in numbers that at least six Learjet charter companies in South Florida served them. The pilots preferred flying the boys because of their generous tips. Drug-trafficking had such a high-profit margin that a $100 bill often served as the standard tipping denomination. The boys would often ask the pilots to do a barrel roll and then reward them with hundred dollar bills. Occasionally, the pilots received $500 tips. Ace was paid the paltry sum of $1100 per month for his Learjet-Captain duties, but his jet-set travels to places such as Las Vegas and five-star vacation hotels in the Caribbean, along with the C-note tips, allowed him to enjoy a quality of life far beyond his income.

The big-money flights did not always center on the *boys*, as there were many legitimate businessmen who despised the idea of paying taxes and, instead, shuffled their monies out of the country into offshore accounts. Many flights to Grand Cayman were flown with the baggage compartment stuffed with large suitcases filled with cash. It was particularly interesting to observe the nonchalant fashion of the airport authorities at Grand Cayman as they opened the suitcases, observed the many millions of dollars, and very expeditiously processed the entry forms for the wealthy tax evader. Grand Cayman was a popular scuba diving resort, but offshore banking was the crux of its economy, and the massive quantities of cash were readily welcomed. The locals enjoyed a relatively high level of economic security and a very comfortable lifestyle. **Money laundering is good work if you can get it!** Ace and his flying companions often got wind of reports of famous and prominent aviation entrepreneurs who took their company to bankruptcy and were later seen taking private jets to Grand Cayman. The U.S. dollars that have been illegally deposited in offshore accounts in the last four decades would pay off the national debt and provide the American citizenry with free medical and dental care for many years.

Countless charter flights flew to many of the Caribbean islands and to Central and South America. Many of these flights involved layovers at resort hotels, and the contrast for pilots with previous freight-dog lifestyle values exceeded profound proportions. Catered flights took off with gourmet food such as shrimp, lobster, and stone crab claws. Flight participants, excluding Ace and his copilot, of course, washed down these delectable tidbits with Dom Perignon champagne. Once the passengers left the aircraft, the pilots then often relaxed in the cabin treating themselves to leftovers. These delightful experiences of conspicuous consumption validated Ace's long-held premise that, *if you don't like hedonism, you've probably never tried it.* The undesirable element of this job was that Ace had a very erratic work schedule and had to carry a beeper at all times since many of the charter flights were "pop-up" flights with an ASAP departure. Appropriate rest or duty time was not a consideration because the needs of the paying customers superseded the pilots' physiological needs by a wide margin.

One prime example of the ridiculously long duty periods involved a late-afternoon, pop-up charter trip to Los Angeles. Ace had been busy all day, enjoying his South Florida playground, when he was summoned for the jaunt to LA. At approximately six p.m., the flight departed for Los Angeles with a required fuel stop in Texas. The arrival in Burbank, CA, was nearly ten p.m. local (one a.m. east coast), and the very fatigued flight crew finally got to the hotel and settled in between the sheets about midnight (local time). Shortly thereafter, the same group of charter passengers, who had identified themselves as participants in the music business but were more likely the *boys*, called Ace to inform him that they had to leave "right away." They would be at the airport ready to go within one hour. Their new destination headed northbound to Reno, Nevada, and upon arrival at Reno the passengers insisted that the flight crew join them in their limousine.

Unknowingly, Ace and his copilot colleague were being hijacked to the world famous brothel, the Mustang Ranch. This would be a unique experience if one were well rested, but in a state of severe sleep deprivation it was just very strangely weird. The boys were regular customers, Ace learned, and were immediately issued carte blanche services, including food, for the duration of the stay. After a nice breakfast, Ace opted to get some sleep for the first time in nearly thirty hours. This type of extended duty-day flight profile was far too common in the Learjet charter business. The accident rate for chartered aircraft is infinitely higher than that of scheduled commercial flights, and in many instances, a very tired flight crew is a contributing cause.

VIEWING VENEZUELA
FROM THE PRISON WINDOW

Nearly half of the charter flights were international—primarily to the Caribbean—but there were also many flights to Central and South America.

They were especially challenging because of the increased paperwork, and at most locations there were no prepaid handling agents. The captain was responsible for rounding up all the customs and immigration forms and getting the appropriate people to stamp them. This was often made more difficult by the local on-the-take authorities, who made subtle requests for an off-the-books pay-off before they would process the required paperwork. Adding to an already unusual situation, it was not uncommon to deal with five or six different airport agencies, any one of which could stymie the departure process by not signing or stamping the appropriate document. Determining how much to give to whom often required a critical snap decision. Then, too, the fuel-truck driver, who also might delay the process until he got his appropriate tip, would occasionally intensify this dilemma. After an hour or two of this airport hoop jumping, the words "gear up" sounded like sweet music since it was now time for the easy part—an airplane ride.

On November 27, 1975, Ace was assigned to pick up a passenger in Miami and to fly him to Venezuela (MIQ-Maiquetia Airport). Ace, and his copilot Jim, had flown this gentleman previously and found him to be a very pleasant, professional and legitimate businessman. The following day, after spending a restful night at the Hilton Inn Hotel, Ace and Jim were ready for a full day of flying. The day's assignment was to take the previous day's passenger, John, and his Venezuelan business colleagues to several locations. Since the first proposed destination was located in Columbia, it was required to file international paperwork, referred to as general declarations, which name the passengers, flight crew, departure point, and destination.

When the passengers arrived at the aircraft, they informed Ace that their first destination had changed, and they now wanted to go to an airport that was located within Venezuela. Since going back to the terminal to engage in a lengthy process of re-filing a flight plan would result in a significant delay, Ace asked the control tower if it would be acceptable to change the destination to a Venezuelan airport. The response was affirmative; N14BC (aircraft tail number and call sign) was re-cleared to the desired destination, and an uneventful flight occurred. This procedure of changing destinations with the air-traffic control tower was common in the U.S., and Ace had previously used this procedure in the Caribbean as well.

The entire day was filled with unique aviation experiences. Destination number two was outside of the Venezuelan radar coverage. This destination was an uncontrolled airport with no control tower, but many cows dotted the landscape. The cows elected to continue to focus on their grazing and wisely stayed clear of the runway. Because no terminal existed, Ace and Jim sat somewhat anxiously in the aircraft, while the passengers went about their business. The next flight had the Venezuelan Guri Dam airport as its destination. Its remoteness and resemblance to a barren, uninhabited desert plateau created a Twilight-Zone atmosphere. Not only did this airport not have a terminal, there were no taxiways, along with a very good probability that not one human life could have been seen within a fifty-mile radius. After the aircraft came to a halt, the passengers were picked up by one of their business colleagues in a large four-wheel-drive vehicle, which then rambled off to the Guri Dam area, a proposed site for a future resort. Ace recalls the unnerving wait inside the aircraft with Jim. Ace's paranoid thoughts drifted to the possibility of an engine-start failure there in that very remote location and their last adventure would have them as nourishment for the circling vultures. Much to their delight, however, the passengers returned, both engines started, and an uneventful flight back to Caracas completed a long day. This was the end of anything uneventful for this particular day as the "feces-into-the-fan" was preparing to rear its ugly head.

The passengers disembarked at the Caracas terminal, and after Ace and Jim taxied the aircraft to the remote parking area, an airport official in a jeep greeted them with a ride to the airport office to pay the appropriate airport fees. As they entered the office, Ace immediately observed an excessive number of "Policia" in the area, finding their glaring gazes very disconcerting. As Ace attempted to pay the fees, he was pointedly questioned about which airports they had flown to that day. The "investigation" rapidly turned into a very stressful situation, made more difficult by Ace's rudimentary Spanish-language capability. The tension was extraordinary, and Ace immediately suggested to Jim to get a taxi, to go into the city, and to return to the airport with the bilingual Venezuelan passenger in order to help negotiate this impending crisis. The negative vibes in the airport office were profound, and Ace had just enough street savvy to deduce he faced a potentially serious problem. Many of the private jets that came from the U.S. to Venezuela were involved in some type of illicit-smuggling activity. Quite surprisingly, much of the contraband smuggled out of Venezuela consisted of emeralds rather than illicit drugs.

The next phase of this operation involved Ace under escort back to the aircraft by several Policia equipped with AK-47 rifles. The officers searched every nook and cranny of the aircraft, including each item in Ace's briefcase and wallet. Since no contraband was found, Ace felt that this little mini-saga would soon come to an end. He was wrong by a wide margin! His next encounter put him behind a closed-door interrogation with Venezuela's drug-enforcement chief. Because of the language barrier, Ace and the chief did not communicate very well. Even though Ace had no interpreter, it was clear that he was being accused of smuggling drugs. After approximately one hour, Ace was allowed to leave the room. While he waited for events to unfold, it was with great relief that he observed Jim and the multilingual Venezuelan passenger arriving in a taxi.

Things then began to look a bit brighter, but even that slightly-less-than-rosy perspective soon changed when Ace, Jim, and the Venezuelan passenger, a gentleman named José, were put into a government vehicle and driven into the city of Caracas. One of the gracious Venezuelan government agents in the vehicle continually reassured everyone, "*No ees problema*"—easy for him to say since he was escorting Ace and friends off to jail. At the jail, Ace and his colleagues had to remove and to relinquish shoes, belts, wallets, watches, and jewelry, still with no explanation why the "gringos" were under arrest. Ace was escorted to a cell. When the door closed behind him, he heard only a tiny clank, but its effect was sickeningly deafening. The cell had one piece of furniture: a single bed with no mattress.

By now it was nearly midnight. Totally exhausted from the long and stressful day, Ace easily fell asleep. Shortly after dawn, a crowing rooster awoke him, followed by footsteps outside his cell door. Just as he had seen in cartoons and in films, a plate of food was extended through the small, swinging door near the floor. This was a nice gesture by the host captors, but Ace soon found the food unfit for human consumption, even though he had eaten very little the previous day. Sitting on his bed with his head in his hands contemplating his plight, he looked toward the plate of food. It was now completely covered with cockroaches!

A few hours later, the cell door opened, and Ace was taken to an area for further interrogation, fingerprinting, and mug shots. Here he was reunited with Jim and José. Jim had a small but noticeable trembling problem. However, in the current circumstances his entire body *vibrated* as he asked, "Ace, what are we going to do?" As he attempted to reduce the tension with a bit of sarcastic humor, Ace responded in jest, "Did you have the eggs Benedict or the blueberry pancakes for breakfast?" Jim shook his head in disgust, followed, by an intensified visible vibration of most of his moveable body parts. A request to call the American Embassy was refused, as was another appeal to call the company back in Florida. Ace was allowed to see a copy of the morning newspaper, which had a front-page picture of the alleged smugglers' Learjet. The knowledge that N14BC, along with Ace and his fellow prisoners created a big news story in Caracas provided at least some consolation for Ace. By mid-afternoon, the appropriate authorities had completed their investigation and determined that the suspected smugglers were innocent. After paying a $400 fine, Ace and his colleagues were released. Around eight o'clock that evening, as Learjet N14BC climbed northbound for Miami, the rapidly dimming lights of Caracas in the distance created a warm, fuzzy feeling. The previous thirty-six hours had been an emotionally charged experience, and all occupants of the Learjet enjoyed a comforting sense of relief. Ace knew that Latin American authorities sometimes impounded private jets and incarcerated flight crews for indefinite periods during the early 1970s.

A few months later, Ace and Jim experienced *another* unique encounter at the Maiquetia Airport (MIQ) in Caracas. As they approached the airport for arrival, the local air-traffic controllers suddenly elected to close the airport for all takeoffs and landings, stating that the closure would persist for an indefinite period. After thirty minutes of holding and several discussions with the air traffic controllers, it finally became necessary to either go to a nearby airport, where no fuel was available, or to declare an emergency and land at MIQ. Declaring an emergency would almost certainly result in the usual airport paperwork as well as a protracted discussion of the reason for declaring an emergency. Nonetheless, the decision was made to declare an emergency and to land at MIQ rather than to head for the small airport that did not have badly needed Jet A fuel available. Upon arrival at the tarmac, government vehicles promptly surrounded the aircraft. After a lengthy discussion, the officials elected to accept Ace's explanation of why it was necessary to declare an emergency and to land at MIQ. The reason for the airport closure was that the Venezuelan president was preparing to depart in his aircraft. This random and unannounced closing of an airport typified the rudimentary air-traffic-control system throughout South America during the early 1970s.

FIVE-STAR HOTELS ON
GARBAGE COLLECTOR'S SALARY

Despite the Caracas fiascoes, most of the flights were uneventful and often resulted in several day layovers at five-star hotels in world-renowned resort areas. A few of the destinations included Grand Cayman, Panama City, Bermuda, Las Vegas, Aruba, and many locations in the Bahamas. In February 1976, Ace's colleagues flew a group of revelers to Rio de Janeiro for the world-renowned, pre-Lent Carnival: the popular musical group, the Carpenters. Ace and Jim were left later with the table scraps when they picked up some passengers in Nassau and flew them to Trinidad for the third-best—New Orleans is second best—carnival in the world. After two days of rum drinks and nearly non-stop dancing in the streets, the vacation continued with some rest and recuperation in Barbados. Nearly half of the trips were to the Caribbean or Central and South America, but many flight destinations were to the Northeast U.S., with layovers in Boston, Montréal, and New York City. Montréal was a very interesting city with its distinctive French flair, but after a three-day layover in January, it was always great to get back to the warm weather, the blue skies, and the white, sandy-beaches of the Caribbean.

This glamorous jet-set lifestyle created some marital discord for Ace, since the "little lady" remained at home and spent about eighty hours a week engaged in employment, child rearing, and household duties. The marital disharmony persisted until Ace learned to fabricate a travelogue explanation of having to stay in an old, dilapidated Motel 6 with no TV, and the closest restaurant was a McDonald's situated more than a one-mile walk from the motel. Aviation marriages are usually tenuous at best, and the average male airline pilot is so vulnerable that during the '60s, '70s, and '80s, it was common for veteran pilots to have been married three or four times with most of their paychecks going to their ex-wives.

A choice dessert topped off the main course of this gourmet lifestyle: Ace remained an avid golfer, and his company acquired, to Ace's good fortune, a contract to provide Jack Nicklaus with Learjet travel. At that time, Nicklaus was the best golfer in the world, unleashing an iconic stature comparable to today's Tiger Woods. The spin-off benefits of flying Jack Nicklaus were multifaceted. Ace and his pilot colleague, Jim, for instance, were able to play Jack's most famous course, Muirfield Village in Ohio. They also attended many golf tournaments, including the renowned Masters at Augusta, Georgia. In early April, the Masters at Augusta is the golf fan's Mecca. Similar to the Grand Canyon, the golfing event is necessary to observe in person in order to experience and to absorb its magnificence.

South Florida, inundated with celebrities, musicians, and showbiz icons, provided the Learjet flight crews with many remarkable experiences. It was no surprise that the casual, offstage-persona of these celebrities was often quite similar to their music and stage persona. A short trip with Olivia Newton John, by way of example, revealed her to be as sweet and as pleasant as her soft and sensual singing. Helen Reddy, too, radiated her free-spirited, feminist personality. After she had just finished a concert in Jacksonville, she serenaded the flight crew on the return trip to Miami with her popular hit, "I Am Woman, Hear Me Roar." There were no microphones, but she sat in the front seat about four feet from the cockpit, and the power of her voice complemented the muscular lyrics of her songs.

On a different occasion, Ace and Jim picked up another interesting celebrity, including the singer's wife, to take them home to Alabama for Thanksgiving. After the plane leveled off at cruise altitude, the wife of Jimmy Buffett requested a sharp knife in order to slice a smoked turkey that they had brought with them. A few minutes later, they began to pass slices of their Thanksgiving turkey to the airplane's chauffeurs, a glaring example of the Jimmy Buffett, "laid-back" lifestyle so often expressed in the lyrics of his music. At the opposite end of the spectrum, hardly a single smile punctuated the face of Secretary of the Treasury William E. Simon and his colleagues during a two-and-one-half hour flight.

(BOB) MARLEY AND ME

Of Ace's many close encounters and varied interactions with the celebrities, the most interesting story involved smuggling Bob Marley out of Kingston, Jamaica. Smuggling Marley from Kingston exemplified a remarkable synchronicity that seemed a common theme in Ace's career. Just a few days prior to this somewhat clandestine maneuver, Ace came across a magazine entitled *High Times* while perusing the magazine rack at the bookstore. It contained an interview with Bob Marley, and Ace found the Reggae legend to be a very intriguing, almost mystical person. A couple of days later, while reading his local newspaper, the *Palm Beach Post*, Ace came across an article that discussed Marley's upcoming concert in Kingston, Jamaica. The article pointed out that Mr. Marley was very politically controversial, and the local police in Kingston were geared up for potential civil unrest. The next day's paper had a follow-up article, stating that gunmen had attacked Bob Marley, his band, his family, and his friends and several people in their home, injuring a number of them. That afternoon, Ace's company received a call from Chris Blackwell of Island Records (Marley's label) to pick up Mr. Marley, family, and friends in Kingston. On duty that afternoon, Ace and Jim jumped into the nine-passenger Lear 25 and headed for Jamaica.

Upon arrival in Kingston, Ace and Jim completed the appropriate airport paperwork and prepared for a departure to Nassau. After several hours of waiting for passengers, Ace checked with the control tower to update their ATC clearance, learning that the airport was now closed for departures until the following morning. Ace and Jim were now stranded between that proverbial rock and a hard place—they had no passengers and they had not been paid for the trip. A few hours later, while hanging around the nearly abandoned airport, Ace and Jim were standing in front of the terminal contemplating an appropriate course of action when two cars approached the area.

The occupants were part of the Marley entourage and immediately recognized that the two white guys, conspicuously dressed in white shirts and neckties, and awkwardly hanging around the airport in the middle of the night, were Marley's pilots. As they disembarked from their autos in full Rastafarian regalia with long dreadlocks and strange looking, multicolored hats, their appearance was somewhat intimidating. They were, however, very gracious, escorting Ace and Jim to a Kingston hotel where they slept for approximately three hours before returning to the airport in order to depart with Mr. Marley and his entourage prior to daybreak. The aircraft was parked in a remote part of the airport where Marley and his colleagues somewhat clandestinely boarded the aircraft and were flown to Nassau.

The flight would have been very uneventful if it were not for the extremely heavy aroma of the Rastafarian sacrament of Ganja. Nearly every passenger enjoyed a classic Jamaican "big spliff, "a large, cigar-sized marijuana joint. It became immediately necessary for Ace and Jim to don their oxygen masks to avoid entering a counterproductive mental state that could be summarized by the lyrics from a Marley song, "Every little thing is going to be all right." The information regarding the arrival of Bob Marley in Nassau was widely disseminated on the small island, and the airport was packed with his fans. In the '70s, throughout the Caribbean, Bob Marley represented a cultural and a musical icon comparable to the Beatles in the '60s or Elvis Presley in the '50s. A return trip to Kingston was necessary to retrieve more of the Marley entourage and to relocate them to Nassau. When Ace and Jim finally returned to West Palm Beach in a severely bedraggled state, they informed their boss that they only had three hours of sleep the previous evening. His response was, "That's good training for you." Unfortunately, this seemingly jokingly sarcastic statement proved to be valid.

Just a few months prior to the Marley adventure, Imperial Aviation was in the process of de-emphasizing and possibly eliminating its Learjet charter program. As a result, a new company called BizJet was formed, and Ace was now with his *fourth employer in four years*. The boss, Captain Bob, previously of World/Imperial Aviation, had now been exposed to the Harvard-business-school mantra of "achieving maximum utilization of the human resources," a euphemism for squeezing as much work as possible out of the employees. Besides the 80 to 100 hours of flying per month, Ace was also required—on those weekdays when he did not fly—to present himself in the office to do paperwork or light maintenance on the aircraft. After nearly a year of living on a beeper and rarely having any genuinely free time, Ace began to burn out. These factors, along with flight operations that often jeopardized safety, forced Ace to seek employment elsewhere.

After giving his two-week notice, he flew his final flight for BizJet on Saturday, April 30, 1977. That last flight was particularly memorable because Ace sat in the right seat, providing ongoing guidance for the left-seat pilot—an elderly but very wealthy Palm Beach mogul—who not only required constant coaching, but was also totally unaware of his advanced level of incompetence. After the flight, the tycoon droned on in boastful fashion about how easy it was to fly a Learjet. Ace, not wanting outwardly to disrespect the rich and foolishly prideful man, politely agreed. Ace also felt strongly compelled to bite his tongue as he rolled his eyes in disgust, allowing his inner voice to sing Johnny Paycheck's famous hit song, "Take this Job and Shove It."

BLIND PIG FINDS ACORN

At eight o'clock on a Monday morning two days later, Ace was planning strategies for the next employment search when the telephone rang. Amazingly, the caller turned out to be his next source of employment! Several months earlier, Ace had flown a charter from Philadelphia to Fort Lauderdale, and one of the passengers was a helicopter pilot. Ace had invited him into the cockpit for a bit of right-seat Learjet time since the passenger also held a license as a fixed-wing pilot. This little gesture of PR work was well remembered, and, when the passenger's boss saw the need for a Learjet to complement his helicopter fleet, the helicopter pilot, a gentleman named Mark, immediately called Ace, a truly extraordinary bit of good fortune for Ace. Stepping toward his fifth piloting job on the Learjet, his salary *doubled* from $1100 to $2200 a month. Ace, representing the interests of his newest employer, Benson and Benson, contacted Duncan Aviation in Lincoln, Nebraska, to make arrangements for a lease/option-to-purchase of a Learjet 25.

Ace utilized Mark, the company helicopter pilot, as his copilot in the Learjet; however, when Mark was unavailable, Ace had to find another copilot. When he contacted his former Zantop-Airways, co-captain-colleague Jim Worden, the timing was right, and Jim joined Ace for some corporate, passenger flying. Between flights the two buddies would wax nostalgic about their radical experiences during the freight-dog days. Jim and Ace now achieved a distancing about as far as humanly possible from the greasy freight ramp at YIP when they dined with the boss and his entourage at the famous Club 21 in Manhattan. They then followed up this bit of high-society hobnobbing with a three-day golf vacation at Hilton Head. The new job went quite well for several months until Mr. Benson's bankers informed him that he couldn't afford the cost of purchasing and operating the Learjet. Ace, forever poised with updated résumés, didn't have real high hopes of this situation becoming a career job, so he happily returned to Florida to join his family.

The major airlines had now finally begun to increase hiring, prompting Ace to conclude that now would be a good time to pursue employment as an airline pilot. Accordingly, he enrolled in a Boeing 727 flight-engineer-training program because most of the airlines required this training before they would consider a pilot applicant for hire. Approximately two months later, Ace completed the program and was newly licensed as a turbojet flight engineer. The training was completed on the morning of December 28, 1977, but Ace was unemployed and now needed to revise his résumé while preparing to carry on the job-search mode. Later that same day, another fortuitous bounce of the aviation employment-ball occurred when Ace received a call from Graff Jets in Fort Lauderdale, informing him that the company had an immediate opening for a Learjet Captain for its Learjet charter operation. Ace accepted the offer and agreed to commence his new employment on January 1, 1978.

On New Year's Eve, the day before launching his next job, Ace, quite by chance, finished the mandatory celebration early and hit the sack shortly after midnight. This proved to be very good fortune since he received a call at a little past five a.m., merely five hours later, to inform him that he was needed ASAP for an air-ambulance charter trip that would likely conclude some sixteen hours later. The trip, initially beginning in Fort Lauderdale, involved the pick-up of a sick passenger at Freeport in the Bahamas for a drop-off in Phoenix, Arizona.

Much more cumbersome than most passenger charters, air-ambulance trips required coordination with hospitals and ambulances, along with stretcher, portable oxygen bottles, and other medical paraphernalia. A nurse would usually accompany the patient, along with members of the patient's family, and occasionally a doctor. The very able assistance of copilot Ron Ragsdale greatly facilitated this particular flight's success. "Rags," as he was affectionately referred to around the hangar, had an outgoing, vivacious personality, along with a Humphrey-Bogart-like "Joe Cool" demeanor. In his mid-fifties, Rags, like many of the older pilots, could apparently survive for weeks on coffee and cigarettes. Fuel stops were necessary, both westbound and on the return flight to Fort Lauderdale, and this lengthy trip—which started in the dark and ended in the dark—required lots of coffee and cigarettes during the last leg of the flight with two tired pilots in the cockpit.

Rags and Ace established an immediate rapport, and this was the first of their many aviation adventures together. Ace was often intrigued as he watched Rags fly an approach with his lit cigarette hanging out of his mouth and an inch-long ash that mysteriously would not drop into his lap. In fact, it was not uncommon for the older, hardcore-smoker captains to have a lit cigarette hanging from their mouths during approach. Wisely, most airlines and aviation departments have now prohibited smoking in the cockpit. This first, very long day on the job for Ace would be an indication of the future workload at Graff Jets. But the extra workload was worth it since Ace was now being paid a salary that represented a fifty-percent pay raise from his previous Learjet charter job with BizJet.

The Graff Jets job proved to be even more dynamic and diversified than Ace's previous Learjet jobs: a larger variety of clients, including *the boys*, air ambulance flights, and CBS news teams to Havana, Cuba. The business flights to other destinations characterized themselves as long weekends with wealthy clients for ski vacations in Sun Valley, Idaho, as well as diving and snorkeling jaunts to Bermuda and Grand Cayman. The boys were great to fly because those C-note tips came out of their pockets with near certainty. On the downside of flying the boys, foreign airport authorities readily recognized rich, illicit-drug entrepreneurs when they saw them, and these authoritarian shakedown techniques, judging by the looks on the faces of the "businessmen," were carried out quite effectively. Ace needed to demonstrate discretion with the dispersal of C-note "tips," or bribes, that were often required to get the reams of required paperwork stamped or signed.

Since most of the flying was "south of the border" to Latin America and the Caribbean, Ace became very familiar with the topography, which greatly facilitated many of the flights. Quite frequently the flights to South America and the Caribbean required overflying Cuba, but occasionally the over flight clearance would not be granted and the flight would then be required to bypass the island. Ace figured out how to "cut the corners" on the inside of the airway without stirring up the Russian Mig-jet fighters supposedly poised to intercept any intruders. Cutting the corner on the inside of the airway would sometimes save just enough time and fuel to avoid an en-route fuel stop.

Many charters actually landed in Havana. The major news networks— CBS in particular—would frequently charter Learjets. The networks packed the aircraft with cameras and a couple of reporters and flew off to Havana to seek their stories. These trips were normally quite uneventful, and the airport authorities graciously and readily processed the appropriate paperwork. It was, interestingly enough, easier getting fuel and effectuating a quick turnaround in Havana than it was in most of the U.S. airports. One of Graff's pilots even found the nearby military airport authorities to be quite accommodating. A very short distance south of Havana's José Marti International Airport was a military airport that had its runways and taxiways oriented exactly like those at José Marti. A Graff Jets pilot accidentally ended up on final approach at this airport, and a few minutes later, on short final, he became aware of this mistake. Rather than executing a go-around and vacating the area, he wisely decided to land and to deal with the potential consequences. To turn tail could make him appear as an invading intruder and potentially get shot down. This turned out to be a very good decision, and after a few questions by the military *"commandantes,"* the aircraft was released and continued on to its correct destination, a few miles to the north.

Other flights to Cuba ended up at the now infamous Guantánamo Naval Air Station (GITMO). These were unique excursions in that Miami Center radar was not available all the way to GITMO. For such flights, a small "twilight zone" existed in which there was not only no radar coverage but also no airway. The weather was usually very VFR (unlimited visibility), and the pilot could proceed visually though carefully to avoid overflying the Cuban mainland until the GITMO radar could see the inbound aircraft. Another variable involved a no-fly area just west of the GITMO airport. Because of this no-fly area, landing on an easterly approach required a very tight pattern with a right turn and rolling out at a low altitude to a short, final approach. This was not a problem with the very maneuverable Learjet, but it certainly did create a predicament for a cargo-carrying DC-8 aircraft that crashed while attempting this challenging and treacherous approach.

While the flights to Bogotá, Santa Marta, and to Cartagena, Colombia, usually passed quite uneventfully, there were a few, small exceptions. The normal arrival at Bogotá resulted in a minimal amount of fuel remaining, and there were very few adequate alternate airports in the immediate area. On one memorable evening, shortly after landing, a fog bank rolled in and buried the airport in London-style pea soup fog. Only ten minutes after arrival, the airport visibility was reduced to a few hundred feet. If the arrival had been fifteen minutes later, it would not have been possible to land. Proceeding to an alternate airport would have resulted, with a little bit of luck, in landing "on fumes." The premise that "timing is everything" certainly applied to this situation.

Yet another notable incident in Bogotá involved a brief but stressful encounter with the local police. The charter passengers (*the boys*) had put their flight crew up for a weekend in a very nice hotel in an upscale part of Bogotá. On Saturday afternoon, Ace decided to go for a walk in the commercial district. In the process of window shopping, he observed a reflection of a police car moving along the street at the same slow speed at which he walked. When he turned to look directly at the police car, the car stopped, and two young Columbian Policia officers emerged with their machine guns held high. Angrily and aggressively, they immediately interrogated Ace, demanding to see his passport. Ace attempted to respond with his very rudimentary Spanish, a mistake because the officers showed even *more* anger and frustration in attempting to understand Ace's unintelligible Spanish gibberish. One of the Policia swung his machine gun in a very aggressive—perhaps trigger-happy—fashion, an act that Ace found particularly disturbing. After about twenty minutes of this harassment, the two Policia apparently decided they had successfully scared the rich American gringo and drove away. During the encounter, Ace entertained flashbacks of his incarceration experience in Venezuela, easily convincing himself that the prison accommodations here in Colombia would be even less hospitable.

After several years of flying throughout the Caribbean, and South America, Ace's familiarity with the lay of the land allowed him comfortably to venture outside of the envelope. Shortly after takeoff on a flight to Columbia both VORs (primary navigation aids) became inoperative. The only remaining navigation aids were the single ADF and the weather radar, which could be used in the ground-mapping mode for identifying islands and distinguishing land mass areas. The flight from Fort Lauderdale to Bogotá succeeded by means of the ADF, the radar, and some good old-fashioned dead reckoning navigation. Twenty-first century pilots, with their very reliable GPS navigation systems, would never consider an extended flight of this nature over water with only ADF and weather radar for navigation. Deviating from SOP (standard operating procedures) was often necessary to get the job done. Learjet charter flying in Latin America and the Caribbean required a great deal of creativity and flexibility.

COPILOT COLLEAGUES CRASH

Extending the normal-operations envelope, however, occurred later on a charter trip from Fort Lauderdale to Bermuda. This venture generally proceeded through the mythical Bermuda Triangle and involved several hundred miles of dead reckoning (no navigation aids available). Two other negative factors came into play that day: sickness and inexperience. The first factor had Ace extremely sick with a stomach virus. Unfortunately, no one else was available to fly the trip, and "calling in sick" would have resulted in the company losing a large sum of revenue. For the second factor, Ace now hit the clouds in the Learjet with a relatively inexperienced, new copilot, a fellow named George. The first hour of the trip went by without event, that is to say, up until Ace's stomach cramps dictated a necessarily rapid maneuver to the very cramped aircraft "powder room," a procedure implemented only in the event of an extreme excretory emergency.

When he returned to the cockpit, Ace immediately observed that the aircraft had exceeded the approved maximum-Mach airspeed by a wide margin. Apparently in a hurry, George had disarmed the switch designed to prevent this over-speed situation. The Learjet had an aerodynamic vulnerability that caused it to go into a steep dive, also known as Mach Tuck, if the aircraft went too fast. George had the aircraft on the very precipice of such a catastrophic nosedive. If Ace had stayed in the bathroom another couple of minutes, the ensuing vertical entry into the Atlantic Ocean would have caused barely a ripple, and the mysterious disappearance of this aircraft would have provided even more "evidence" to bolster the great Bermuda-Triangle myth. And, of course, the emotional turmoil that would have pervaded the cockpit and cabin prior to impact would have been immeasurable.

In addition to his inexperience, copilot George had a certain flair for the bizarre that would sometimes exhibit itself in dangerously daring activity. George once invited Ace and his family to his home where he demonstrated how he and his young sons would jump off the roof of their house into the swimming pool. A slip or a slight miscalculation would have resulted in very serious injury. On a weekend layover at Grand Cayman, George introduced Ace to the exhilarating joys of snorkeling. His extraordinary derring-do involved swimming twenty feet below the surface and then entering a tunnel underneath the coral reef. Ace waited nearly a minute for him to reappear, and, as he feared for George's well being, he finally looked up from the reef to observe George on the surface nearly one hundred yards away! He had exited the reef on the opposite side from where he had entered. During later flights, George would seemingly take personal mental excursions unrelated to the business of the cockpit. Finally, and to draw this particular account to a dead end, George managed to get himself killed when his aircraft, an MU-2, struck the ground at a high rate of speed in the Florida Everglades, apparently in an out-of-control situation.

Graff Jets kept Ace very busy with nearly one-hundred hours of flying per month, along with maintaining several sets of Jeppesen air-navigation manuals that required fifteen to twenty hours of office work per week. Normally, this would be a copilot function, but the only copilots employed at Graff were part time employees, so the responsibility fell to Ace. Nevertheless, the extra workload paid large dividends later. When Ace returned from a trip on Christmas Eve, for example, he checked his mailbox to discover that Santa Claus had, indeed, arrived. As Ace viewed his Christmas bonus check for $2,000, he was only disappointed that his boss and fellow Learjet captain, John Coe, wasn't there for a hug. This substantial Christmas bonus was a huge surprise, and Ace felt immensely grateful. When he informed Mr. Coe of some lucrative job offers from other potential employers a few months later, Ace was immediately rewarded with a fifty-percent pay raise. Despite the lack of free time and the need to live with a nerve-jangling beeper, Ace had a congenial relationship with his employer and fellow employees, and he happily remained at Graff Jets. He now had nearly 5,000 hours of flight time in Learjets, and with the exception of a few demanding situations, the actual flying was relatively easy work.

Many of the flights to more distant destinations required a fuel stop that was not only a major inconvenience but also quite costly. Rather than the normal .80 cruise Mach that most Learjet pilots would use, Ace chose a much slower cruise speed in order to significantly extend the aircraft's range. This technique resulted in about ten percent more flight time. Then, too, the slower rate of speed eliminated a fuel stop, saving one to two hours overall. While working for a previous employer, Ace and his copilot, on one particular occasion, flew a Learjet 25 from Palm Springs, CA, to Palm Beach, FL—a distance of eighteen-hundred miles during which they kept the aircraft airborne for four hours and twenty minutes. This likely record-breaking flight for a General Electric-powered Learjet was made possible by using the angle-of-attack gauge and by flying at L/D max (the speed that creates the most lift in relationship to the drag). Amazingly, the remaining fuel in the aircraft after landing *exceeded* the required FAA reserve. The Learjet, a very fuel sensitive airplane, burned twice as much fuel at low altitudes than it did at its normal 41,000 ft. to 45,000 ft. cruise altitude. This often necessitated delaying the descent for landing as long as possible. Since the introduction of the Learjet in 1964, there have been thousands of Learjet landings with low-fuel lights glaring with only a few minutes of fuel remaining in the tanks.

THE LEGEND

Ace accumulated a plethora of unique Learjet experiences, but his stories are likely kindergarten stuff compared to the prominent pilot of the Learjet charter community, Harvey Hop. Prematurely bald and a former Navy pilot, Harvey Hop stood six-foot-five inches tall. Both his personality and his energy over-shadowed his much-larger-than-normal stature. He began flying Learjets in the late 1960s and was amongst the first type-rated Learjet captains. He may also have been the first pilot in South Florida with a Learjet charter operation. As a result, he developed such a large clientele that he would often fly 140 hours a month, once informing folks listening on the Miami Center ATC frequency that he had flown 180 hours the previous month. Ace retired with 18,000+ hours of actual flight time, of which approximately 2,000 hours were spent "recharging the batteries" with mini power naps. It is entirely probable that Harvey Hop may have exceeded Ace's estimated cockpit time spent in the snooze mode. In the late 1980s, Harvey had accumulated over 22,000 hours of Learjet time, and he was still flying! It is also highly likely that Harvey amassed more time in a Learjet than any pilot has ever acquired in any single type of aircraft. Considering the astonishing number of flight hours as well as the wide variety of challenges that occur in an on-demand jet-charter environment—not to forget the numerous international flights to short runways with poor or no approach aids at all— Harvey Hop's lengthy career could put him in a category as one of the world's greatest pilots. He assembled a total career flight time of 37,000 hours without an accident. Although Harvey's astounding flight time included a stint as a Navy test pilot, he spent most of his time flying the Learjet for the very demanding and high-risk environment of the on-demand charter business.

"THE MAN"

WHO HAS THE MONEY?

The South Florida Learjet charter experience was filled with odd financial experiences since there were high rollers everywhere with their piles of $100 bills. On one particular charter, while taking a group of young people on a weekend party excursion, Ace received a very generous tip amounting to $300. The trip returned Sunday evening, and, when Ace went to the office the next morning, he was informed that the trip was paid for with $100 bills that were all counterfeit. Much to his chagrin, Ace's C-notes were also counterfeit.

While working for BizJet at PBI a few years earlier, Ace was sent to the airport on a Friday evening at about eleven p.m. to facilitate a Learjet charter to Las Vegas. An earlier call requesting a jet charter came to the company from a local watering hole at the peak of happy hour. It was a near certainty that these rowdy partiers did not have the $7,000 to pay for the flight. How wrong Ace was! Not only did they show up for the flight, but they did it in grand fashion with two car loads of raucous revelers, the convertible tops down, and nearly everyone wielded his or her own bottle of liquor. When Ace sarcastically asked, "Who has the cash?" bank bags with large quantities of $100 bills appeared. This disheveled group of fast-lane party people was led by one of the many wealthy heirs in the local area.

The Ben Franklin bills flew in a ubiquitous manner in the South-Florida, fast-lane party scene. Since con artists and scammers lurked behind nearly every palm tree in South Florida, Mr. Coe, the Graff Jets owner, wisely established a policy to ensure payment prior to flying the charter customers. He did, however, let his guard down on one particular occasion when he launched Ace and copilot Cheney for a passenger pickup in Aruba, informing them that he had a "bad feeling about this one." He had agreed to allow the passenger to pay for the flight when he was picked up in Aruba. After the arrival in Aruba and the rendezvous with the passenger, Rodney, the allegedly rich racehorse owner from Kentucky, Ace promptly discovered that Rodney did not have the money to pay for the trip. The con-game story continued when Rodney asked to be flown to Nassau where he said he could acquire the trip-payment funds from his business colleagues. Since the return flight to Fort Lauderdale went directly over Nassau, Ace took the bait and flew Rodney to Nassau. In the taxi ride from the Nassau Airport to the hotel, Rodney expressed his great admiration for the American financier-con man, Robert Vesco, who had left the United States with millions of illegally acquired company funds. **Rodney was no Vesco**, Ace concluded to himself, but the situation began to reveal Rodney as an accomplished con man. Shortly after checking into the hotel, Ace received a call from the front desk informing him that Rodney's credit card had expired. To make matters worse, the con man had put all of his room charges on Ace's credit card that was on file at the hotel desk

The following day, when the situation became more and more evident in their minds that this Rodney character functioned as a con man, Ace and Cheney hastened to Rodney's lavish suite to confront him. They were in turn confronted by two hookers who also had not received their payment and they insisted that Ace should pay them. Ace and Cheney empathized with the hookers since they had also been screwed—**both literally, and figuratively**—by the smooth-talking con man. A moment later, Ace and Cheney found themselves in the room alone with Rodney. They quelled their initial instinct to toss him off the tenth-floor balcony to see if he could con his way out of the Sir Isaac Newton's unforgiving law of gravity. Although a "culling of the herd" might have been appropriate, they elected to spare his life. A telephone discussion with the Graff Jet office revealed that Rodney worked as a minimum-wage stable boy at the famous Calumet horse farm in Kentucky. His total assets, likewise, probably would not cover the bottle of Dom Perignon Champagne that he had charged to his hotel room. Ace and Cheney returned to Fort Lauderdale with no passenger and no payment.

Cheney owned a Citabria, a very maneuverable aerobatic aircraft, and he *finally* talked Ace into going for a ride with him. The flight scenario occurred at very low altitudes just east of the Fort Lauderdale pier, and Cheney's boldness presented a disconcerting problem for Ace. The U.S. Air Force policy for aerobatics in a jet aircraft required the plane to be fully recovered from its maneuvers at an altitude of no less than 10,000 feet above the ground. Ace had been accustomed to seeing a lot of space between his aircraft and the ground during aerobatic maneuvers in his Air Force jets and was not comfortable with pulling out of loops just a few hundred feet above the water. He informed Cheney that he was not feeling well and requested to return to the airport to land. With a different passenger in the back seat a few weeks later, Cheney was doing aerobatics in the *same area* and crashed into the ocean, killing both occupants. This accident had a particularly gruesome twist to it: the passenger was the daughter of the Learjet FAA examiner who had just recently given Cheney his type rating and captain's check ride in the Learjet.

While on a charter trip passing through Detroit in late June of 1979, Ace had a few hours of layover. A spontaneous impulse led him to phone Zantop Airways, and, quite by chance, his former associate, Rick, was in the office, so he and Ace exchanged a few stories. Ace, now experiencing another burnout from the heavy workload and the erratic charter schedule, half jokingly asked Rick if he needed a pilot to fly one of the company's G-159 cargo aircraft, a Gulfstream. Astonishingly, Rick responded that the company did require a captain for the new Miami base and offered Ace the job. Once again, the uncanny intervention of the aviation-employment Gods smiled down upon Ace. He would soon be off learning how to fly a turboprop aircraft but again with one of his former employers.

THESE GIRLS WILL SPIN YOUR PROP

CHAPTER FIVE

An Accident
Looking For A Place to Happen

JET PILOTS IN PROP PLANES

Before turning to Ace's turboprop-airplane experiences, we must regress in order to explore the topics of jet pilots and small propeller-driven aircraft. Many aviation skills are common to successful flight in both jet aircraft and small propeller planes. Basic eye-hand coordination, along with stick and rudder skills, is required to fly any aircraft, including today's high-tech computerized jets. However, transitioning from jet aircraft to reciprocating-engine propeller airplanes is quite difficult for most jet pilots, unless they have had lots of previous experience in small, single-engine airplanes. Furthermore, the accident rate for smaller planes, even with experienced and skilled pilots, is infinitely higher than that for jet aircraft—even for jets flown by relatively inexperienced pilots.

During his T-41A (Cessna 172) Air Force training, Ace was quite comfortable in his little prop plane. Nonetheless, even after nearly forty years of flying and 18,000 hours of flight time, he found that both fear and tension severely cast a shadow over pleasure whenever he climbed back into a small, prop-driven Cessna.

JET JOCKS ATTAIN NEAR-DEATH EXPERIENCE

During Air Force pilot training in Phoenix, a few of Ace's colleagues rented Cherokee 140 aircraft to fly their wives and girlfriends to Las Vegas. Since they had no experience with small-prop airplanes in high-density-altitude airports, their takeoff roll on that hot day was a long, grueling, eye-opening experience. They were barely able to get high enough to climb over the mountainous terrain between Phoenix and Las Vegas. There were later stories of a stall-warning horn activating as they fought for a few more feet of altitude. High-density airport accidents have killed hundreds of pilots in small reciprocating engine planes. The degradation of airplane performance between sea level and 5,000 feet above sea level is surprisingly significant, and many new or poorly trained pilots only learn of this as their aircraft splatters uncontrollably into the terrain with insufficient flying speed. Ace's training colleagues all went on to become successful Air Force pilots, but they unanimously agreed that their Vegas venture in the Cherokee 140 brought them perilously close to the brink of disaster.

During F-4 training at MacDill Air Force Base in Florida, one year later, Ace and his F-4 GIB colleagues would rent Cherokee 140 aircraft to fly low-level formation. Ace now had a total of nearly ten hours of flight time in the Cherokee 140 and felt reasonably comfortable flying this severely underpowered airplane. His sense of competency was not based on reality but rather came as fallout from the omniscient, omnipotent attitude that often afflicts inexperienced, rookie jet pilots. When they now reflect upon this extremely dangerous, low-level maneuver, they can only scratch their heads in amazement at their folly.

Shortly after Ace completed F-4 Phantom GIB training, he took a few days of leave to return to Upstate New York, where he once again demonstrated his delusions of immortality by renting a Cherokee 140. Ace wanted to demonstrate to his father that he really could fly an airplane. It was a hot summer day when he departed the 7,000-foot runway at Syracuse. The airport where he intended to pick up his father was a cute little grass strip measuring 1,800 feet long and 40 feet wide. The runway at MacDill Air Force Base, where Ace had been landing the Phantom, measured 14,000 feet long and 500 feet wide. The contrast was so great that it took Ace three approaches before he could manipulate the Cherokee to the ground. His 240-pound father jumped into the right seat, and Ace provided him with the most exciting takeoff of his life. Partial flaps were extended, a rolling-around-the-corner alignment with the runway was executed, and Ace was now, quite reluctantly, performing his very first grass-runway takeoff. The wind was calm, the temperature was nearly ninety degrees, and the slow acceleration was disconcertingly uncomfortable. As the fence at the end of the runway loomed large, Ace pulled back on the yoke even though he had not reached the recommended liftoff airspeed, and—with his stall-warning horn blaring—climbed over the fence with only a few feet to spare. Ace had once again successfully demonstrated the severe disconnect between flying high-performance jets and underpowered prop planes.

After Ace received his Air Force discharge four years later—honorably, amazingly enough—he returned to Upstate New York where, foolishly, once again, he tried to fly a small prop plane. It was a brisk spring day. A cold front had passed through the area with winds gusting to nearly twenty miles an hour. Not a good day for flying small airplanes, but Ace attempted to get a checkout in a Piper Tri-Pacer. The Tri-Pacer is a short-winged airplane, squirrelly even during calm conditions, and after two failed approaches to a short runway in heavy crosswinds, Ace was happy to turn the controls over to the experienced instructor pilot, who landed the aircraft.

A few years later, when Ace flew Learjets in Florida, he befriended a private pilot, who owned his own airplane, a Mooney. Ace assisted his newly acquired friend, named Dennis, with his instrument-rating training. Because Ace observed how easily he could manage this aircraft, he suggested to Dennis that he might rent it to take his family up North for a vacation. Dennis readily acquiesced since he had the usual private pilot's respect and trust for this experienced jet-jock

During a pleasant, calm Florida morning, Dennis put Ace in the left seat for a quick aircraft checkout. The first landing at the Lantana Airport verified the cliché that "even a blind pig can find an acorn," as he made a ridiculously smooth, grease-job landing. As a consequence, Dennis came to the conclusion that Ace knew what he was doing. He was wrong by a wide margin, as Ace would later demonstrate. The checkout flight returned to PBI, where Ace then stuffed his family and baggage into the Mooney's tiny cockpit.

The first leg of the journey brought the flying family up the East Coast of Florida, where Ace foolishly attempted to out-climb the rapidly rising cumulus clouds. The Learjet, by comparison, would climb from sea level to 41,000 feet in the same amount of time that the Mooney would take to climb from 9,000 feet to 11,000 feet. Landing for a fuel stop at Charleston, South Carolina, Ace flew the approach with a little extra airspeed. As aviators say, "A few extra knots for mom and the kids." This resulted in the dreaded nose-gear-first touchdown, followed by the very uncomfortable nose-gear-to-main-gear oscillation. Ace, much to his relief, executed a go around and managed to get the tricky Mooney on the ground on the next approach.

After a fairly lengthy fuel stop, the second and final leg began. As Ace estimated his arrival time, he realized that it would be getting close to sunset for the landing at Pennridge Airport, located about thirty miles north of Philadelphia. Ace had failed to purchase a flashlight during the fuel stop, and this oversight would be a factor on the next landing. As a result of excessive off-course vectoring by air traffic control, it was well past sunset by the time Ace had found the destination airport. On the downwind leg, all of the instrument and cockpit lights failed. Since it was not possible to read the airspeed indicator on approach, he added a lot of extra airspeed—*for mom and the kids*—which resulted in a nose-first touchdown, followed by a large bounce. A go around was not a consideration, and fewer than 1,000 feet of runway remained when the aircraft returned to the beloved terra firma. As Ace mashed the brake pedals, he was able to stop the aircraft with only a few feet of remaining runway. The tiny cockpit was filled with very loud and uncensored sighs of relief and varied expressions of deep concern as Ace sheepishly parked on the tarmac.

Ace managed to continue this aviation escapade with no other dangerous encounters. A few years later, long after he had recovered from this small airplane trauma, Ace once again ventured off into that otherworldly realm of propeller airplanes: a family ski trip to Gatlinburg, Tennessee. Flying over the mountains of southern Tennessee, Ace encountered icing conditions and was unable to climb above or to descend below the icing level. The rented Cherokee Six had no deicing equipment, and after a VOR approach to very low ceiling and with visibility near minimums, the family exclaimed *another* great sigh of relief during the taxiing to the tarmac.

For nearly twenty-five years, Ace had carefully avoided a mid-air collision with the "bug smashers" (big airplane pilot's slang for small, propeller-driven aircraft) in his Boeing 727. As he approached the mandatory retirement age of sixty, he decided it might be fun to get checked out in a Cessna 172 to do a bit of pleasure flying in New York State's scenic Finger Lakes region. Ace's check-pilot instructor had him do some air work—stalls, steep turns, etc. This went well, but then it was back to the 3,400-foot aerodrome to do some touch-and go-landings. On a hot summer day with lots of thermals creating unstable air and gusty crosswinds, the five touch-and-go landings resulted in very unpleasant experiences. After each touchdown, Ace was totally relieved that he hadn't damaged the aircraft. However, as he attempted to retract the flaps with the cumbersome manual flap handle during a go-around maneuver, the trees at the end of the runway getting closer and seemingly taller, and adrenalin raced through his sweat-soaked body.

"You are signed off and good to go. Whenever you want to rent the aircraft, just call the airport office," the young instructor commented after the flight. Ace was amazed that the instructor would consider him safe in this aircraft, and he silently stated to himself; "Thank you, but I won't be back," vowing never again to fly small airplanes as he drove away.

The FAA has on file several hundred, perhaps even several thousand accident or incident reports of experienced jet pilots flying small, propeller-driven airplanes. It is quite common to see a newspaper report of a retired airline pilot who crashed his homebuilt or experimental aircraft. However, no group of professionals can top the medical doctors for their propensity to crash small aircraft. The Beechcraft Bonanza V-35 was, for many years, the most popular method of increasing the numbers of doctors' widows. As this chapter title says: an accident looking for a place to happen.

CHAPTER SIX

From Learjet Chaos To The Boring Whine Of The Turboprop Freighter

Returning now to Ace's homecoming with Zantop, the Grumman G-159 (G1) aircraft was a very popular corporate aircraft that Zantop Airways had converted to a cargo-carrying air machine. It was time for Ace to reacquaint himself with the bleak lifestyle of the freight dog. Yet the sacrifice was well worth it, since he now had, for the first time in his aviation career, a defined schedule with weekends off. He had reunited with the folks who had previously treated him very well, and he considered them not only friends but good friends as well. This very rare relationship with a previous employer would endure well past his employment at Zantop.

The first day of class for new hire training is always interesting, and this was no exception. The company maintained a progressive and open-minded management style, hiring two very low-time, male flight attendants, who had taken leave from Eastern Airlines to become entry-level commercial pilots. The commercial pilot's requirement of operating under the rules of FAR 121, the same parameters that governed the large airlines, would play a significant role in Ace's next job. Another of the company's new hires was a middle-aged Trailways bus driver, a man named Bill Hurd, who had not flown airplanes in a few years and actually had to take a pay cut to get back to aviation. The former bus driver would eventually become Ace's good friend and cockpit companion, ultimately progressing upwards first to become a 747 Captain flying worldwide before he then evolved into an FAA examiner on the 747 aircraft. An instant camaraderie overcame this class of new-hire training pilots, and everyone looked forward to flying this unique turboprop airplane.

Two weeks of ground school cruised along quite smoothly—with the exception of concern for the complexity of the specialized propeller system. After completion of ground school, it was off to Milwaukee for aircraft training. There was no simulator available, so Ace was given a quick six hours of training in the airplane and then sent off to face the FAA for a type-rating check ride. The check ride went well, and Ace was deemed by the examiner to be a certified G-1 captain. Just a few days later, Ace was in Miami to initiate IOE (initial operating experience) training. After a short time into the flight, the check airman (sitting on the jump seat), and the FO lit up their cigars. Ace had long ago abandoned cockpit smoking and was quite amazed to see two people smoking in the cockpit. His first thought concluded that this might be a form of *psychological* hazing to complement the *actual* hazing of the cockpit itself. Since he was the new guy on the block and he wasn't technically the pilot-in-command until he finished his IOE training, Ace elected to endure the eye-and-throat-burning cockpit pollution. To display his disgust for the toxic cockpit air, nonetheless, Ace frequently coughed and choked (faked, of course), while he sarcastically asked the copilot to refer to the cockpit smoke and fire checklist.

JUST LIKE A REAL AIRLINE

The IOE training mandated by FAR 121 (commercial airline parameters) was soon complete, and Ace settled into a comfortable life style with plenty of time off and relatively stress-free flying. The Learjet trips had always seemed on the verge of running out of fuel, but the G-1 could carry nearly twelve hours of fuel, and most of the trips rarely exceeded two hours, a reassuring detail for Ace. Ace also enjoyed the pleasant company of copilot Tim, one of the Eastern Airline flight attendants based in Miami. Ace and Tim were both voracious readers, and as soon as the aircraft reached cruising altitude, the flying duties were relinquished to the auto-pilot, and the cockpit lights were turned on bright to facilitate the pilots' number one priority—finishing the most recent Kurt Vonnegut or Tom Clancy novel. Although getting the aircraft safely from point A to point B was the real number-one priority, Ace always embraced the concept that creating the most comfortable work environment possible was a major consideration.

One small downside of this operation had the crew flying at night, usually between nine in the evening and seven in the morning, though the flight crew's rudimentarily rustic rest room at the hub airport in Smyrna, Tennessee did provide for a bit of shut-eye. Trying to get a couple hours of sleep in a small room overwhelmed by snoring, farting, and belching pilots was, to understate the sight, smell, and sound, anything but pleasant. Another minor downside was that the maximum altitude of the G-1 based on normal payload was about 25,000 feet. Ace had been used to flying over thunderstorms at 41,000 feet, but penetrating a squall line at lower altitudes was much more problematic. In addition, the noisy and chaotic ramp activity at Smyrna simulated a scene out of a sci-fi horror movie: high-speed lift trucks, complemented by ramp rats scurrying from aircraft to aircraft and cargo "igloos" moving about in a seemingly out-of-control fashion. This cacophony of men and equipment was punctuated by the ear-piercing high-pitched scream of turboprop engines. In freight-dog terminology this ramp scenario could only be described as a "clusterf__." It was, amazingly enough, functional, and by 5:30 a.m. the ramp had magically transitioned to an area of desolation, and the Emery Air Freight boxes were enroute to their destination.

Another odd dimension of the upside-down sleep schedule was that when the freight dogs arrived at their hotel at about seven a.m., they had finished work, but everyone else was headed off to work. This allowed the pilots to wash down their scrambled eggs with a couple of beers before retiring to their hotel rooms to rest before "hauling some boxes" that evening. Ace recalls a flight in which he was administered his annual line check with the chief pilot, and the debriefing was completed during breakfast while he quaffed down a few cold brews. Since the FARs only required eight hours between the *bottle and the throttle,* the thirst quenching, was perfectly legal. The breakfast beers were needed to assist with the pilot's trip to "slumber-land." Attempting to sleep in a hotel during the day could be very trying, and despite a large "DO NOT DISTURB" sign on the door, the maids would insist on regularly entering and shouting, "Do you need anything?" The maids also insisted on vacuuming the hall floor as close as possible to any "DO NOT DISTURB" signs. There were reports of pilots going to the hall to snatch the vacuum from the maid and then locking it in their room.

Despite the comfortable work environment and conditions of flying a G-1 with a known schedule (sans beeper) and lots of time off, Ace was unable to wrest himself away from the ever-so-luring siren song of the Learjet charter world. The South Florida Learjet charter operators needed part-time, day-rate pilots. Ace couldn't resist the amenities of the charter world, including generous tips, leftover stone crab claws, and Dom Perignon to wash down the seafood— not to mention the always-enticing possibility that an air-ambulance nurse might show an interest in joining the eight-mile-high club on the deadhead flight back to Fort Lauderdale. The mile-high club is quite popular amongst young pilots in their small propeller airplanes, but the eight-mile-high club was extremely exclusive since only the very wealthy or the Learjet flight crews would have access to the required 41,000-foot altitude as well as to the privacy of the entire cabin of a jet airplane. A few of the Learjet pilots had custom-made "eight-mile-high pins" that provided a bit of the impetus for this unique venture as they could be worn with pride by the daring, young ladies seeking a bit of status amongst their envious and promiscuous friends.

TIRED PILOTS AND THUNDERSTORMS

It was Ace's week off from his G-1 flying, and in the late afternoon of September 24, 1979, he received a call requesting his services to fly a charter that evening to Guatemala City. He arrived at the airport at approximately nine p.m., and as he was preparing the aircraft for the flight, the owner of the company, Mr. Bill, arrived on the scene. Mr. Bill announced that he was very tired, having just returned from an air-ambulance trip to Cairo, Egypt. He said he would sit in the right seat and pull gear for Captain Ace. Mr. Bill was actually captain-qualified in the Learjet, but he wanted to sit back and relax. He picked the wrong trip, as this one would be filled with many challenging encounters.

Two captains flying together often created havoc on the flight deck. This was, however, an exception, as both Bill and Ace had their hands full, dealing with the many problems that they encountered on this flight. Shortly after departure, near Key West, a forecast for a large area of embedded thunderstorms turned out to be accurate. Ace and Mr. Bill were very busy monitoring their aircraft's weather radar in an attempt to avoid one of these level-five, mature thunderstorms, when the weather radar decided to go on the fritz. Mid-way between Key West and the Yucatán Peninsula, one of the normally reliable GE engines also elected to take some time off. The single-engine operation in embedded thunderstorms without radar was quite challenging. A descent to a lower altitude was necessary, but it was not possible to get an altitude-change clearance, since the air-traffic control folks had also taken the night off! It was necessary to descend to 24,000 feet before the flamed-out engine would reignite. Although air traffic control was not available to guarantee a safe separation from other aircraft, Ace and Mr. Bill had no choice but to climb back to 41,000 feet in order to have enough fuel to reach their destination. Finally, communication was reestablished with ATC, and the most recent weather forecast for Guatemala City indicated low ceiling, low visibility, and thunderstorms in all quadrants.

The arrival in the Guatemala City area confirmed the previous weather information, and with just enough fuel remaining to go *not very far*, the VOR approach, namely the *only* approach available, to runway 35 was initiated. On the final approach at the designated MDA (minimum descent altitude) and missed-approach-point DME, there was no runway in sight. Therefore, an immediate decision was made to cheat by a couple hundred feet in the hopes of finding a runway. After breaking out below the overcast, the runway was spotted and some low-level, maximum-performance maneuvering allowed Ace to land the airplane in the heavy rain and wind. While the plane taxied to the ramp, the cockpit and cabin were filled with the silence of people issuing thanks to their chosen object of worship. Upon reaching the ramp, Ace set the parking brake, and Mr. Bill opened the cabin door to allow the passenger to disembark. Ace remained in the cockpit since he was experiencing Parkinson's Disease-like symptoms with quivering legs that felt like jelly as they failed to respond to his desire to get out of his seat. Ace's body was adrenaline-depleted, and a portion of his autonomic nervous system had shut down. Ace's final flight in the 727 was punctuated with a few seconds of intense turmoil, but the Guatemala trip wins the prize for Most Harrowing Aviation Experience (MHAE).

The immediate aftermath of this trip involved sleeping in the humidity-soaked, mosquito-infested airplane. A major earthquake had occurred the previous day, and no hotels were available. Most of the windows in the terminal were broken, and the floor was littered with stranded passengers. Ace and Bill were just happy to have their own space. When they awoke, they were lucky enough to find a few packages of stale crackers for breakfast. The hedonistic, jet-set existence that is the norm for Learjet charter flights was clearly not accessible, and Ace yearned for his comfortable recliner chair at Zantop operations, where he snoozed while he waited for his G-1 aircraft to be loaded with freight.

ZANTOP AIRWAYS SOLD TO TAG (ORION AIR)

Back at Zantop, meanwhile, everyone enjoyed the good life of stable employment. However, if everything is going along smoothly in aviation, it is probably time to fasten the seat belt, because some invisible CAT (clear air turbulence) is imminent. Zantop Airways functioned very efficiently up until a midweek bulletin was issued to all the pilots, announcing a mandatory pilot meeting in Detroit on the upcoming Sunday. The meeting was so important that the company bought airline tickets for the majority of those pilots who did not live in the Detroit area. As the pilots gathered in the large conference room of the Ramada Inn, there was a sense of impending doom, since everyone knew that whatever was "coming down" was pretty significant, and the results might not be pretty. Lloyd introduced the pilot group to some very professional-looking businessmen in Brooks Brother's sharkskin suits. The pilots developed an immediate dislike for them. When they then spoke of their firm's purchase of the quaint little mom-and-pop company, it became readily apparent that the good times would soon be all gone, and the sense of "family" would soon fade into the annals of aviation. The new employer, The Aviation Group (TAG)/Orion Air, was a quasi-Wall-Street investment operation, and it was quite clear that the company had intentions to adopt the Harvard-Business-

School mantra of "maximum utilization of human resources," even though they spoke of a "harmonious and synergistic transition."

A few weeks later, Ace was designated as the captain-pilot representative who would meet with the Orion management to ensure that the pilot force would not undergo exploitation. He and his copilot colleague, John Bilo, ventured off to corporate headquarters to take on this potentially draconian management team and to let them know up front that the pilot group was a force with which to be reckoned. Ace and John were quite pleased with the compensation package that Orion presented to them, reporting back to their pilot colleagues the seemingly positive results of their meeting. Unfortunately, Ace and John were well over their heads in naïve acceptance of the new conditions. When the complex pay program had been investigated more closely, it was soon discovered that the pilots might actually take a small pay cut. Ace and John had been hoodwinked by the smooth-talking "suits." Union cards were circulated, and the lengthy and difficult process of organizing for union protection began. The likelihood of an unfavorable future at Orion sent Ace back to the typewriter to revise his résumé and to seek employment as a corporate pilot.

Although a few attractive employment situations appeared on the horizon, Ace was headed for the exit door at Orion when he received a call from Chief Pilot Rod Swank, informing Ace that he was scheduled for B-727 captain's type-rating training at Braniff Airlines in Dallas. The company had garnered a contract with UPS to operate Boeing 727s for the package-delivery giant. Ace *re-evaluated* the situation and voted unanimously to grab hold of this big brass ring. Quite coincidently, Ace had also been invited to his first major airline interview with Braniff Airlines. The interview seemed to be going quite well until Ace naively asked the question, "Would I be able to continue flying Learjets on my off days in order to maintain my flying skills, since I would be a flight engineer at Braniff?" The response from the panel of senior captains was an array of raised eyebrows since it was taboo to show anything other than devout commitment to the company. By not knowing the rules of the game Ace had disqualified himself, and the interviewing curmudgeons immediately terminated the conversation. This later proved to be a blessing in disguise in light of the fact that the rising super star of the airline world, Braniff International Airlines, would soon come crashing down like an out-of-control asteroid as its rapid over-expansion managed to destroy the airline.

CHAPTER SEVEN
If It Ain't a Boeing, I Ain't Going

The 727 training nearly brought on the demise of Ace because he initially struggled severely. He had excelled in ground school and scored the highest grades on all the aircraft-system tests. He then headed off to simulator training with the idea that flying a 727 would be extremely easy for a pilot who had flown high-performance fighter jets and the sensitive, unstable Learjet. But on the first simulator session, he discovered that the 727 "sim" acted as if it were on the end of a bungee cord. The solid, honest feel of the Gulfstream turbo-prop was now replaced by what seemed like a squealing greased pig that wanted to bury Ace in a large pile of its manure. Simulator ride number two wasn't much better. His traumatic sense of incompetence was intensified as Ace watched his simulator partner named Todd fly the "box" with near precision. Ace later discovered that, while he himself had only a few hours of jet-simulator experience, Todd had been a C-141 simulator instructor in the Air Force and had flown jet simulators for hundreds of hours. After the second simulator ride, Ace went back to his room and seriously considered tearing up his pilot's license (airman's certificate) since he was convinced that he was a totally incompetent pilot. It has been theorized by many pilots that flight simulators are the key element in a sinister plot by engineers to humiliate pilots.

ACE FINALLY FINDS THE HANDLE

The third simulator session had a few bright moments as Ace seemed to be getting a handle on this unstable, electronic torture device. Things started coming together during the next two training sessions, and the sixth simulator flight was a type-rating check ride with the FAA examiner sitting behind Ace to determine if he was going to be a competent Boeing 727 captain. After a normal takeoff and climb to 5,000 feet, the first maneuvers performed were the steep turns. Ace managed to "wire" the steep turns with no loss of altitude and airspeed, and the FAA examiner responded with a highly congratulatory comment that greatly alleviated the "check-ride-itis" that Ace was experiencing. The rest of the check ride went well, and Ace successfully completed this difficult portion of the qualification procedures.

A few days later, Ace and two of his colleagues-in-training went for their aircraft check ride. Getting out of the simulator and into the aircraft was very relieving. Ace did his "bounces" first, and after three *firm* landings, the FAA check pilot deemed the landings to be acceptable. Ace's first encounter with the left seat of the real 727 was a success, and he retired to the cabin to revel in his personal glory. Braniff Airline's 727s were the most elegant in the world with their all-leather interiors and uniquely stylish, single-color paint job. While sitting in the soft, sensual leather seat as the other pilots performed their bounces, Ace gained a sense of overwhelming fulfillment as he reflected on the fact that he would soon be functioning as the captain on one of these glorious air machines. His smug sense of pride was enhanced by the fact that a few weeks previously he had felt unworthy to fly *any* airplane after being severely beaten up by the "box."

The following week Ace headed to Seattle where he rendezvoused with a Braniff check airman to begin his IOE (initial operating experience) training. Ace was still on cloud nine as he climbed into the big, sleek Boeing "3-holer" and headed for ORD (Chicago's O'Hare airport). During one of the legs of the IOE training, it was required that an FAA examiner sit in the cockpit jump seat to evaluate the new captain. At ORD the FAA check pilot entered the flight deck and joined the flight crew for his evaluation of the rookie captain. The enroute phase from ORD to Worchester, Massachusetts, proceeded quite uneventfully, but the approach to the runway called for an ADF approach to circle for landing with a low ceiling. This presented a real handful for Ace, and the night landing to a strange runway had him on the edge of his seat trying to determine if the wheels were ten feet or ten inches off the runway. Suddenly, the wheels magically started rolling on the runway. Once again, "the blind pig had found the acorn." The sheer, dumb-luck, "grease-job landing" deluded the FAA examiner into the notion that perhaps Ace was an ace. Ace soon completed his IOE training and was given a few days off before assimilation into the regular flight schedule.

THE MAGNIFICENT 727 "THREE-HOLER"

During this period of time, Ace had been socializing with some pilots employed by Ryan International Airlines. These pilots informed him that Ryan intended to acquire 727 aircraft to operate for Emery Worldwide Air Freight, and that the company would have an aircraft based in Miami. His current employer, Orion Air, hinted that it might be necessary for their pilots to live in the area of Louisville, Kentucky, the location of the UPS hub airport. Ace did not want to relocate his family to Louisville.

Ace sent a résumé to Ryan International informing the company that he sought employment for the Miami base. He immediately received a response and was invited to Wichita for an interview. Ryan offered him a position as a training captain (check airman) to help train the pilots who would be assigned to fly the 727 for the new Emery contract. Ace's two previous airline employers, Zantop and Orion, were FAR 121 operations, and Ryan needed a pilot with FAR 121 experience to function as a check airman to train the new pilots. The salary offered nearly doubled the amount he was receiving from his Orion employer. Ace would be based in Miami, but occasionally he would be required to fly with a first-class pass on United Airlines to Denver, where he would administer simulator training since Ryan had a contract with United to provide training for the new Boeing pilots.

The decision to leave Orion for Ryan constituted an absolute "no brainer." Ace was grateful for the free training in the 727, but it would have been demeaning to work for the pathetic sum of $26,000 per year as a 727 captain. Ace gave his employer, Orion, the recommended two-week notice, and he was rewarded by not being called to fly during this period. The Orion management team had apparently viewed him as a despicable ingrate, since he was resigning after having just finished his expensive flight training and the company did not want him around the other pilots. Perhaps there was a premise that he would symbolize the proverbial "rotten apple in the barrel" and contaminate the rest of Orion's pilot group. The Orion management team was incensed, and the chief pilot added to Ace's infamy by expressing to as many people as possible his disdain for this ungrateful turncoat.

Since Ryan International had not yet begun to fly the 727 for Emery, Ace traveled to the United Training Center in Denver (DENTK) to begin check-airman training. He would then be assigned the task of administering simulator training to the Ryan pilots who had been flying the company's Learjets and Cessna Citations. He would also administer aircraft training and IOE for both captains and copilots. This was a very curious situation, in that Ryan's 727s would be piloted by a group of pilots who had never flown large jets, particularly the 727. The trainees would also receive most of their training from a check airman (Ace), who had *very little* experience in the 727. Amazingly enough, and despite the minimal level of experience in the cockpit, Ryan never had an accident or a significant incident as long as the company operated 727 aircraft.

A major contributor to this success was that a majority of the flight engineers were furloughed United Airline pilots, most of whom had several years of experience in the 727. Their advanced knowledge of the aircraft and the expert assistance that they provided to the window-seat pilots proved invaluable. Another contributing factor to the impeccable safety record of the program was the world-class training facility provided by United Airlines. One more additional bonus was that the aircraft Ryan operated for Emery were ex-United 727s, and this helped provide continuity of training. But the major reason for the excellent safety record centered on these young, extremely talented aviators. One of the young pilots, Bob Walker, had to wait until he had reached twenty-three years of age to become a captain (FAA stipulation). In spite of his youth and inexperience, his performance in the simulator upgrade training stood at a level that exceeded the norm by a wide margin. Ace often attempted to test Walker by loading him down with multiple emergencies, but the youthful trainee handled every situation with great ease and competence while maintaining nearly perfect aircraft control.

Ace received a refresher ground school, followed by simulator training and check ride. Upon completion of this phase of his certification as a check airman for the 727, he then had to administer a simulator check ride and an aircraft check ride for one of the new pilots. The simulator check-ride training came off without a glitch, but the aircraft training revealed Ace's inexperience and thus led to 727 war-story number one, with *hundreds more to follow!*

Ace jumped into the left seat of the 727 with a soon-to-be-Ryan first officer for a copilot-certification check ride. The standard terminology for the airline crew is captain, FO (first officer/copilot) and SO/FE (second officer/flight engineer). Along with Ace and the Ryan FO trainee on this flight were the SO, a veteran United Airlines flight-engineer instructor, and the United Airlines Director of 727 Training, Captain John Perkins, who sat in the jump seat to evaluate Captain Ace's check-airman capability. This copilot check ride, also referred to as "bounces," would involve a short flight to the Pueblo, Colorado, airport. After three or four approaches with touch and go landings, the flight would then return to Denver's Stapleton International Airport.

With approximately 10,000 pounds of fuel remaining in the aircraft, Ace very foolishly requested one more ILS approach. The decision to fly that approach elicited gasps of concern from Captain Perkins and the United Airlines flight engineer. They were both very concerned about arriving back at Denver in a low-fuel state during the busy afternoon arrival rush. Ace's inexperience in the 727 was clear from his lack of awareness regarding the aforementioned low-fuel state; as a consequence, the landing at Denver occurred with slightly less than 7,000 pounds of fuel aboard. During the debriefing session, Captain Perkins justifiably admonished Ace for choosing to fly the additional approach with so little fuel remaining. Nevertheless, he agreed to sign off Ace, as a "good-to-go-train-them" check airman for Ryan International Airlines. In his 727 career of 11,500 hours of flight time and at least 10,000 landings, only twice did Ace land the 727 with less than 7,000 pounds of fuel remaining.

The following day Ace went to Ryan headquarters in Wichita to pick up a 727 that he and his crew would fly to Dayton, Ohio, the location of Emery Airfreight's "super hub." At approximately four a.m. the next morning, he departed Dayton for Miami with the inaugural Ryan Air/Emery 727 load of freight. The backside of the clock and the usual diminished functionality that occurs with lack of sleep revealed its insidious effects on this maiden flight. The tired-pilot syndrome was an-all-too frequent event throughout Ace's career. Ace sat in the right seat, administering IOE training to a new captain.

This should have been a relatively easy task since Captain Rick already had a few hundred hours of flight time in the aircraft. As the aircraft passed by Jacksonville, the flight crew's brains began to clear away the cobwebs of the dastardly "O-dark 30" hours as the morning dawn peeked over the horizon of the vast Atlantic Ocean. This flight appeared to be a cakewalk as the Ryan freighter had been cleared direct to Miami. The entire Florida peninsula came into view, and it was difficult to find even a small cloud. The tired, hungry cockpit crewmembers focused on their upcoming breakfast at Denny's.

Ace then decided to take a look at the flight engineer's panel to check the fuel status. This proved to be a very timely action since the FE had been feeding all three engines out of tank number two. Bob, the FE, had followed proper fuel-management procedures by feeding all three engines out of tank number two until the three tanks had an equal amount of fuel. However, he had failed to switch back to the normal "tank to engine" mode, and since he had been feeding all three engines from tank two, it now had less than 4,000 pounds remaining. If the flight crew did not reset the fuel panel, within another few more minutes tank number two would be empty and all three engines would then flame out. FE Bob re-established the fuel switches to their proper position, and the possibility of the Ryan 727 briefly becoming a jet-engine-equipped glider was avoided. Upon arrival in Miami, Ace made a telephone call to Ryan headquarters in order to relay the message that the maiden Ryan 727/Emery Air Freight flight had safely arrived. Not surprisingly, he did not volunteer the information regarding the near flameout of all three engines over Jacksonville.

Ace and his 727 Ryan pilot colleagues, with their new $450 airline-pilot uniforms, would perform their duties with great enthusiasm since they had just made a quantum leap in their status as professional pilots. They were scheduled for one week of work (Monday thru Friday), followed by nine days off. It was quite common during his non-flying weeks for Ace to show up at Denver for simulator training and check rides for the new pilots. Occasionally, he was sent to Wichita to administer aircraft training and aircraft type-rating rides. The best aspect of his extra duty as a training pilot was the aircraft training for those new copilots who had just completed their simulator training. This involved a daytime flight from Miami International to the nearby TNT airport (Dade-Collier Training Airport), which lay in the middle of the Everglades about thirty miles west of Miami. The aircraft was filled with fuel, and the pilots flew ILS and visual approaches to touch-and-go-landings until their level of proficiency deemed them ready for "the line," namely regularly scheduled flights.

Ace often brought along his private-pilot neighbor to ride in the cockpit jump seat, and on one fortuitous occasion, he was able to take along his father, the original rogue aviator, in the cockpit jump seat for a training flight at TNT. On another occasion, Ace's twelve-year-old son climbed into the jump seat. On the brief return flight to Miami, Ace put him in the copilot seat and let him actually fly the aircraft for a few minutes. While this was a great thrill for his son, the flying experience did not hook the youth on flying; instead, he wisely entered a career path in the high-tech field. Yet another fun-filled training adventure involved barrel rolls over Denver in the 727 simulator. Ace did, however, demonstrate unusual restraint: during his twenty-two years of flying the highly maneuverable three-holer, he never did roll the actual airplane in flight.

The Miami-based Emery 727 normally departed Miami at nine p.m. for a nonstop flight to the Emery hub at Dayton, Ohio. After four or five hours of hanging around the hub, during "the sort," the Miami crew would depart at four a.m. to return to Miami. The copilot always flew this return flight at this most awful hour in order to permit the captain to rest up for another day of fun and sun in Florida. Ace usually stayed awake for the first ten minutes of flight, but there were instances of deep snoring before the flaps were completely retracted. The return flight to Miami was extremely boring, and with the circadian-rhythm monster exhibiting its intractable influence, it was very rare that this two-hour flight concluded without a brief nap. During the longer days of summer months, a beautiful sunset was in view during the northbound flight while the early-morning return flight to Miami would often provide a spectacular sunrise over the Atlantic. The visual aesthetics of aviation frequently trump all other considerations.

The grandeur of the beautiful sunsets was totally negated by the exposure to the noisy and jarring activity on the Emery ramp. The Emery ramp at Dayton fostered a level of chaos that superseded the previously described Emery ramp at Smyrna. Still worse was the crew lounge, a large, uninviting room filled with bleak plastic tables and chairs. The so-called lounge had the function to serve as break room for the ramp rats and Emery "sort" employees, a place fully equipped with vending-machine "food simulators" that would dispense non-nutritional, food-substitute items. The noisy commotions, adding an unpleasant ambience somewhere in the 110-decibel range, emanated from the sort area. This nerve-rattling environment was created by the assembly-line apparatus that moved the freight along conveyer belts, sending freight to the correct aircraft. This high-pitched screeching noise was often outdone by the clatter of lift trucks and other freight-moving vehicles and screaming jet engines. Only a seasoned freight dog would be able to enjoy his tasteless machine coffee and stale pastry while engaging in woeful aviation tales with his colleagues. All commercial pilots who fly passengers should experience the night "sort" of the freight carriers in order to find out how the other half lives. In fact, longevity research has discovered that a group of pilots who spent most of their careers engaged in night freight had retired at sixty and died at sixty-three. These ugly actuarial results reveal the effect of poor diet along with working at night and attempting to sleep by day.

While Ace's training duties presented challenges, normal line flying represented boredom and lifelessness. A few instances of wintertime ground fog resulted in a necessary diversion, usually to Indianapolis. Occasionally, it would be necessary to penetrate a line of thunderstorms, sometimes offering a particularly challenging scenario because the old freighters had antiquated and marginally effective weather radar systems.

PRAY FOR A SECULAR PILOT

One of the more interesting airplane anecdotes from the Ryan-aviation-early-1980s era involved a Ryan captain nicknamed "the Reverend." Reverend Steve, a born-again Christian, frequently engaged in proselytizing. It was reported that he read his Bible while attempting to penetrate a squall line of thunderstorms. The copilot, according to the reports, worked diligently with the airborne weather radar in order to find a soft spot through the possible severe turbulence when the Reverend Steve, as the story goes, looked up from his Bible and stated, "God will help us through."

Such faith is not confined to one religion alone. A major aircraft accident in the Middle East involved a Muslim captain engaging in prayer and accepting that his fate would soon unite him with Allah. As the cabin crew awaited his command to evacuate the burning aircraft, he failed to respond. *The passengers and the flight crew all died in the inferno.* There are very likely many other aircraft accidents aided and abetted by the captain surrendering his duties to God's will. The author suggests that, if you board an aircraft whose pilots are referring to their religious texts rather than to their flight manual, the *only* prudent course of action is a quick "one-eighty" (reverse course) to travel via another flight.

The owner of the company, Mr. Ryan, also a born-again Christian, created great problems for the flight crews. A Boeing 727, the layman must understand, has numerous nooks and crannies in the cockpit, seemingly designed for the stowing of pictures of scantily clad women. The pilots would graciously share their women by leaving these salacious photos on exhibit for the next flight crew. This was negated, however, by Mr. Ryan's strong and seemingly overzealous anti-cheesecake stance when he instructed the maintenance personnel to remove and to destroy the pictures. The pilots, not to be denied their prurient pleasures, would soon replenish the discreetly located photos. Unfortunately, Mr. Ryan, who had a succession of very attractive young wives, did not understand that the male freight-dog's girlie *pics* represented a critical element to his well-being. At three a.m., as the pilots gathered together in flight operations waiting for their load sheets and flight plans, the missing pictures would come to the forefront as one of the more advanced topics of discussion. The effervescent Robert La Rue, who had a personality that could turn a chain-gang-forced march into a joyously carefree stroll down a scenic rural country road, usually led this discussion. His fun-loving personality and great sense of humor created such a positive environment at flight operations that the dreaded two-thirty to four-thirty a.m. time-frame became tolerable.

La Rue's sense of humor, moreover, was so adventuresome and radical that during an airline interview, he was asked the standard question, "Have you ever smoked marijuana?" His response was the obvious "No!" Upon completion of the interview, he asked the interviewer to meet him in the parking lot during lunch hour in order to "burn one" (slang for smoking marijuana). Another unverifiable anecdote has La Rue ditching an aircraft in the Florida Straits and then swimming to shore. One might speculate that this aircraft could have contained contraband.

Throughout most of the '70s, drug dealers were seemingly behind every palm tree in South Florida, and any mention of being a pilot would quite frequently result in an offer from a perfect stranger to "make a run." The East Coast of Florida in the '70s was comparable to the Mexican-American border in 2010. On weekends, the intra-coastal waterway was over-run by expensive drug-smuggling "cigarette boats" that could out-run the Coast Guard's boats. Old, propeller-driven cargo airplanes laden with bales of marijuana were flown into remote airports during the middle of the night. A few of the pilots Ace had encountered as casual acquaintances at the airport did spend some jail time for seeking the easy dollars of drug running.

Ace wisely avoided this temptation of easy money, but he did get caught in the middle of a DEA sting operation while flying his Emery Air Freight 727. As he and his fellow crewmembers sat in the cockpit during the loading process at Miami, two men entered the cockpit with a small package, informing the flight crew that this package would have to be carried in the cockpit. Ace then asked the question, "Who are you, and what's in the package?" The two men finally identified themselves as DEA agents, saying that the package contained cocaine. Because Ace wanted no part of being in the middle of a drug sting, he informed the DEA agents that the only way it, the package, could be carried on his airplane would be to have it loaded in the freight igloos with the other cargo, thus relieving Ace and his fellow pilots from any involvement *with* or any awareness *of* the movement of the illegal drugs. Ace also considered one possible outcome of his refusal to go along with the DEA agents: the suspected drug dealers on the other end of the flight might seek out Captain Ace and his crew as collaborators and attempt to inflict retribution. Prior to the use of trained drug-sniffing dogs, Ace entertained the probability that several billion dollars worth of illicit drugs traveled by air from point A to point B on the numerous package-carrying airlines.

Despite occasional challenges like the drug-sting operation, the freight-run life style flew onwards relatively uneventfully with nearly eighteen days per month free of duty. Therefore, Ace elected to remain current and qualified in the Learjet, and very pleased that several South Florida charter operators would occasionally call him to assume the captain's seat of the Learjet on chartered trips. The continuing Learjet opportunities signified a nice diversion from the other world of night freight even though the transition from ten feet above the runway during touchdown in the 727 to four feet above the runway in the Learjet proved to remain quite a challenge. Another challenging element of the Learjet diversion put Ace flying for several different operators, and nearly every Learjet had cockpit-configuration differences. Ace had flown mostly model 23, 24, and 25 Learjets, but he had approximately one-hundred hours in the Lear 35, a longer-range, more fuel-efficient aircraft.

LINBERGH DID IT IN A PROP PLANE— IT WILL BE EASY IN A LEARJET

On the Friday evening prior to Memorial Day weekend of 1981, Ace's previous employer, BizJet, contacted him to fly a Learjet trip the following day to Zürich, Switzerland. He was informed that his copilot, JB Barnes, had flown across the North Atlantic, and his experience in the cockpit would be most helpful. While Ace had never flown across the North Atlantic, he welcomed the challenge. When he met JB at the airport the following morning, Ace immediately noticed an absence of the Lear 35 on the tarmac and soon discovered that he and JB would instead pilot the Lear 25 to Europe, the start of another day dominated by Murphy's Law.

The Lear 25 had a shortened range capability, which would make the trip much more challenging. Ace and JB stopped to pick up a passenger in Fort

Lauderdale, made another stop in Pennsylvania to fetch an additional pilot, and refueled at Goose Bay, Labrador. After Goose Bay, one more refueling stop at Keflavik, Iceland, would be required prior to the final flight to Zurich, Switzerland. The departure from Goose Bay was put on hold for a few hours because of the weather at Keflavik, Iceland, the only acceptable refueling stop, was WOXOF (zero ceiling and zero visibility). One of Ace's Learjet colleagues previously had the very uncomfortable experience, he told Ace, of occupying the right seat with a rich, very elderly, marginally competent Palm-Beach-socialite pilot while landing his Learjet at Keflavik. The pilot-owner flew the airplane through severe weather and crosswinds, and with minimal fuel remaining, the pilot's "pucker meter" pegged out to its maximum level until the aircraft was safely on the ground. Ace wanted no part of such a precarious scenario. Because the computer flight plan indicated minimal fuel remaining upon arrival, he closely monitored the weather situation at Keflavik until the revised report finally showed CAVU (clear and visibility unlimited).

The aircraft was then "packed" with as much fuel as possible since the computer flight plan indicated a very minimal 1100 pounds of remaining fuel at destination. After only thirty minutes of a three-and-one-half-hour flight, the navigation had deteriorated to dead reckoning only, because navigation aids would not be received until approximately 200 miles from Iceland. This "twilight zone" element was accentuated by the fact that there was also no radio communication available. The computer flight plan provided appropriate magnetic headings based on the forecast winds at 39,000 feet. During this seemingly pre-historic era of aviation navigation, the wonderful concept of GPS was not yet available. To add to the drama, there were two significant glitches in the computer's flight-plan information. First, the forecast of a slight *tail wind* was in error since there was actually a slight *head wind*. To further exasperate this tenuous trip across "the pond," the outside air temperature was abnormally warm, resulting in additional fuel consumption. The navigation problem was easily solved when the weather radar used in the ground-mapping mode revealed the southern coast of Greenland and the West Coast of Iceland.

The destination was in sight in the aircraft's electronic eye—the radar—but the fuel situation remained tenuous, and this concern intensified as the rare easterly headwinds increased. On the final approach to Keflavik, the remaining fuel on the aircraft stood at approximately 400 pounds, and when the landing gear would not extend on the initial attempt, there was a brief moment of disbelief and advanced alarm. At this point the cockpit hyperventilation intensified, afflicting the three pilots with the "deer in the headlights" blank stare as they briefly contemplated this complication. A recycling of the gear handle caused the illumination of three green lights, indicating the landing gear was down and locked, resulting in a loud sigh of relief for all concerned. An uneventful landing was made. A missed approach or go-around might have resulted in fuel starvation and a ditching of the aircraft in the bitter cold seas off the coast of Iceland.

Because of the northern latitude and the long days of late May, the eastbound flight created a very short night. The departure from Goose Bay had occurred just after sunset, and the plane landed at Keflavík with the bright morning sun in the bleary-eyed pilots' eyes. The following flight from Keflavik to Zürich, Switzerland, went by without incident although highlighted by a descent past the verdant German countryside on a perfect summer day amid a sky filled with multi-colored hot air balloons. The cockpit crew, with Bill, the additional pilot, had now descended into a state of advanced sleep-deprivation euphoria, and this idyllic setting seemed to act as a cleansing dream after the nightmare of the previous flight. After landing in Zürich, the flight crew helped the passengers off-load their very heavy, cash-laden suitcases into a limousine. The passengers then drove off to their actual destination, Liechtenstein. Liechtenstein, adjacent to Switzerland, engaged itself during those years in the lucrative business of "off-shore banking." The passengers' risky, uncomfortable trip in the cramped Learjet was offset by the saving of a few million dollars of income tax money that would not be paid to the IRS.

Ace and his fellow pilots snatched a few hours of sleep in the hotel in an attempt to fight off severe jet lag and the accompanying sleep deprivation. It was now twilight in Zürich, and the jet-lag monster held its nasty fingers on the severely confused minds and bodies of the pilots as they ate their first meal in two days. Since it was pilot Bill's birthday, the decision to celebrate his birthday—and the successful excursion across the Atlantic Ocean—with a few drinks, was readily agreed to by all as the only proper course of action The party began in Bill's room since his refrigerator was well stocked with a fine complement of alcoholic beverages. After Bill's refrigerator was emptied, the restless aviators had more stories to tell and capitalized on the generous supply of beverages in JB's refrigerator. In what seemed like only a short period of time, they disbelievingly observed what they thought was a very premature sunrise: their little birthday party had extended from twilight to dawn. After a few hours of sleep in a bed that seemed to be spinning, it became necessary to go to the airport to plan for the return flight to the U.S. Because the taxi ride was a bit unstable, Ace's equally unstable stomach required purging. JB laughed uncontrollably as his captain endured the humiliation of tossing his cookies alongside the airport's entry road. Despite this disgracefully ignominious situation, the required international paperwork and other flight-required logistics were completed, and the pilots returned to the hotel.

After a few more hours of rest and recuperation at the hotel, the westbound trip along the famous "Blue Spruce Route" would get under way. Leg one was an uneventful flight to Shannon, Ireland, for a quick and efficient refueling for the next leg to Keflavík, Iceland. It was very pleasant to arrive at Keflavík with *more* than a few gallons of fuel remaining. The third leg went from Keflavik to Goose Bay, Labrador. From Goose Bay, it was on to Allentown, Pennsylvania, to drop off Bill, and then back to Fort Lauderdale to return the charter passengers with their empty suitcases. Ace and JB finally ferried the empty aircraft back to West Palm Beach.

After an extended recuperative rest, Ace went to the BizJet office on the following day to relate this adventure to his colleagues and to collect his pay. As a part-time pilot, Ace was paid the going rate of one hundred dollars per day. Captain Bob, the owner and sole proprietor of BizJet, engaged in some self-serving, creative calculations that determined Ace and JB should be paid for only two days of work. Yet, in slightly more than forty-eight hours, Ace had flown twenty-seven hours and had created approximately $30,000 worth of revenue for the company. Without fanfare, Ace accepted the $200, a sum that represented a wage scale of $4.00 per hour for Captain Ace. When he walked out of the door at BizJet, he vowed never to return for additional exploitation. Captain Bob was equally adept in the extortion of salary from part-time copilots. If, for instance, one of the other Learjet operators in the area needed a copilot, BizJet would send the company a part-time copilot. He then paid the copilot $50 and billed the other Learjet operator $100 for his services, while pocketing half of the copilot's salary. Captain Bob greatly increased his personal wealth while operating BizJet. On the other side of the coin, he died in an untimely boating accident at an early age.

After this brief "European vacation," Ace made the commitment not to accept less than minimum wage for his pilot services, choosing only to fly the 727 for the next decade. The employment situation at Ryan was quite stable. In fact, many of the passenger airlines began to hire more pilots as a result of deregulation. A few of the more experienced pilots employed with some of the other Emery-contract carriers discovered a start-up airline by the name of Air Atlanta. Ace and Dwane, one of his Miami-based pilot colleagues, managed to garner an interview with this new and uniquely singular airline.

CHAPTER EIGHT

Pilots' Nirvana

(A SCHEDULED PASSENGER AIRLINE WITH HOT MEALS AND FINE FLIGHT ATTENDANTS)

Air Atlanta facilitated the interview with a free pass to Atlanta on one of its scheduled flights. With only ten other passengers aboard the aircraft, three stunningly beautiful flight attendants pampered Ace and Dwane with gourmet food and first-class service. After enjoying some freshly squeezed orange juice, complemented by Eggs Benedict and Belgian waffles with Vermont maple syrup, their decision to accept an employment offer was now predetermined. Air Atlanta had at least three remarkable qualities: the entire aircraft spoke volumes of first-class service with its large first class seats; passengers dined on top-quality food and fine wine, served by the "crème de la crème" of Atlanta-area debutantes. Both Ace and Dwane warmly embraced their new job, and the horrors of the Dayton freight ramp soon receded into the remote crevices of the memory bank. The gourmet meals served in the cabin on every flight were also provided to the cockpit crewmembers. The dreadfulness of the noisy break room and the unpalatable machine food at Dayton also became distant memories

Although hired as captain for the rapidly expanding airline, current staffing required Ace to begin his employment as a flight engineer. The flight engineer training proved to be quite challenging because Ace fell under the delusion that his left-seat experience in the 727 would provide an easy transition to the 727 flight engineer's seat. However, Ace needed to put his full attention towards the task in order to complete the training successfully and to win approval as a competent Air Atlanta 727 flight engineer. Since the company anticipated that his services would soon be required in the window seat, he also became qualified as both captain and copilot. This triple-threat qualification that allowed him to fill any of the three seats in the "three-holer" was a crew scheduler's dream. Ace had a "crash pad" on the airport perimeter, and, since a free meal was a certainty, he made himself readily available for any trip in any one of the three seats. Ace's status of current and qualified in all three seats, an advantage that allowed Ace to frequently bounce from the FE panel to the captain's chair, played a significant role in providing him with stimulating and interesting challenges.

The core of the Air Atlanta pilot staff, particularly the captains, were former Continental pilots, who had gone on strike after the infamous aviation entrepreneur, Frank Lorenzo, had *once again* threatened to reduce the pilots' salary to a paltry sum. The experience level of the veteran 727 captains, complemented by the first-class cabin amenities, generated a top-quality product, making Air Atlanta the darling of the startup airlines. The pilots immediately voted to be represented by ALPA, the largest and most effective pilot union. The ex-Continental pilots displayed intense hatred towards the scab pilots who had crossed the picket line to fly the Continental aircraft. Exposure to the vehement and bitterly striking pilots would later play a part in Ace's employment decisions.

Air Atlanta, a feeder airline for Pan Am, had several daily flights between Atlanta and Miami, including flights between Atlanta and JFK Airport in New York. The chief pilot had a liberal jump-seat policy that permitted the authorization of several cockpit jump-seat passes as long as there were empty seats in the cabin. Word of this very benevolent policy traveled fast; as a consequence, many commuting pilots and flight attendants soon enjoyed the benefits of traveling first class on Air Atlanta. The recognized record for jump-seat passengers on an Air Atlanta flight was thirteen, despite the fact that there were only two cockpit jump seats. In addition, all passengers aboard Air Atlanta took advantage of one particularly significant aspect of the first class service: unlimited free alcohol. This is to say that Air Atlanta stood out as a party airline. Since all the employees could partake in free travel, it was not uncommon for the seven p.m. ATL to MIA flight to have ten to fifteen "non-rev" passengers congregating in the aft section of the aircraft with the commuting pilots and flight attendants. With the free alcohol and the free food, everyone had a good time. On top of all that, because there was no required inventory of the alcohol supply on the aircraft, the flight attendants frequently provided free layover libations for the flight crews. Most of the pilots abided by the "eight-hours-between-the-bottle-and-the throttle" FAA requirement; however, the Miami layovers enticed many of the young, fast-lane flight attendants to venture to the world-renowned party spot: South Beach, Miami. Flight attendants working the seven a.m. Miami to Atlanta flight would sometimes return to the layover hotel just in time to freshen up, to put on the uniform, and to work the one easy flight of the day back to Atlanta.

PILOTS ARE LIKE SNOWFAKES: NO TWO ARE ALIKE

One of the leaders of the party pack, a young pilot named George Zifferblatt, possessed an outgoing, flamboyant personality. "Ziff," as he was affectionately referred to, didn't have a lot of polish, but he did have a lot of pizzazz, and his exuberant personality led to considerable comic relief. As is often the case with advancement, the comical side of his personality crossed over to the negative side when he received an upgrade to captain's status, instantly turning into an omniscient, omnipotent, tyrannical commander. At that time, Air Atlanta was expanding rapidly, thus resulting in relatively young and inexperienced copilots upgraded to captain. A number of these newly upgraded captains compensated for their lack of experience and security with sometimes disgusting displays of power and control. George, however, elevated this concept to its highest level whenever he barked orders and berated gate agents. Most of his victims would simply shake their heads and laugh at him, since to them he was only a big man acting like a yapping puppy dog. Someday, they knew, or at least hoped, he would become a mature, cool captain like the ex-Continental pilots, easy and secure in their competence.

A great example of the quiet but competent captain was one of Ace's favorite pilots, Ted McClard. Very slight of build and perhaps no more than 5'7" tall, Ted always maintained a pleasant and gracious demeanor. His wisdom was clearly revealed by a remark he once made about flying with many different captains. He said, "Every copilot should have the opportunity to fly with an asshole. Then he won't be one when he gets to the left seat," a simple, a useful, and a significant perspective. Ted had several thousand hours in the left seat of the 727, and the normally difficult-to-attain-grease-job landing in the 727 was a routine accomplishment for him. However, even experienced veterans occasionally make a hard landing.

Ace sat at the FE panel and Ted was in the left seat for a night landing to runway 9R at Miami International. A bit of wind shear over the threshold resulted in a very atypical hard landing with Ted at the controls. When the aircraft had cleared the runway and the flight attendants had opened the cabin door, the passengers' distress over the hard landing pervaded the cabin. Ted then picked up the PA microphone and, in his best gravelly-voiced captain dialect, made the following announcement: "Folks, I want you to know I've been flying these big jets 20 years, and that was the very best landing I ever made." The passengers, to the smiling relief of the flight crew, enjoyed this light, self-deprecating humor with which the diplomatic Ted had creatively defused the tension of the passengers in the cabin.

Of the many unforgettable characters at Air Atlanta was Ted's ex-Continental colleague, "high-speed" Harry Brown. Harry was like Ted, slight of build, soft-spoken, and unassuming. Air Atlanta was the first black-owned and black-managed airline, and Harry was one of several black pilots employed with the company. His slow talking, slow walking, cool demeanor made him susceptible to lighthearted comparisons to the black-media phenomenon, *Super Fly*. Harry had come a long way in a life that began in the cotton fields of the Florida Panhandle. The Vietnam War provided him with an escape route, and he performed service time as a helicopter pilot in that conflict. His survivability factor was evidenced by the fact that he had been shot down twelve times and rewarded with innumerable military service citations and awards.

One of his legendary deeds at Air Atlanta occurred on a layover. According to the story passed along through the rumor grapevine, the Air Atlanta pilots sat next to a table of Continental scab pilots who spoke disparagingly of Air Atlanta. This discord then ratcheted the hatred for Continental scabs up a notch. When one of the scabs went to the men's room, Harry discreetly followed. He then—equally discreetly—rearranged the scab's facial structure. Of course, this story could well represent a bit of cautionary folklore, fabricated, in other words, to illustrate the possible side effects when hungry-for-work pilots turn into scabs. But for Ace, the story solidified one good reason not to cross a picket line. Interestingly however, Harry's normally cool demeanor contradicted itself by his very noticeable fear of a mature thunderstorm. By way of example, while returning on a flight from Miami to Atlanta through clear air underneath a thunderstorm "anvil," his aircraft was pelted with heavy hail that produced severe damage. After this experience, Harry very judiciously avoided thunderstorms by an unusually wide margin.

To complement high-speed Harry, Air Atlanta was gifted with a "Sky God." Ron Arnold was 6'2", weighed 220 pounds, and displayed the chiseled features of a movie star. With his four stripes and confident demeanor, he personified the image of the airline captain. His colleagues and co-workers respectfully tagged him with the moniker, "Sky God." He also functioned as a check airman, who exhibited advanced understanding and knowledge of the 727, along with equally superlative stick-and-rudder skills. Ron had an outstanding aviation résumé, which included employment as check engineer at Western airlines, from which he had been furloughed. Ron then applied for employment at United Airlines but was unaccountably rejected in favor of another Air Atlanta pilot, a low-time, inexperienced copilot who exhibited a less-than-scintillating persona of a reclusive accountant.

Airline-hiring policies were often bizarre and inexplicable. According to legendary accounts, the Delta Airlines interviewing process involved the applicant sitting in a rocking chair. The great debate, *should the interviewee rock or should he or she not rock,* would echo in airplane cockpits for decades. The airlines would also require a battery of tests, including the Minnesota Multiphasic Personality Test, which had little, if any, bearing on one's aviation skills or aptitudes. Given such absurd attitudes and practices, it was common enough for a Casper Milquetoast—a pear-shaped figure who found it difficult to "walk and chew gum at the same time"—to be hired, while the Sky God-like exquisite aviator encountered rejection.

Air Atlanta's pilot management consisted primarily of ex-Continental pilots and other highly experienced aviators. As a result, pilots rather than personnel managers or quirky psychologists controlled the pilot hiring process. Also, Air Atlanta, a minority-owned airline, was very receptive to hiring minorities. The company employed six African-American pilots and three female pilots amongst the 120 pilots on the seniority list. Continuing on as a very desirable popular start-up airline, Air Atlanta attracted quality pilots, who received training from an experienced training department that insisted on high standards. The only anomaly amongst the quality aviators was a black flight engineer named Jerry, who continually exhibited ongoing incompetence at the FE panel and was regularly "written up" by the captains. Jerry was required to receive some remedial FE training. When he returned to the "line," his performance did not improve, and he soon found himself unemployed, the only Air Atlanta pilot ever to receive the pink slip. After the flight training management staff reviewed his background and flight time, they discovered that he had entered into his logbook a significant amount of "Parker Pen" flight time. "Parker Pen" is aviation slang for falsifying one's flight logbook. By a surprising coincidence, Ace would reconnect with Jerry at a later date.

Air Atlanta steadily increased its passenger loads and expanded its route structures, requiring additional aircraft to the fleet. Ace received promotion to the status of captain-check airman, and the influx of new pilots kept him busy administering IOE training. He couldn't wait to get to work because the upbeat attitude of the airline employees, combined with gratitude expressed by pleasant and gracious passengers, resulted in an extremely high level of job satisfaction. The minor downside was that the pilot salary ranked well below the industry norm. Pilot compensation, in fact, was so low that the beautiful flight attendants would rarely pay any attention to the pilot group. Many of them held to a passenger-screening process directed at the young male business executives, mandating that any male passenger who might try to seek their companionship had to wear Gucci loafers and a Rolex watch.

Ace was presented with an opportunity to become part of the Gucci-loafer-Rolex-watch crowd when United Airlines called him with a hard-to-refuse offer. On May 17, 1985, United Airline pilots went on strike. Ace had an application on file with United, declaring him a current and qualified 727 Captain. An unsolicited call from United informed him that he could immediately become a United Airlines 727 Captain with an annual salary of $125,000. Ace then asked the caller, "What will happen to me and what will my status be when the striking United Airline pilots return to work?" The answer came in the form of a lengthy and revealing silence. Ace could have immediately *tripled* his salary, but crossing the picket line was never a consideration. Not accepting this position cost Ace at least $2 million in potential salary and retirement funds!

He did, however, retain his dignity and was able to avoid the sinister hazing that the scab pilots experienced. Both Continental and Eastern airlines personnel departments would later attempt to entice Ace across the picket lines after their pilots, too, went on strike. Although unemployed during both of these job opportunities, he once again, unequivocally, said "No thanks." ALPA, also known as the Air Line Pilots' Association, was a very strong union, and its solidarity and its effort for reform not only resulted in better salary and work conditions for all pilots but also contributed in a paramount way to the outstanding safety record of the major U.S. airlines. ALPA, furthermore, initiated progressive training policies, along with very important restrictions to maximum flight and duty times. Pilot fatigue is a frequent contributing factor in airplane accidents and incidents. The fact that ALPA addressed this issue has probably saved thousands of lives. There is, however, more work to accomplish on this issue.

The major airlines were stepping up the hiring significantly, and several of the Air Atlanta pilots sought employment with the larger, more stable "legacy" carriers. Ace's roommate and colleague, Dwane, was hired by United and sacrificed his captain's chair at Air Atlanta to labor at the third seat (the flight engineer's panel) at United. Ace, in the meantime, picked up an interview with UPS, which began to form a flight department to operate its own fleet of airplanes. Ace was not hired, but in retrospect, this was a blessing, since the corporate culture at UPS was incompatible with his own value system. The UPS flight department gained the demeaning moniker, "Sky Nazis." This reputation will be elaborated on later in this chapter. While at Louisville for the UPS interview, Ace had a chance encounter with one of his ex-Air Atlanta colleagues, Jerry. The same "Parker Pen" Jerry who had been fired at Air Atlanta was now working at UPS—and that's not the last chapter of this particular story.

CINDERELLA STORY ENDS IN UGLY DIVORCE

The Air Atlanta pilots had unanimously voted to become an ALPA airline, but the pilot's association had not yet negotiated a functioning contract with the airline management. By December 1986, the company had ten 727 aircraft, and the future looked bright. A gala Christmas party was held and Michael Hollis—CEO, founder, and owner—sent a 727 to Washington, DC, in order to provide first-class travel to wine and dine many of his past government colleagues, including other significant associates. The cost of the flight, the lodging at the Ritz-Carlton, and the extravagant Christmas party totaled well over $100,000 of company funds, a short-lived though generous display of company well being. A few weeks later, company scuttlebutt indicated that Air Atlanta found itself in serious financial difficulties to the point that the airline might soon cease operations despite its strong load factor and outward appearance of success. The employees, led by the pilot group, became very proactive in attempting to save the company. A great sense of pride in their world-class product resulted in a deep desire to keep Air Atlanta alive. There were vociferous denunciations of Michael Hollis, but demands that he step down were unsuccessful.

Michael Hollis, on the brighter side, had received many plaudits as an up-and-coming, African-American aviation entrepreneur, and Air Atlanta personified the cover story for the burgeoning-airline-start-up phenomenon. Hollis was able to capitalize on the unbridled cooperation of the powerful Atlanta-area black political structure. The death of Air Atlanta in mid-February, 1987, (Feb. 19, 1987, *USA Today* newspaper article) aroused intense animosity in the dedicated employee group. When company employees found their health insurance cancelled and their paychecks bounced, no one had to tell them that Air Atlanta had taken a nosedive into oblivion. Ace lost over $5,000 in unpaid salary and per-diem expense compensation. He and his associates held strongly to the belief that Michael Hollis "took the money and ran," although this was impossible to validate since the company was privately held. Yet circumstantial evidence, based particularly on the large sum of investor money that Air Atlanta had absorbed, indicated the likelihood of foul play. Despite owing the employees at least a quarter of a million dollars in unpaid salary, Hollis then proceeded to purchase a radio station in Atlanta and sold it a short period of time for a very large profit. There were absolutely no reports of any attempts to pay his ex-employees the money they had earned. Despite pleas from the employee group, Atlanta-area media sources failed to engage in what should have been some very aggressive investigative journalism.

CHAPTER NINE

THE TURBULENT TEN
(1987 thru 1997)

"WILL FLY FOR FOOD"

Deregulation had opened the doors for aviation entrepreneurs to create start-up airlines with minimal capital and minimal aviation experience. When a pilot's resume indicated he or she had worked for one of these poorly run companies, major airlines would frequently reject them as candidates for employment, despite their experience and aviator skills. Numerous sad stories of the rise and fall of a new airline, such as the Air Atlanta travesty, were widespread in the aviation community. Ace returned to Florida, and while waiting for the next flying job to land in his lap, he attempted to fend off the bill collectors by engaging in manual labor. He found employment with his former golf buddy, Vinnie, in a nursery-irrigation-system endeavor. For a few weeks his work positioned him a couple of miles from the Palm Beach International final-approach fix. After eight hours of "chain gang" manual labor, the sight and the sound of the overflying 727s became emotionally debilitating for Ace.

But Ace kept the faith, and it became clear that UPS would soon initiate its own airline and discontinue its previous policy of having contract carriers fly the company's packages. Ace was given an inside track, with direct communication to the pilot who would serve as director of training for this long awaited, pilot-coveted, massive aviation operation. Ace's experience in the 727, together with background as a training-check airman, had opened the door to a potentially lucrative job. During the telephone interview, Ace informed the director of training that he was very interested in the management/check-airman position, but Ace went on to declare, "After a couple of years in the training department, I would like to become a line pilot." Responding straightforward, the UPS director of training said, "That is not possible because once an employee has worked on the *inside* (management), he would never be allowed to work on the *outside* (labor)." The term *outside* in reference to the bulk of the work force did not set well with Ace. He sensed a corporate culture that was not compatible with his values, and he politely said, "No thanks." He had, once again, looked the gift horse in the mouth and stepped away from potential employment that might have created several million dollars of income and stock options. He solaced himself by recalling one of the numerous stories relating to the quasi-fascist management tactics of UPS.

This "O-dark thirty" anecdote involved an overzealous ramp supervisor at the sort in Louisville when he entered a cockpit and observed that the captain was not wearing the company necktie. This Gestapo-like, uniformed policeman then informed the captain of the requirement to dress himself in proper uniform if he wanted to continue flying cargo for UPS. The captain, most likely in a state of sleep deprivation irritability, did not share this sense of need for a professional image in the cockpit at three o'clock in the morning. The intruding wardrobe-ramp cop placed the captain into a state of disbelief with such a meaningless demand. As the story goes, the captain calmly picked up his personal baggage, exited the aircraft, and headed for the passenger terminal to catch a commercial flight home, concluding, of course, his UPS career. After a few decades of reflection, Ace resolved that flying an airplane painted the color "baby-shit brown" and wearing a uniform of the same hue would have been an ignominy to which he felt fortunate to have avoided.

MARYLEE AT THE 727 FE PANEL

After only a few more months of groveling for survival with physically demanding part-time jobs, Ace received a call from his former Air Atlanta aviatrix colleague, Marylee. She informed him that her new employer, Sun Coast Airlines, was hiring. She did issue the caveat, however, that the Sun Coast was not a great place to work when compared to Air Atlanta, but it *was* a flying job, and the only crew base was located in nearby Fort Lauderdale, thus eliminating the need to commute and to remain away from home for an extended period of time. Then, too, there were several ex-Air Atlanta pilots at Sun Coast, and Ace thought it would be nice to reconnect with them and to share the camaraderie of venting their combined anger towards Michael Hollis, the Air Atlanta CEO. Ace was hired at Sun Coast, and shortly thereafter it became apparent that he had stepped into a quagmire. The airline operated on a shoestring budget, and aircraft maintenance was marginal at best. In addition, paychecks were issued from several days to a few weeks late. The company CEO, Byron Ellison, embodied the convincingly eloquent prognosticator of eternal green pastures just around the corner. He conducted open-house, company-management meetings and encouraged the employees to attend in order to elaborate on potentially new contracts and grandiose plans for the future.

WHERE'S MY PAYCHECK?

For each trip the captain was given a sum of cash to pay for fuel, catering, landing fees, etc. Sun Coast was so severely over-extended that the various vendors providing goods and services to the airline would no longer extend credit. Many of the flights went to South America and the Caribbean, and the increased workload of an international flight was intensified by the captain's additional duty of managing the money. As the situation deteriorated, the pilots' pay became more than a month in arrears, and many of the pilots refused to fly unless they were paid with cash prior to the trip.

Byron Ellison then issued a mandate requiring all of the company employees to attend a very important meeting. This meeting was co-hosted by an investment broker, Rosemary Grady. The purpose of the meeting was to inform the employees that their company intended to go public. After a presentation regarding the mechanics of the public offering, the employees were informed that they would be able to purchase the stock at a discounted price. Along with this *dog-and-pony-show* presentation came a gentle coercion for the employees to purchase stock in order to save their fledgling company. Unfortunately, many of the employees, including Ace, did not understand the basic nuances of the penny-stock game and its potential to bamboozle the novice investor. Ace succumbed to the propaganda and "maxed out" his charge cards to purchase $10,000 of company stock. Less than a month later, after Ace had gained more insight into this *public-offering* scam, he attempted to sell his stock, only to be informed by Rosemary Grady that there was no market for it, and he would not be able sell it.

Despite this premeditated $10,000 fleecing, Ace continued to fly for Sun Coast Airlines because he had no other aviation job readily available. Many of the flights flew from New York's JFK airport to Georgetown, Guyana, with a fuel stop in San Juan, Puerto Rico. The usual modus operandi of the captain's cash pouch did not apply on these flights, and the fuel stop in San Juan was particularly challenging because the captain had to get the cash from a San Juan business associate of Byron Ellison. This situation was quite tenuous: if the cash had not been available, one-hundred-and-seventy passengers and a flight crew of seven would have to sit stranded in a Boeing 727 at a remote parking area of the airport.

FROLICKING ON THE TARMAC AT GEORGETOWN, GUYANA

The holiday season of December 1987 was extremely busy for Sun Coast Airlines as it acquired some additional flights between the Caribbean and the Northeast U.S. However, the operational problems encountered by flight crews, as a result of the ongoing credit problems, frequently resulted in a cabin full of extremely angry passengers. It was not uncommon for passengers to have been stranded at a terminal in the Caribbean for two or three days. They would then get on an airplane with the understanding that their flight would take them on a non-stop flight to the JFK airport in New York. However, for company logistic purposes it was necessary to divert the flight to Fort Lauderdale for a fuel stop. The pilots were instructed to inform the passengers *after* the flight was underway that they were encountering unusual headwinds and would be forced to make a fuel stop. The passenger frustration was frequently intensified by the fact that there might be an inadequate catering supply in the cabin, and the unfortunate flight attendants would not even have drinks available for the passengers. The pilots could keep the cockpit door locked, but the flight attendants were trapped in the cabin and had to deal with the wrath of the justifiably angry and abused passengers.

The many new start-up airlines had resulted in an abundance of discount charter flights to various vacation spots in the Caribbean. Many of these carriers were small, two-or-three-airplane operations. When an airplane was grounded for maintenance, the airlines would have to find another airline for "sub service." Quite frequently the communication and coordination between the two airlines would misfire, and the flight crews would encounter major logistical problems. A great example of this took place on January 3, 1988, when Ace was called to the Fort Lauderdale airport to finish a trip that had originated in Martinique and was destined for Philadelphia. The passengers had been stranded at the Martinique terminal for an extended period of time and were planning on a non-stop flight from Martinique to Philadelphia. They were now trapped on an airplane at Fort Lauderdale exhibiting, understandably so, a near riotous state of disgruntlement. When Ace arrived at the aircraft, he was met with nearly uncontrolled chaos in the cabin. Because of the nearly intolerable passenger animosity the flight attendants almost walked off the job rather than continuing the flight to Philadelphia. Byron Ellison happened to be in the area with a fistful of cash, and he made the flight attendants an offer that they couldn't refuse.

As the aircraft was readied for its flight to Philadelphia Ace was informed that he could not purchase fuel because none of the fuel vendors in Philadelphia would extend credit to Sun Coast Airlines. The only viable solution was to fill the aircraft with fuel in order to "tanker" the fuel for the return trip to Fort Lauderdale. This would require an overweight takeoff, but that very slight degradation of flight safety was overruled by the need to prevent a potential riot by the irate passengers. Approximately one hundred miles south of Philadelphia, the Sun Coast flight was issued a holding clearance as a snowstorm in the Northeast U.S. slowed the air traffic flow into Philadelphia. After only twenty minutes of holding, Ace landed the Sun Coast aircraft. Thus ended the passengers' nightmarish "Caribbean vacation flight from Hell."

Unfortunately, the additional fuel burn during the holding resulted in an insufficient amount of fuel for the return flight to Fort Lauderdale. Ace did not have a company cash-stash, and it was confirmed that the only available fuel vendor in Philadelphia would not extend Sun Coast Airlines any further credit. The brief consideration of parking the aircraft and finding a hotel was rejected since there were no company credit cards available and several hundred dollars worth of crew rooms would have to be paid for by one of Ace's credit cards. In the "non-sked charter" aviation environment, the captain is responsible for his crew. The continuing snowstorm dictated a rapid decision or it would be necessary to de-ice the aircraft before departure at an expense of several thousand dollars. The aircraft was scheduled for another trip as soon as it returned to Fort Lauderdale, and as a devout and foolishly loyal company man, Ace pulled out his own charge card to pay for the necessary fuel to return to Fort Lauderdale. His first officer, a very experienced veteran captain, was familiar with the volatile nature of the non-sked aviation environment, and he strongly advised Ace against spending his own money for company operations.

FO/Captain Satterwhite's advice was not followed, but the old sage's wisdom would be revealed on the following day. After the four a.m. arrival in Fort Lauderdale, Ace got a few hours of sleep and then went to the corporate office with the intention of receiving his long-overdue paycheck, along with compensation for the eight hundred dollars that he had put on his charge card to pay for fuel the previous evening. When he entered the office, he was surprised to see a large group of company employees. He was then informed that the company had just "shut down" and was in the process of declaring chapter-eleven bankruptcy. The possible loss of the eight hundred dollars of fuel money created a near rage, and the normally mild-mannered Ace exhibited a visible and vocal agitation. Ace immediately looked for the company officer who often dispensed the cash required to keep the company afloat. Ace's intense desire to recover his fuel money was immediately recognized by this man, who then issued eight hundred-dollar bills to compensate for Ace's fuel expenditure.

Four days later, Ace's son was severely injured in an automobile accident, and, to pile misfortune upon misfortune, when he called his insurance company regarding the health insurance policy that was supposedly provided by Sun Coast Airlines, he was informed that the policy had been cancelled because the premium had not been paid in several months. Many other employees encountered similar problems and would be forced to pay huge medical expenses out of pocket. Devious underhandedness of this nature was quite common during this incredibly unstable era of de-regulation that resulted in third-world-quality airlines emerging in the U.S. A common theme during this unprecedented era of new airlines involved the entrepreneurs defaulting on their financial obligations while siphoning money out of the coffers and stashing it into offshore accounts. Unpaid FICA and health insurance premiums extracted from the employees' paychecks served as a popular method of scamming the workers.

Sun Coast Airlines resumed flight operations a few weeks later, and Ace elected to return to fly a few trips on a cash-up-front basis only. Ace flew his last trip for Sun Coast on February 17, 1988. The employees, who had been severely stiffed by the owner-CEO Byron Ellison, were encouraged to attend the bankruptcy hearings. The interaction among the judge, Byron Ellison, and Ellison's attorney reeked with gracious congeniality. The judge did not show any interest in receiving input from the company's bitter and angry employees. Ace soon discovered that the entrepreneur is usually a benefactor of bankruptcy proceedings at the expense of the employees who are relegated to a few crumbs—if any remained at all. This airline-scam scenario was quite common after the airline industry took advantage of deregulation in 1978.

In less than a year's time, two smooth-talking aviation entrepreneurs had scammed Ace. He once again returned to the Florida State unemployment office, where he began to acquaint himself with office personnel and the appropriate filing procedure. He complemented his unemployment check with various part-time-cash jobs. He had his feelers out in all directions to seek income-producing events, when, out of a clear-blue sky, his old Learjet colleague and good friend, Jim Keeling, called Ace to offer him a one-day copilot job.

WILL FLY FOR FOOD AND/OR ALCOHOL

Ace jumped at this opportunity to make a few easy bucks "riding shotgun" and talking on the radio while Jim flew the aircraft. Jim and Ace caught a commercial flight to Baltimore, where they were assigned to pick up an old Jet Star aircraft and to fly it to Long Island's Islip airport. On the surface this appeared an easy task. However, this particular Jet Star aircraft had not flown in more than one year. Captain Jim had not flown any aircraft in recent months, and his very limited experience in the Jet Star aircraft would necessitate studying the flight manual for an informal and brief refresher-training program. Jim's total flight time in the Jet Star aircraft amounted to only twenty hours, but Ace knew Jim was an experienced and adaptable pilot who had flown several different types of aircraft in his career. Therefore, Ace had plenty of confidence in his good buddy Captain Jim and the antiquated Jet Star. However, as the afternoon thunderstorms built in strength, and the immediate weather observation evolved into *thunderstorms in all quadrants*, the two severely under-qualified "migrant aviators" suddenly acquired some good judgment: they unanimously decided to cancel the flight and to fly the airplane to Islip the following day.

The canceled flight led to a rapid lunge for the aircraft's liquor cabinet. The functionality of the old Jet Star was still unknown, but the quality of the top-shelf liquor supply revealed itself as both excellent and pleasingly consumable. As unemployed pilots, Ace and Jim attempted to hold their own entertainment costs to a minimum, so they immediately capitalized on this opportunity to eliminate happy-hour expenditures. The following morning,

Jim and Ace launched the Jet Star from Baltimore, and Jim showed off his aviator skills by making a perfect landing in an airplane that he had not flown in over a year. Jim was still trying to get even with Ace. About a decade earlier, when Ace had a total of nearly 5,000 hours in the Learjet and Jim had only a few hours in the airplane, they departed Boston's Logan Airport in the Learjet for a short ferry flight to Providence.

Jim sat in the left seat on his first actual operational flight, and—as is quite often the case with new Learjet pilots—the aircraft seemed determined to get away from its pilot. When he tried to level at 11,000 feet, he ended up about 300 feet high. Ace said, "Jim, I've got the aircraft." Ace, flagrantly showing off, took the flight controls and immediately performed a gentle barrel roll with the aircraft finishing at 11,000 feet. Jim's response consisted of a few friendly expletives. Jim responded brilliantly by executing a perfect grease-job landing at Providence. Jim had a distinguished and pleasant demeanor about him, and as he gained copilot experience with BizJet, he often jokingly referred to himself as a "grunt" while he engaged in the copilot's non-flying duties of cleaning the aircraft, dumping the chemical potty, and taking care of other janitorial tasks.

AIRLINE INTERVIEW
OR CHINESE WATER TORTURE

Ace felt gratified by the easy two-hundred-dollar copilot pay, but he now prepared himself for a really big event, since he had finally been invited for an interview with United Airlines in Denver. Upon arrival at DENTK (Denver training center), he immediately observed that he was the only pilot candidate wearing a brown suit. He asked the receptionist if a blue suit was mandatory. Her response clearly communicated to Ace that she had never seen a pilot show up for an interview in anything other than a blue suit. Ace, it seems, had not gotten the word, and now faced a serious dilemma. He responded immediately by renting the receptionist's car to dash off to the closest Wal-Mart, where he bought the cheapest blue suit available.

Phase one of the interview involved a group meeting with eleven other pilot applicants. Ten of these applicants were female pilots, most of whom had very little experience with fewer than 1,000 hours of total flight time. One other applicant, a Latino male, had nearly 2,000 hours of flight time. Ace, by contrast, had already logged over 11,000 hours of PIC (pilot in command) flight time in jet aircraft. Along with a flight engineer's rating, 5,000 hours of flight time in the 727, and check-airman experience, he felt quite confident that he would be hired.

Ace returned a few weeks later for phase two of the interview, which seemingly went quite well, and—based on the positive response of the four pilots who conducted the final interview—he was near certain that he would receive an offer of employment. A short time afterward, he received a postcard from United, indicating that he would not be considered for employment. Perhaps he was over qualified for the job, but it is a near certainty that filling government quotas would bring about his demise, at least with United.

A very relevant sidebar to this story involved a second trip to Denver, where Ace once again ran into Jerry the previously fired African-American pilot from Air Atlanta. Jerry had left UPS and was now employed by United. Ace (and many of his highly skilled and veteran non-sked pilot colleagues) had fallen victim to a recently implemented program by the EEOC (Equal Employment Opportunity Commission), mandating that United Airlines would have to ensure a significant increase in the number of minority pilots. The old cliché about the three biggest lies—one of them, "I'm from the government and I'm here to help you"—proved sadly applicable in this instance. Apparently, United Airlines employed very few minority pilots, and the company came under pressure to achieve the appropriate government-mandated percentage quota as soon as possible. During this period of government mandate to fill quotas, thousands of experienced and qualified corporate pilots, commuter pilots, cargo pilots, and non-sked pilots received rejection notices despite their excellent background and aviation experiences.

Several volumes could be written about the anomalies of major airlines' hiring procedures, but the United Airlines minority-hiring program unmistakably stood out as *the* most unfair, counterproductive hiring policy in the history of major airlines. Numerous reports told of minority hires receiving extended *and* additional training until they could meet the minimum standards required by the DENTK training staff. Many of the minority hires had adequate aviator skills, but the anecdotes of *incompetent* performance by minority hires circulated throughout the pilot community. The only comparable legacy of incompetent pilots emanated from the Continental Airlines scabs hired to fill the seats of the striking pilots. Many of the scab pilots were *severely* under qualified, but they reacted with great enthusiasm for a chance to fly the big jets without considering the potential consequences of their inexperience during an emergency situation. Although there were hundreds of reported incidents, quite miraculously, no fatal accidents took place during this period of inexperienced pilots in the cockpit at Continental Airlines. If an airline hires "replacement" workers to fly its airplanes, the safety factor plummets. The likelihood of dying on a flight flown by "replacement workers" is increased considerably.

A few months later, Ace was invited for an interview at Eastern airlines. Eastern, like many other airlines, experienced great turmoil during this period, eventually shutting down and ceasing operations. Ace's interview process, however, proceeded to the second phase, and during the follow-up interview with Eastern's director of training, the director asked, "How do you feel about being based in New York?" Ace responded with his best honest answer, "It would create a hardship for me since my family is settled here in South Florida." The interviewer immediately closed the folder and terminated the interview. Once again, Ace did not know how to play the game. He later discovered that the only correct answer was, "No problem sir. I'll go anywhere for Eastern Airlines." Another rejection of good fortune had ironically occurred when Eastern Airlines, too, soon began rapidly to accelerate into its own terminal-death spiral. Eastern closed its doors a short while after Ace's interview—another fortuitous rejection.

Ace also interviewed with US Airways and was *again* fortunate enough to be rejected. Within a year after his interview, US Airways began furloughing its pilots. If Ace had accepted an employment offer with US Airways, he, too, would have been furloughed, with no recall rights, since he would not have completed the one-year probation period. Because Ace admitted to a light cigarette-smoking habit on an application with American Airlines, the company turned him down as well. American Airlines would not hire any person for any position if he or she lit up those cancer sticks. Once again, Ace had not gotten the word, and it seemed that he was destined to remain a career non-sked pilot.

Ace kept his ear to the ground, and as always, a new employer appeared on the horizon: Gulf Air in June, 1989. This particular Gulf Air airline was headquartered in New Iberia, Louisiana, rather than in the Kingdom of Saudi Arabia. Upon completion of FAA-mandated training for ground school and simulator check rides, Ace had his Gulf Air job temporarily interrupted by a classic golden opportunity. His old colleague from Zantop Airways, Jim Worden, called to request his services on his corporate Learjet. Jim's regular copilot had just been hired by a major airline, and in a few days the aircraft owner and his new wife were going to commence a one-month vacation throughout Europe. Jim had never flown to Europe, and he felt that Ace's experience might be of value in this venture across the Atlantic Ocean. The timing came like perfect clockwork since Gulf Air was actually a bit overstaffed, and a one-month leave of absence was readily granted.

JUST ANOTHER EUROPEAN VACATION

Jim's Lear 55 had a considerably extended range compared to the Lear 25, which Ace had previously flown in crossing the North Atlantic. Moreover, Ace experienced little or no concern about running out of fuel over the frigid North Atlantic Ocean. After arriving in Edinburgh, Scotland, Ace and Jim reset their body clocks with eight hours in the hotel and then walked across the street to what is regarded as one of the most interesting tourist points in Scotland: the historic Edinburgh Castle. The castle is similar to the Grand Canyon: you must experience it firsthand to even start to grasp its magnanimity. The breathtaking aesthetics of this overwhelming scene came to the forefront when a large group of Scottish bagpipers, clad in their stunning uniforms of kilts and other accoutrements, appeared on the scene. It was a rare but gloriously sunny day, and the beautiful landscaping of lush green grass, flowers in full bloom, and perfectly manicured foliage surrounding the area of the castle—complimented with bagpipe music—resulted in an incomparable, idyllic scenario.

But this event was completely overshadowed the following day when the gracious honeymooners, Marilyn and Bob Fisher, requested their pilots to join them at the Old Saint Andrews golf club for a round of golf. Ace and Jim, prepared for this contingency, had wisely stowed their golf clubs in the back of the aircraft's cargo compartment. The day after the Saint Andrews golf outing, Ace and Jim received an invitation to join the honeymooners for dinner at their rented castle. In order to enjoy the unique ambience of Scotland, ideally, one should spend some time in one's private, fully staffed castle. Two months earlier, Ace had been slaving in the hot Florida sun, trying to make a few extra bucks with some good old-fashioned manual labor. The random swinging of the pendulum had once again propelled him over to the bright side and to the good life.

Phase two of the European vacation involved a short flight south to London, where the vacationers enjoyed the very rare phenomenon of five perfect sunny days. They enjoyed the usual tourist activities, along with the Paris Air Show, which was being held at Farnborough, England. The Paris Air Show is hosted in Farnborough every other year. It was soon apparent that this aviation extravaganza functioned primarily as a "show and sell" of military aviation hardware. The pervasive American military-industrial complex paraded its diversified wares for sale to the Middle East as well as to other Third-World countries. As Ace watched the Russian Mig-29 fighter jets turn on a dime, and, recalling his military-service years, he was glad that he didn't have to tangle with them in his old, far-less-maneuverable F-4C Phantom. The behemoth-like Soviet freighter, the Antonov 225, was parked next to a U.S. Air Force C-5A. The Soviet Antonov aircraft dwarfed America's largest cargo jet, the C-5A .

Upon completion of activities in the UK, the vacationers headed to France. They arrived at LeTouque, a popular resort along the West Coast of France. Day two of the French vacation broke out into a warm, sunny Saturday. Jim and Ace walked to the beach to see if these Frenchwomen really did engage in topless sunbathing. The answer was a rousing affirmative, and as they marveled at the many mammary glands, they jokingly postulated that perhaps topless sunbathing was mandatory in France. Two days later, they climbed back into the Learjet for a short flight to Caen, the airport closest to Normandy Beach. The Normandy Beach excursion turned into a life-changing event for Ace. His exposure to the magnitude and the significance of D-Day on a first-hand basis resulted in a sense of responsibility to gain further insight and understanding of world history and the nuances of geopolitics. Every American and European citizen should visit this profoundly historical site to partake of the tourist area referred to as The Memorial. This indoor exhibit about twenty miles from Normandy Beach provides the viewer with an in-depth description of European events that preceded the D-Day invasion, to include a jaw-dropping, split-screen video that was filmed during the early stages of this profoundly significant battle. Based on these videos shot during the actual event, the scenes depicted in the popular movie, *Saving Private Ryan*, loomed realistic.

The high point of this priceless saga positioned the honeymooners and their well-kept airplane chauffeurs in Paris. The vacationing honeymooners, who may well have been the nicest rich people in the world, frequently invited their pilots to join them for dinner. Both honeymooners had studied French, and they enjoyed displaying their linguistic expertise by ordering unique gourmet appetizers for their pilots. Carte blanche dining in a Five-Star Parisian restaurant, and the knowledge that the boss would pull out the platinum American Express card, was a privilege normally experienced only by the rich and famous. Jim and Ace visited the Palace of Versailles, the Eiffel Tower, and numerous art museums including the Louvre. They were, however, somewhat negligent in their tourist duties: they failed to visit the famed Crazy Horse Saloon and the Moulin Rouge. These two iconic night clubs were world renowned for their stage shows with stunningly beautiful women. Jim had lived in Las Vegas, and Ace had visited America's gambling Mecca many times. Perhaps, after watching the many stage shows they had developed a somewhat blasé attitude about viewing a large stage filled with near-nude women with perfect bodies.

Ace provided frequent comedy relief by attempting to banter with the Parisians utilizing his pathetic French-language skills. Ace foolishly tried to learn French from his little guidebook, with no awareness of the near impossibility of this task. Jim had formulated some very simple insight into getting around Paris, as he would constantly mutter, *"C'est bon, C'est bon"* (that's good). Ace was fortunate enough to visit most of the large cities in the world, but Paris took the top prize by a wide margin.

The return trip to Detroit began with a heavy heart for Ace, knowing that this remarkable experience would most likely represent the high point of his aviation career. As the flight passed south of Iceland, the honeymooners entertained the pilots with off-color, sheepherder jokes that did not reflect well on the men back in the Scottish Highlands. Bangor, Maine, was the required fuel stop and customs clearance point of entry. From there it was on to Detroit, home for the honeymooners. For Ace, the cultural shock upon returning to Detroit resulted in an immediate urge to immigrate to France. In a one-month period, Ace had made more money (five thousand dollars) than he had earned in the previous five months—while *also* indulging in a five-star vacation filled with gloriously grand experiences. Keeping in touch with one's ex-pilot colleagues, as was the case for the European vacation, would prove to be invaluable for Ace during the remainder of the turbulent ten.

25-HOUR DUTY DAYS/GOOD TRAINING!

Ace returned to the non-sked charter world of Gulf Air, and his first IOE trip out of Philadelphia consisted of a classic *goat rope.* The eight a.m. show time resulted in information that the aircraft scheduled for this trip to Mexico's West Coast would not arrive at Philadelphia until ten-thirty a.m. When it did finally arrive, it had a minor maintenance problem requiring another two-hour delay. The aircraft was not ready by two p.m., and crew scheduling advised the flight crew to go to the hotel to rest. Two hours later, which happened to be only a few minutes after getting settled in the hotel room, Ace received a call from crew scheduling advising him to gather his crewmembers to head for the airport. At approximately six p.m., the flight took off for Puerto Vallarta,

Mexico, with a required fuel stop in Texas. The return flight to Philadelphia also required a fuel stop, and the severely fatigued flight crewmembers did not finish their duty day (and night) until the following morning at nine a.m. When Ace suggested to the company check airman that a twenty-five-hour duty day was pretty ridiculous, the check airman responded, "I couldn't agree more, but you're singing to the choir."

Gulf Air, a worldwide charter operator, had achieved the status of a "Flag Carrier." According to the Federal Aviation Regulations that govern both flight-time and duty-time limitations for flag-carrier operations under FAR 121, there is no requirement for a rest break. The FAR states that the flight crew must not exceed twelve hours of flight time in a twenty-four hour period, but there is no stipulation that mandates a requirement for rest. The twenty-five-hour duty day was perfectly legal, according to the FAA, since this flight was technically considered an international flight, even though the aircraft required a domestic fuel stop in Texas. This is a little-known loophole provided by the FAA for the International-Flag-Carrier-certificated airline. Although the loophole certainly saves a lot of money in crew expense, utilization of the loophole occasionally results in a flight crew whose advanced sleep deprivation severely compromises safety. A few weeks later, Ace had an FAA inspector in the cockpit jump seat for the purpose of a routine line-check evaluation. Like most of the FAA inspectors, this "Fed" came across very friendly and gracious, and Ace queried him regarding his thoughts on the above-mentioned FAR loophole. His response! A silent *no comment.* Since the FAA usually operates from a reactive rather than from a proactive position, it is likely that only a fatal aircraft crash piloted by a severely sleep-deprived flight crew will have to occur to rescind this absurd regulation. Pilot fatigue has very frequently been a contributing factor in aviation accidents and incidents, and the FAA has shown complicity with the airlines by not demanding more restrictive duty-and-flight-time restrictions. "I'm from the government and I'm here to help you,"—unless you are a flight crewmember who would like to get some rest.

The pilot fatigue factor played itself out during the February 12, 2009, Colgan Air crash in Buffalo, New York, precipitating federal government action to implement long-overdue rule changes.

Sadly, the rule changes came "too little and too late" largely because the recently published (September 14, 2010) NPRM (Notice of Public Rulemaking) has been deemed by commercial aviation pilots to be totally inadequate, perhaps even counter-productive.

FLYING WITH THE "FONZ"

Based out of Philadelphia, Ace flew vacation group-charter flights to the West Coast of Mexico, to Cancun, to Aruba, to Montego Bay, to Jamaica, and to other prime vacation spots in the Caribbean. Occasionally, Gulf Air would hustle gambling-junket charters to Atlantic City from various cities in the Northeast U.S. It was a dark, and depressingly dreary, rainy night at the overseas terminal at Philadelphia International when Ace first met the cordially ebullient Mike Scala, aka "The Fonz." With an infectious, upbeat personality regardless of the circumstances, all of the flight crew members enjoyed working with the Fonz. He was incapable of anger. His moniker, "The Fonz," was quite appropriate since he was a dead-ringer for TV's famous Fonzi. In their first meeting, Ace entered the cockpit, and the Fonz greeted him with the following statement: "Hey cap'n! What's happ'n? I've got the NAV computer loaded, I'm picking up the clearance, the fuel truck is on the way, and we're gonna launch this rocket on time. Grab a coffee and kick back! I've got you covered, skipper." From that point on, Ace and the Fonz had more fun in a Boeing 727 than should be allowed, while following each other from one fly-by-night airline to another and establishing a lifelong friendship.

Except for the occasional extended-time duty days, Gulf Air proved to be a reasonably pleasant, non-sked, employment situation. Ace was quite comfortable on the job; until he was assigned to pilot a charter from BWI (Baltimore) to St. Thomas, in the Virgin Islands, followed by a very short flight to St. Croix to refuel and to add additional passengers for the return flight to BWI. Ace had flown Learjets into St. Thomas, but this very first excursion to this very intimidating airport with a 727 aircraft had his full attention. The landing on the relatively short runway posed no problem even though the aircraft's weight was close to the maximum permitted. Departure, however, was fraught with fear and trepidation. Because of the short runway and the rapidly rising terrain to the east of the airport along the departure path, this 727-200 aircraft was confronted with severe limitations in the take-off and departure. With forty passengers, minimal baggage, and just enough fuel for the 12 minute flight to St. Croix, the performance tables revealed the aircraft takeoff weight to be exactly the maximum allowable for the prevailing conditions.

When Ace taxied onto runway nine for takeoff and departure, the short runway and the steeply rising terrain to the east created the classic "pit of the stomach" sensation. The "sight picture," (seemingly large mountains in the takeoff flight path) was not a pretty one and Ace was reluctant to push the thrust levers forward to make the takeoff. He had a strong urge to taxi back to the ramp, to park the aircraft, to walk across the street to the beach area, and to start quaffing down tropical rum drinks. Despite the feeling of enclosure in a "box canyon," he entrusted the highly reliable GE JT 8D-15 engines to faithfully perform their duties, and with that in mind, he initiated the takeoff. In fact, both takeoff and departure occurred uneventfully with Ace breathing a sigh of relief as his aircraft climbed over the high terrain on the departure path.

The winter of 1988-89 was followed by a special gift for the spring of 1989. Gulf Air had accepted a contract with Air Malta to operate a 727 based in Malta to fly European tourists to this very popular Mediterranean vacation spot, a particularly good duty because most of the trips departed Malta at mid-morning and returned from Europe in time for happy hour. The first radio communication that Ace experienced with air traffic control over Rome convinced him that he had made contact with Father Guido Sarducci, the famous *Saturday Night Live* priest, whose pronunciation certainly caused many viewers to fall off their chairs. Responding to Ace's initial transmission, the controller asked, "This'a Romah Controlah…and'ah…what'sa you'a positione?" The French were probably equally amused when Ace would check off from Paris Control with his bumbled, "Bon Jour, Monsieur." The American pilots enjoyed the European flavor of Malta as they evolved into enthusiastic consumers of Guinness beer and actually put vinegar on their French Fries. They also embarrassed themselves as ugly Americans when they went to the swimming pool and rudely gawked at the topless, sunbathing women. Ace had already "been there and done that" in France, and he walked away in disgust when Gulf Air pilots took pictures and engaged in very loud-spoken comparisons. The demure bare-breasted ladies would look up from their books and immediately conclude that these crass *male boobs* must be American pilots.

BEWARE THE CARNIVAL BARKER

Ace returned to the U.S. after one month and continued to fly with Gulf Air until July 14, 1989, at which time he was furloughed. Gulf Air succumbed to a similar fate as the pilot from Greek mythology, Icarus, who flew close enough to the sun only to have his wax wings melt. Likewise, Gulf Air went too far in attempting to expand its charter market by operating DC-8 aircraft in order to capitalize on the long-range, worldwide charter market. Shortly thereafter, the company went out of business. Meanwhile, Ace received a call from Marylee, a former aviator colleague during their days with Air Atlanta and Sun Coast airlines. She now worked for Carnival Airlines in Fort Lauderdale. The information that the company was getting ready to hire pilots was warmly received, and Ace then pursued his next aviation gig with Carnival. He soon found out that Carnival Airlines was aptly named: management's modus operandi resembled carnival barkers, who would con fairgoers into a game they could not win.

The owners of Carnival Airlines also possessed a hotel, the Crystal Palace in Nassau. A large portion of the Carnival Airlines business involved flying passengers from several different locations in the U.S. for vacations at the Crystal Palace. As Ace and several of his fellow pilot employees would discover, Carnival not only engaged in the process of gaming their customers at the Crystal Palace, they would also "game" their own employees. An example of this involved the purchase of uniforms by the flight attendants. They were required to buy their uniforms through their employer, Carnival, rather than from the supplier that sold them to Carnival. When a flight attendant went to the supplier to purchase the uniform for a price considerably less than the price charged by Carnival, she was severely chastised. A memo was then sent to all flight attendants, informing them that they must buy the uniforms from the company. Obviously, a company management employee happily pocketed the markup profit, only one of many examples of Carnival Airlines exploiting its employees.

On Ace's first captain's trip with Carnival, flight operations informed him that the Crystal Palace Hotel, which normally provided lodging for the flight crews on Nassau layovers, was oversold. His crew would have to lodge at the Casuarinas Hotel. During the aircraft turn-around in Fort Lauderdale, Ace learned from the disembarking captain that the Casuarinas Hotel had neither air-conditioning nor hot water, an almost uninhabitable setting, indeed. Upon arrival in Nassau, Ace led his crew straightaway to the Crystal Palace, where the front desk informed him that many rooms were available. Ace then called the Casuarinas Hotel to cancel crew reservations there, and he and his crew stayed at the Crystal Palace. When Ace received his next paycheck, however, he noted an extra, unspecified deduction totaling $240. When he queried the accounting department regarding this deduction, he was informed that the Casuarinas Hotel had billed Carnival this amount. Since Ace had made the decision to take his crew to the Crystal Palace, he would have to pay for the Casuarinas Hotel's bogus bill even though he had cancelled the reservations.

Several of Ace's pilot colleagues and good friends from previous airlines were fired by Carnival, including the "Fonz," usually for very petty infractions. Pilots had no union protection and if for some reason a check airman, a chief pilot, or any other management person didn't like someone, he could be fired without just cause. During a pilot meeting, the pilot group was informed that each pilot would have to share a hotel room with another pilot during overnight trips. Ace, immediately established himself as a thorn in the side of the Carnival management, as he stepped forward to inform management that this would *not* be a consideration for the pilot group and that they would *not* share rooms.

Despite such independent exclamations, Ace managed to keep his nose clean and would at last settle in and "get with the program and go with the flow." The winter of 1989-1990 passed by quite smoothly with mostly Caribbean flying along with many laid-back layovers in Nassau. Flight 711, one of the very popular trips, departed Fort Lauderdale at about seven p.m. for a thirty-five minute flight to Nassau. The flight crew would then avail themselves of the Crystal Palace amenities, including a free buffet dinner, usually followed by a few hours of sleep in the hotel until the return flight to Fort Lauderdale at three a.m. Other trip "pairings" involved an "inside turn." After the Fort Lauderdale to Nassau flight, the same crew would go to a Northeast U.S. city or to a Mid-west city to return passengers to Nassau, where they would rush to the casino to make their contributions to the gambling gods. During the southbound trip to Nassau, the passengers were filled with anticipatory joy and exuberance—laughing, smiling, and joking. A few days later, after leaving behind the sobering reality of their gambling losses, they would board the aircraft with their heads drooped, uttering discontented, guttural, grumbling sounds.

It was another sunny day in Nassau, and Ace and his crew reported to the airport for their eight a.m. departure to Miami. Ace was greeted by a mechanic who informed him that the L2 window (captain's left-side window) had been replaced. He showed Ace a maintenance logbook with the appropriate entries clearing the aircraft for flight. He also pointed out the appropriate page in the MEL (minimum equipment list) and indicated that the maintenance performed and the logbook sign-off fell in line with FAA procedures. Ace flew the airplane to Miami, where he was then assigned to another aircraft for a full day of charter flying. The next aircraft that he was going to fly had several deferred maintenance items (DMIs), so Ace called the director of maintenance to seek some clarification regarding these items.

The director of maintenance immediately responded with shock that Ace had flown aircraft 609 from Nassau to Miami. His understanding of the situation differed from that of the mechanic in Nassau. The director thought the L2 window installed originated out of a 727-200 aircraft and, therefore, was not compatible with his 727-100 aircraft. The MEL page presented to Ace by the maintenance rep at Nassau had not indicated this. Further research into the ambiguously written MEL (that was stamped as approved by the FAA) disclosed that the maintenance rep was in error and that the aircraft was technically not certified for flight based on the conflicting and nebulous fine print.

The director of maintenance immediately called the FAA to inform himself of the recently implemented policy of "self disclosure." Here is the gist of this policy: if you did a "bad" but went ahead and told the FAA about it, exoneration would likely be granted. Ace did not capitalize on this loophole, and he soon received a letter from the Atlanta District Office of the FAA, stating, "Certificate action is pending." In civilian terms, the FAA was engaged in a process that would punish Ace by suspending or terminating his pilot's license along with possibly imposing a $10,000 fine. This harsh action was brought about by the fact that the L2 window heat was inoperative for the short thirty-minute flight to Miami. On a thirty-minute flight conducted primarily in day VFR (visual flight rules) conditions, as was the case in this flight, window heat for the L2 window would be totally unnecessary. Once again the multiple-choice question must be asked, "I'm from the government and I'm here to (1) Help you? (2) Or to screw you?" The answer to this scenario is quite clear.

Ace then sought assistance from the company's pilot-management staff and was very politely informed that this was his problem, not theirs. He would need to seek his own attorney at his own expense to represent him in the hearing with the FAA. Ace went to the hearing with an attorney at his side, but it soon became clear that the attorney was unnecessary. The very intelligent and clear-thinking lady from the Atlanta FAA office briefly looked at the facts of the case and immediately dismissed it, indicating that she was appalled that the government wasted time and effort on such a meaningless case. Ace returned to the cockpit with his airman's certificate intact. There is a multitude of self-serving politics that describes the FAA, particularly at the higher management levels, but most of the inspectors and examiners exhibit good judgment and fairness regarding the many issues that they are required to resolve.

The pilot staff at Carnival was relatively stable, but there was a large turnover amongst the flight attendants, and this made it difficult for the crew-scheduling staff. In one instance, Ace, assigned a lengthy daytime charter, learned that one of his cabin crewmembers had spent all night working another flight. When Ace asked to have this flight attendant replaced, he was first told to allow the crewmember to sleep in the back of the airplane. As Ace became more insistent upon having a rested flight attendant in the cabin, he was informed that he would continue the trip with this flight attendant or he would be fired. Perhaps surprisingly, Ace survived several more months at Carnival before he did receive the pink slip.

ANYONE FOR AN EXTENDED MIDDLE EAST DESERT VACATION?

The rate of pilot firings would increase as a result of a significant change in primary-duty location. The Carnival management had negotiated a contract with Air Egypt to operate a 727 out of Cairo, Egypt. *There were no volunteers for this duty.* Since Ace held a position relatively junior on the captain's seniority list, he was assigned to the first group of crewmembers to serve in Cairo. At about mid-day on May 29, the flight crews and the maintenance-support people gathered for a photo-op scenario on the ramp next to the Carnival 727 that would soon be ferried across the North Atlantic and across Europe to Cairo. Shortly thereafter the adventurous crossing over the Atlantic Ocean commenced. Ace relaxed in the cabin as a passenger for the first flight. All went well until approximately abeam Jacksonville the captain made a PA announcement that the flight would return to Fort Lauderdale because the aircraft's maintenance logbook was not aboard. This logbook must be aboard for all flights, but the previously mentioned preflight chaos, had apparently led to the oversight of this critical item.

Several hours later, by which time most of the aircraft occupants had not slept in twelve or thirteen hours, leg number two prepared for departure from Goose Bay, Labrador to Keflavik, Iceland. Ace and his assigned copilot, Jeff, were scheduled to fly the last two flights from Keflavík to Cairo with a fuel stop in Milan, Italy. Jeff and Ace were the only two company pilots who had flown in Europe, so they were assigned these last two flights. As they busied themselves in the cockpit prior to the departure to Keflavik, they noticed that the flight crew for this over-water journey planned to depart with a minimum fuel load. Jeff and Ace, familiar with the potential for rapid change of weather conditions at Iceland, would have to make a diplomatic suggestion to carry some additional contingency fuel. This particular crew was quite experienced in the 727 but had never flown across the Atlantic or to Europe. They had not experienced the traumatizing consideration of ditching in the frigid waters of the North Atlantic Ocean and bobbing about on twenty-foot waves in a small raft. Fear can often be a valuable contributor to more prudent and cautious pilot decisions, and in this case the diplomatic move resulted in added fuel for the flight. The age-old pilot axiom that the only time you have too much fuel is when your airplane is on fire.

The flight to Keflavik went smoothly, and after a brief nap in the cabin, Jeff and Ace flew the next flight to Milan, arriving approximately twenty-four hours after the initial show time in Fort Lauderdale on the previous day. Since Ace and his crew had technically just begun their duty day with the flight to Milan, the flight was considered legal, according to the appropriate flight-and-duty-time FARs. However, *all* crewmembers were extremely tired. An attempt to get hotel rooms in Milan to recharge the batteries did not succeed, and so the "goat rope" to Cairo continued. In the process of utilizing his seat's full recline position and "evaluating his inner eyelids" somewhere just north of the Mediterranean Sea, Captain Ace was awoken by the flight engineer, who informed him that engine number three was rapidly losing oil. A few minutes later, engine number three had to be shut down. Since there were only forty-five minutes of flight time remaining to Cairo, Ace decided to push on, and he soon viewed the pyramids on the approach to Cairo. The uneventful engine-out landing was accomplished, and the tired and bedraggled Carnival Airlines entourage found their way to the airport hotel to begin their Middle East stint.

Upon arrival at the hotel, Ace noticed that one of the destinations on the Air Egypt flight schedule was Baghdad. Ace decided that if he were assigned to fly a Baghdad trip, he would declare himself to be extremely sick and unable to fly. Ace had held a top-secret security clearance as an Air Force pilot, and he surmised that Saddam Hussein might detain him to pick his brain regarding nuclear weapons. As it turned out, he did not have to fake an illness because, unfortunately, he and a few of his Carnival colleagues had come down with dysentery. Ace was sickly as a youth and suffered nearly all of the illnesses the western world had to offer, including hepatitis and two bouts of pneumonia, but he discovered that dysentery would make all those other illnesses seem like kid stuff. Somewhat alarmingly, given Ace's condition, Jeff informed Ace that on a previous Middle East aviation excursion, his fellow pilot had contracted dysentery and died in his hotel room from severe dehydration—clearly the kind of news Ace did not want to hear. Jeff did not want another dead captain to deal with so he checked on Ace every few hours.

After about a week, Ace regained his strength, now ready to dash about the Middle East in his beautiful Boeing air machine. He flew to Tripoli but was unable to establish contact with his look-a-like, Colonel Moammar Quadafi. There were also trips to Algeria, Luxor, Saudi Arabia, and Sudan, though Ace had one Sudan trip cancelled as a result of a dust storm that reduced visibility to below landing minimums. The view from the cockpit while flying around the Middle East can only be described as quite colorless, but the view from poolside at the hotel was quite pleasant since it was a layover point for many other international flight crews. Many of the young female flight attendants enjoyed the carefree, playful atmosphere as they exchanged their formal work attire for a string bikini. The actual duty was quite comfortable, but the high point of this venture occurred when Ace was issued a first-class ticket on Air Egypt to go from Cairo to JFK in New York. The long-range 767 remained airborne for a seemingly endless fifteen hours; however, the flight's first-class amenities nearly offset wasting the equivalent of two full working days engaged in a state of boring nothingness trapped in this high-speed cocoon.

THE PINK SLIP IS IN SIGHT

After a few days off in Florida to decompress, Ace was sent to JFK to fly charters to Cancun and other vacation spots. On the first flight from Cancun to JFK, Ace and his fellow crew members relaxed with the autopilot engaged somewhere over the Gulf of Mexico when they heard a stunning, bizarre announcement over the PA. A passenger, who apparently had acquired false courage (stupidity) as a result of too much tequila at the terminal, had decided to grab the flight attendant's microphone to make a declaration. Normally, such behavior would have been a mild transgression, but this particular announcement was laced with obscenities, implying, too, that the captain had the intention to crash the airplane. Ace, startled into action by this lunatic's ramblings, immediately leaped out of his seat to assist the cabin attendants. He then observed the lead flight attendant in the back of the cabin professionally removing the PA microphone from the passenger's grasp. Ace promptly made a PA announcement, "Interfering with a flight crew member's duties in the cabin is a federal offense and punishable by law."

The lead flight attendant communicated to Ace that she had chastised the offender and felt the situation was under control. She also informed Ace that the wife and the two young daughters accompanied this despicable hooligan. Ace discussed the incident—and the audacity of the arrogant orator—with his fellow cockpit crewmembers, and they decided to take action. They forwarded a message to JFK airport requesting that law enforcement officers meet the aircraft. When they landed, four large New York police officers entered the cabin before any passengers were allowed to disembark. The offending passenger was then identified, handcuffed, and escorted off the aircraft by the policemen. The previously brave and foul-mouthed lout exited the aircraft in a scared, wide-eyed, state of shock. It was later discovered that his proclivity towards pompous pontificating was a result of the training for his chosen profession. **He was an attorney!**

A few days later, as Ace was relaxing in his airport hotel in New York, preparing for a weekend of flying charters to Cancun and Montego Bay, he received a call from crew scheduling to inform him that, when he returned from New York on Monday, he should pack his bags for a return trip back to Cairo on Tuesday. Ace's son, who had been previously severely injured in an auto accident, was in dire need of his father's care and support. A letter to the company management from an attorney regarding this situation was ignored. Ace then had to inform crew scheduling that he would be unable to go to Cairo on Tuesday. Crew scheduling advised Ace to call the chief pilot. It was clear to Ace that this conversation would be very simple and straightforward, that the chief pilot's likely response would declare, "Go back to Cairo on Tuesday or you're fired." With this awareness in mind, Ace did not speak to the chief pilot at all. When he returned to Fort Lauderdale on Monday, he went to his mailbox to get his paycheck, only to discover that, instead of a paycheck, he had been presented with the dreaded "pink slip." Ace had just been sucker-punched by the Carnival management, but he knew "when push came to shove," he would be shoved out the door.

As a side-note, Ace, ironically, had just been nominated for Employee of the Month. Nonetheless, he was fired, and he had never before been actually fired from *any* job. Ace's new, non-negotiable status struck initially in quite a debilitating way. In later years, Ace's good friend, Marylee, who would *also* frequently bump heads with management, gained one-upsmanship on Ace by getting herself fired twice. She accomplished something even more momentous—she was re-hired twice. Amongst people familiar with the corporate culture at Carnival Airlines, it was a badge of honor to be fired.

IF IT HAS TWO WINGS, I'LL FLY IT

Ace soon found alternative employment as a day laborer for a lawn maintenance service. The cold-cash payment of fifty dollars a day complemented his unemployment check and aided in fending off a few of the onerous bill collectors. After two months of hard manual labor in the Florida summer heat and humidity, Ace was anxious to hear from the next aviation-employer-benefactor. And, indeed, the inevitable occurred. Ace received a phone call from Larry Erd, whom he had met at a golf driving range, where they had discussed corporate aviation. Larry operated a Cessna Citation jet for Broward Yachts, and his regular copilot had just gone to one of the major airlines; as a result, he needed someone to sit in the right seat to talk on the radio. Larry also said that this assignment involved ferrying the airplane to Orlando for some required maintenance. It was going to be a three-day trip and Larry informed Ace that he could only pay him $250 a day. After recently spending most of his days on a tall ladder operating a noisy, cumbersome hedge trimmer for $50 a day, Ace felt that the prospect of $250 a day—times three—was as good as winning the lottery.

This ridiculously easy duty became even more appealing when Larry requested Ace to "bring the sticks." Upon arrival in Orlando, the Lincoln Continental rental car went straight to the aircraft, the golf clubs were loaded in the trunk, and the severely underworked flight crew members spent the next three days playing golf and living large on the company's credit cards at the famous golf resort, Greenleaf. This combination of easy money with an all-expense-paid golf vacation greatly diminished Ace's enthusiasm for returning to lawn maintenance. Larry indicated that he might utilize Ace's marginal Cessna Citation piloting skills again and would probably call him for another trip in the near future. A few days later, in the heat of one Florida August afternoon sun, Ace reluctantly found himself back at the lawn maintenance job. The boss, a lady who owned the company and functioned as his immediate supervisor, returned from a lengthy lunch in a state of "tipsy" after a "three-martini lunch." She immediately chastised Ace for his poor job performance, and Ace, not one to take a chastisement sitting down, responded: he turned in his hated lawn-maintenance tools and sang a few lines from the great C&W classic by Johnny Paycheck; "Take this Job and Shove it!"

During the last three months of 1990, Ace did some occasional part-time copilot work for Larry and an ex-Learjet colleague who operated a Hawker 700 aircraft. Ace had no training in these aircraft, but he read the aircraft flight manuals and gained a rudimentary understanding of the systems. If his captain became incapacitated, he would have been able to get the aircraft safely on the ground. Ace and his buddy Mike (the Fonz) were beating the bushes for another 727 job. The laissez-faire aviation deregulation had created an environment in which startup airlines emerged like mushrooms from manure, and most of them would evolve into pretty shitty deals. Many of these operations, in Ace's esteemed view, were so despicable that they would stink worse than manure and not even be worthy of the demeaning status of "fly by night." Ace and Mike attended one mass-hiring briefing for a new 727 airline, and after receiving their manuals and projected base and route information from the director of operations, the company CEO addressed them. The CEO did not mince words: the prospective new hire pilots, he said, had the function to "Move airplanes and not to write up discrepancies in the maintenance logbook." Adding insult to obviously potential injury or worse, he stated, "If any of you pilots do not want to work with management in that regard, you should then turn in your manuals and seek employment elsewhere." The message was very clear: *If you want to work here, you will sacrifice safety by flying poorly maintained aircraft.* Shortly thereafter, Ace and the Fonz picked up their manuals, returned them to the desk in the front of the room, and left the area without one look back.

THE MAIL MUST GO THROUGH

In the middle of January, 1991 the underground network of unemployed 727 pilots revealed a new opportunity. The U.S. government had decided that passenger-carrying airlines would no longer be allowed to carry mail for the U.S. postal system. Ace's previous employer, Ryan International Airlines, had received a large contract to move this mail around the country with 727 aircraft. So Ace and Mike went back to work, along with forty or fifty other pilots, mostly ex-Eastern pilots. Eastern airlines had just ceased its operations, and many current and qualified 727 pilots eagerly looked for employment. Many of them, unfamiliar with the nature of "non-sked/freighter" airline operations, shook their heads in disbelief at some of the more unsavory elements of the operation. Having spent most of their life as major airline pilots, the exposure to the "dark side of aviation" was quite eye opening for them. But they rapidly assimilated and began referring to themselves as "freight dogs." They also made the adjustment from warm meals, served by attractive flight attendants, to prepackaged, vendor machine "food simulator" cuisine. They were just happy to have a job flying airplanes during this time of commercial airline instability.

Moving the mail from A to B was a relatively easy job despite the all-night flying and restless days while attempting to sleep in a third-rate hotel. A bag of burgers for dinner highlighted the day. The circadian rhythm monster has long embedded its claws deeply into the homo-sapiens critter, and the efforts to reject the monster are usually fraught with folly. Ace was lucky enough to get some good layover stations, including San Francisco, Los Angeles, and San Juan. San Juan, not the "Jewel of the Caribbean" as the Puerto Rico marketing propaganda stated, certainly outclassed Peoria, Illinois, by a wide margin. The USPS (United States Post Office) management folks overseeing this contractual mail program concerned themselves only with an on-time operation, mandating, too, that the pilots fly as fast as possible. Therefore, Ace and many of his colleagues would fly the aircraft on the edge of the "barber pole" at the maximum allowable airspeed. They frequently violated the FAA's speed restriction of 250 knots below 10,000 feet altitude. The air traffic controllers would occasionally ask the offending speeder, "What's your airspeed?" The cockpit response would always be, "We're right at 250," even though the aircraft flew at 350 knots. It is quite likely that in most cases the air traffic controllers preferred the high-speed arrivals, effectively, quickly, and efficiently clearing the air space for other aircraft.

Another element of the operation enjoyed by everyone centered on the comfortable, flight-operations-pilot-hangout area at the operational hub in Indianapolis. In addition to extraordinarily high quality, microwaveable machine food, the smell of popping popcorn, a popular snack then, created a homey sensation whenever the pilots entered the facility. Mike "The Fonz" Scala enhanced the ambience when he would amiably spread his effervescent personality around the room. His upbeat presence there at the Indianapolis-hub easily compared with Bob LaRue during the previous Emery-hub days at Dayton, Ohio.

In nearly a year and a half of this contract employment, Ace "bumped heads" with the management only twice. The first incident involved a flight to Los Angeles with the normal early-morning forecast: low ceiling and visibility with the usual morning "marine layer" at LAX. The postal people wanted to put on a few extra thousand pounds of mail, which would have mandated a reduced fuel load to make room for the additional weight. Ace did not want to arrive in LAX neither with minimum fuel nor with most of the airports socked in with morning ground fog. The various management pilots, in their attempts to appease the USPS people, engaged in sometimes-heated coercions to force Ace to reduce his fuel load to a level he considered unsafe. Ace would not budge. He insisted that his aircraft and flight crew would not be put into a precarious situation for a few extra bags of mail.

A few months later, Ace was flying for Ryan in the Emery system. He departed Norfolk, Virginia, with a scheduled stop in Roanoke to add a few thousand pounds of freight before continuing on to the Emery hub at Dayton, Ohio. The weather at Roanoke was right at the minimum required for the approach, but Ace had already experienced Roanoke in good weather, finding Roanoke's airport very challenging even under perfect conditions. The available runway was quite short and the tower was reporting heavy rain and poor braking action. The limited instrument approaches available would have necessitated a landing onto a short, wet runway with a tailwind. Once again, Ace favored a more prudent course of action and decided to overfly Roanoke. Upon arrival at Dayton, his flight-operations management people informed him that the Emery folks were very upset by Ace's decision to overfly Roanoke. In a casual tone of voice, he responded, "They'd be more upset if their aircraft were rolled up in a ball off the end of the runway at Roanoke."

Aviation in itself is not inherently dangerous. But to an even greater degree than the sea, it is terribly unforgiving of any carelessness, incapacity or neglect.

A PERFECT "TREE"-POINT LANDING

On May 10, 1992, Ace flew his last flight for Ryan, which had to furlough most of the contract pilots hired the previous January. Again without an aviator's position, he briefly beat the bushes in search of an aviation job. When not even one airline opened its door to the rogue pilot, he headed for upstate New York, where he spent the next six months eating Mom's home cooking while supplementing his income as a freelance golf instructor. After most of autumn's leaves had fallen to the ground, Ace looked around, and observed a few snowflakes falling. He remembered all too well those harsh winters during his youth, and hit the ground running for South Florida! The infamous "corrosion corner" at Miami International Airport might possibly have an old, junk airplane that Ace could fly. Based on his previous good fortune in finding obscure airline jobs, Ace once again launched an optimistic search for aviation employment.

COLLUSION AT CORROSION CORNER

Ace received a call from Mike on a Saturday morning to inform him that Arrow Air in Miami was looking for 727 pilots. That afternoon, Ace called the chief pilot at his home, and after about a three-minute interview, Ace was hired over the phone and told to report for training on Monday morning. As had been the case for the previous several jobs, the start of class would be "like old home day," as the pilots who had worked together at previous airlines would reconvene. At the start of class, the instructor asked each pilot to share a brief verbal résumé regarding his or her background. One pilot, who had a flair for the absurdly satirical, related a bit of his background and then stated, "I'm just proud to be here and to be an Arrow Air pilot." The room full of pilots exploded in laughter since Arrow Air was not highly regarded as an aviation employer. Its location was the famous "corrosion corner" on the northwest side of Miami International Airport. Corrosion corner, an area of nearly one square mile, was cluttered with numerous old, junk airplanes, most of which would never again fly, including aircraft formerly operated by Arrow Air, Rich International Airlines, and Fleming International Airlines.

During Ace's piloting duties at Arrow Air, he was fortunate enough to fly a relatively late-model ex-Eastern Airlines 727-200. Throughout the first months of his employment, he and his favorite copilot, Mike, The Fonz, enjoyed the ease and the comfort of flying day cargo flights to Port-au-Prince, Haiti. At a later time during their gig with Arrow Air, it would be necessary, as a result of an airplane maintenance problem, to experience a layover in Port-au-Prince, offering Ace an opportunity for the first and only time to leave the airport to view first hand the saddening and despicable poverty of this third world country.

Along with the sleek jets operating out of corrosion corner, there were also numerous old DC-6 aircraft as well as World War II aircraft employed to fly cargo to the Caribbean and to other destinations in Latin America. Many of these aircraft were marginally maintained, and some of the "old salts" who flew them insisted that engine failures were very common. An integral part of this aviation lore included a bar named Bryson's, just off 36th Street on the north side of the airport, a hangout for many of the pilots who flew these old birds. Legend has it that the crew schedulers for many of the corrosion-corner operators would make a telephone call to Bryson's bar when they sought the services of a DC-6 engineer or some other type of pilot needed for a flight.

Perhaps the most unlikely non-occurrence in aviation history relates to the idea that none of these old aircraft crashed into the tall buildings in downtown Miami. Ace had one nerve-rattling experience in a DC-6 as a jump-seat passenger on a flight out of Willow Run Airport on a hot summer day, and he vowed never again to ride in a DC-6 aircraft. The very minimal climb rate, combined with the aircraft's vibration and the clattering of four engines struggling to produce the maximum power available, was quite unnerving. As Ace watched the DC-6 cargo flights depart MIA, he would say a little prayer for each of those four old engines. A veteran DC-6 pilot on one occasion told Ace that flying one of these aircraft was like managing a large, nineteenth-century-airborne factory.

Ace and Mike functioned together as the proverbial dynamic duo, and soon their gravy-train trips to Port-au-Prince ended when they started flying trips to Latin America and to other spots in the Caribbean. They hit the jackpot when they received scheduling for a very rare layover in San Jose, Costa Rica. The Arrow Air cockpit jump-seat policy was quite liberal, so Ace took his new girlfriend, Bebe, for an all-expense-paid trip to one of the most popular vacation spots in Central America. After two days of vacation, the return trip to Miami zoomed pleasantly along during the night, although the first 500 miles of the northbound flight transited through an area of embedded thunderstorms. Ace wanted to make sure that Bebe would be able to experience some window-seat time, so he invited her up into the copilot's seat. Shortly after she fastened her seatbelt and shoulder harness, the aircraft entered an area of moderate turbulence with lightning and audible thunder. As the hail pounded the aircraft and Saint Elmo's fire amassed itself on the windshield, the wide-eyed and normally reticent Bebe made a pleading request to have Mike return to the copilot seat.

WILL SOMEBODY PLEASE CLOSE THE BACK DOOR!

The work conditions at Arrow Air were surprisingly reasonable, and other than the very marginal maintenance, "the Big A" was not the onerous employer that Ace and his new hire colleagues had anticipated. Maintenance problems did seem to be intensifying, and the pilots often commented that every flight was like a simulator check ride with multiple emergencies. Arrow Air soon became engaged in passenger service, along with its continued air-cargo service. The airline company, a multi-faceted aviation operation, complemented Batch Air, a parts and aircraft-sales company. Batch's owner, George Batchelor, was a renowned aviation entrepreneur and very generous philanthropist in the Miami area. The Arrow Air 727 aircraft were being maintained by very inexperienced mechanics, often with replacement parts that quite frequently did not effectuate the repair.

Arrow's maintenance situation, if truth be told, resulted in an interesting experience for Ace, his fellow flight crew members, and a nearly-full planeload of passengers when an unusual airframe vibration accompanied their departure from Mexico City. Ace immediately checked the engine gauges to determine that the aircraft had no engine problem. After a few seconds, the vibration diminished, and all appeared okay for a few minutes, that is, up until Ace noticed that the aircraft was not climbing at its normal rate under the prevailing conditions. Shortly thereafter, the lead flight attendant excitedly entered the cockpit and blurted, "The aft air-stair is open," an important piece of information met with utter disbelief by the cockpit crewmembers, including a company maintenance representative situated in the jump seat! The rep *immediately* proceeded to the aft of the aircraft cabin. He returned to the cockpit and assured the crew that this seemingly impossible occurrence had, indeed, occurred.

The 727's aft air-stair is often used for passenger loading and disembarkation; however, when it is in the closed position, it is held closed by mechanical latches called up-locks. Prior to the flight, the Miami maintenance personnel worked on the "rigging" of this mechanism. This factor, along with a DB Cooper vane that had not been lubricated, explained the present dilemma. The DB Cooper vane, a modification for the 727 aircraft, took its name from the famous aircraft hijacker, Mr. DB Cooper, who exited an airborne 727 by opening the aft air-stair in flight and stepping into the airstream with extorted money and a parachute. The legend of DB Cooper lives on. The Cooper vane had been designed to prevent the aft air-stair on the 727 aircraft from ever again opening while airborne, that is to say, until this particular flight captained by Ace took place. When Ace called the Boeing engineers the following day to elaborate on this radical anomaly, they stated that an inadvertent, partial extension of the aft air-stair during flight had *never* before occurred.

The lead flight attendant on this DB Cooper flight, an ex-Sun Coast Airlines employee named Andrea, had also flown with several other non-sked airlines. Her Boeing 727 experience and savvy now came into play. She provided an original and a courageous solution to the problem. The flight crew descended to a lower altitude in order to depressurize the aircraft. Andrea then opened the cabin's rear-entry door and—held firmly by the big, strong maintenance rep—reached out to activate the lever that would raise and mechanically lock the aft air-stair in the up-and-closed position. She next made use of a seat-belt extension to tie the lever in the closed position to guarantee that the door would not re-open in flight. Had the door not been secured in the closed position, it would have dragged on the runway during landing. The accompanying noise, along with sparks flying and significant damage to the air-stair, would have frightened Orville and Wilbur out of their peaceful repose. Hundreds of thousands of current and ex-Boeing 727 pilots will scratch their heads in amazement at this radical aviation aberration.

While phase one of this multifaceted aviation saga came to a happy conclusion, phase two posed the next problem: the significantly increased fuel burn prevented the flight from continuing to Miami. The only viable course of action was to land at Merida in the Yucatán Peninsula. Ace executed this landing with extreme gentle care because Ace still entertained the notion that the door might re-open if he made a hard landing. The maintenance rep soon ascertained that he would be unable to repair the aft air-stair. Thus, the airplane sat grounded until parts could be sent from Miami. The passengers, who had already encountered a significant delay at Mexico City, were anxious to get back to their original destination of Miami, or to get off the airplane if they could not journey on to Miami. The airport authorities initially refused to permit disembarkation because this trip was not a scheduled flight, advising the passengers to stay aboard the aircraft. Several hours later, during which the flight crew assiduously attempted to placate the angry passengers, they were finally allowed to go to a holding area inside the terminal.

As a result of some unique and creative communication between Ace and Arrow Air operations, another aircraft over-flying Merida would land there to pick up the stranded passengers. The Arrow's flight crew, on the other hand, would have to stay with the aircraft until it was repaired the following day. The varying logistics of the situation precluded the possibility of hotel rooms, so the flight crew spent the night at the "Hotel Boeing."

In the course of his career, Ace spent almost as much time sleeping in the cabin of the 727 as he did in the cockpit. A few hours of sleep across the uncomfortable seats created a feeling of having just been run over by a car after finishing a fifteen-round bout with a body puncher. Many of the charter flights in the non-sked environment required flight crews to ride in the cabin for eight to ten hours and then to go to the cockpit to fly for another eight to ten hours, a maneuver clearly designed to circumvent the problems of maximum flight time and required rest for the crew. Crunched into a coach seat in the cabin for several hours could—just barely—be construed as crew rest, another example of how the nebulously written FAA regulations would give the airline an option to stretch the rules.

Ace encountered one more interesting aircraft malfunction during his stint at Arrow Air. He and his crew were sent to Arizona to retrieve an airplane from the "bone yard." The bone yard is an airport (Marana Air Park) near Tucson, Arizona, inundated with hundreds of "moth-balled" aircraft. The plane in question had been sitting in the desert for several years and would undergo refurbishing under the terms of sale to an African company. After a several-hour delay, the maintenance folks put the paperwork together, cleaned up a few loose ends, and finally announced that it was time to launch the old "clunker." The first engine to be started, number three, immediately indicated very high oil pressure and had to be shut down. The maintenance rep removed the engine cowl and determined that the oil line had been crimped. This was soon repaired and the old "desert-rat Boeing" launched for Miami. However, after a little over one hour in the air, the flight engineer observed that engine-number-three oil was diminishing quite rapidly, most likely created by the rapid "de-crimping" of the oil line prior to departure. Ace then made a phone patch to Arrow Air flight operations personnel in Miami to inform them that the engine would likely have to be shut down soon. The response was something like, "No problem, just bring the airplane back to Miami, and we will fix it when you get here." The thought of flying for three more hours, including an extended overwater segment across the Gulf of Mexico with one engine shut down, was not a consideration for Ace. He responded by informing flight operations that he would divert to San Antonio and have the aircraft fixed there. Upon arrival at San Antonio, several 727 mechanics met the aircraft on the ramp and accomplished the repair within one hour. This particular aircraft would later find itself employed for passenger trips out of Miami. Nearly every flight involved some type of aircraft malfunction.

There were numerous other maintenance stories until—eventually—FAA authorities started paying closer attention to the maintenance procedures at Arrow Air. When they did, they discovered ample reason to ground the airline by suspending its operational certificate. An article in The Washington Post, on March 25, 1995, elaborated on this issue. The local newspaper, The Miami Herald, also engaged in some significant investigative reporting, revealing that a major contributing factor for the Arrow Air shutdown was the use of bogus aircraft parts.

INTERNATIONAL INTRIGUE—HIDE THE JET

But, for Ace, it was not to worry, since he lived less than a mile away from the Florida unemployment office. He was now on a first-name basis with most of the employees in the office, and they would often make joking comments like, "Which airline did you run out of business this time?" Ace soon reconnected with as many of his 727 pilot colleagues as possible, and a couple of months later he found yet another unique and challenging situation through an international employment agency. Strong Field Aviation offered what was projected to be a short-term contract to fly out of Europe and to be based in Athens, Greece. The money was good and Ace didn't hesitate. He met his captain colleague, Rick, and flight engineer, Joe, at Miami International and boarded a Delta Airlines flight bound for Athens, Greece. The $4,200 one-way, first-class ticket immediately endeared Ace to his new employer since he had anticipated a long, cramped flight in "steerage" with the teeming masses of humanity battling for elbow room.

This singularly unique aviation opportunity with Strong Field Aviation turned out to involve flying an ex-Lufthansa 727 for a South African company by the name of Safair. Strong Field, a company based in the UK, had hired Ace, and Safair was doing sub-service charter for a Greek company. This mixture sounded like a potential "sticky wicket," and it soon proved to be just that. The Lufthansa 727 had been impeccably maintained by the Germans, and though the aircraft had reached nearly twenty years of age, it clung to a fresh-off-the-assembly-line look. The work schedule was quite comfortable, including daily flights to Europe, primarily to the UK, and side trips to one of the Greek Isles, Iraklion. This new gig moved along nicely until Ace received a call from the company, advising him to get his crew together immediately, to check out of the hotel, and to leave nothing behind because they would not be returning to Athens. Some behind-the scenes, international diplomacy had failed, and the Greek authorities were getting ready to impound the airplane as a result of some an international red-tape paperwork snafu. Ace and his crew members, including the flight attendants, flew the aircraft to Oostende, Belgium. After hiding the airplane in Belgium for a few days, the next destination in this cloak-and-dagger operation brought Ace and everyone else to Basel-Milhous, located in the southeast corner of France.

Strong Field's operations then settled into some semblance of sanity as passenger charters were flown from Basel-Milhous to European vacation destinations such as the Canary Islands. The panoramic views during these flights were spectacular. The departure routing resulted in a flight path that came so close to the Matterhorn that you could almost see the extreme-sport lunatic climbers trying to scale the face. The total view of the Swiss and the French Alps would occasionally be complemented by over-flight of Lake Geneva, Switzerland, which surely lies there as one of the most beautiful places on planet Earth. The Canary Island flights also rewarded everyone with spectacular views over both Gibraltar and the northwest corner of Morocco.

Such stunning panoramas disappeared during one return flight to Basel-Milhous when the area was fogged in with less than a quarter mile of visibility. In addition, fuel was low after the long flight from the Canary Islands, and Ace would have to get right on the edge of his seat for what he knew would be a demanding approach. At the DH (decision height), there were no runway lights in sight, but the needles were centered and the airplane was stabilized so Ace elected to "break minimums" and to continue the approach. A few seconds later, with Ace's emotional intensity maxed out as he worked hard to keep the needles centered, Ace's swelling tension melted away when the copilot called out, "runway lights in sight!" As the aircraft was on its landing roll, the sighs of relief and reduced hyperventilation were audible. The after-landing checklist was accomplished in a celebratory fashion.

A mere twenty-four hours after this contract job had initially presented itself to Ace; he was bound for Athens, Greece. This flying assignment, too, would end with similar swiftness. After arriving back at the hotel from a Canary Island trip, Ace was informed that the contract had just come to a rapid conclusion, and the aircraft would have to be returned to South Africa. Ace's captain colleague, Rick, drew the short straw and would be leaving shortly to ferry the airplane back to South Africa, a flight that was going to require a fuel stop somewhere in the middle of darkest Africa in the middle of the night.

When Ace imagined himself the captain on this dubious mission of uncertainties, he experienced a severe spike in blood pressure and rejoiced in the awareness that he would not serve as the captain on this trans-African adventure. As Ace and his flight crew colleagues lounged in the hotel drinking fine French wine and enjoying exquisite cuisine, they heard the loud sound of their 727 departing for "someplace in Africa." Ace reveled in the good fortune of being able to return to the United States with a first-class ticket on a major airline. He and his crew drank a toast to their departed friend, the beautiful Lufthansa 727, and, since there was no flying the next day, they got *toasted.*

Ace returned to the U.S., and with no flying job immediately appearing on the horizon, he took a job as a starter-ranger at a local private country club. Although the golf course job paid only seven dollars an hour, the work did provide free food and golf. At the time, Ace shared a $300-per-month rental condominium with his girlfriend, Bebe, and he was getting burned out on chasing airplanes around the world trying to make a few bucks. Just when enthusiasm for a return to aviation reached its minimum, Ace received a call from a previous 727 colleague, letting him know of a job opportunity for a new airline based in Miami. As a Miami-based pilot, he would avoid the slings and the arrows of commuting to work to some distant Midwest or Northeast city and evade the discomfort in a sleazy "crash pad" on the wrong side of town. For many pilots, the hassle of the commute is far more stressful than the actual job, since a failure to get to one's duty station for an assigned flight usually results in termination. Then, too, sharing a "commuter pad" is only slightly better than a homeless existence.

THE WINTER OF DISCONTENT

Ace would next "hire on" with Prestige Airways and return to the uncertainties of the non-sked, passenger-charter world. Upon completion of training, he was assigned to fly charters out of Cleveland, Pittsburgh, and Chicago. After a pleasant summer in the Midwest, he returned for a couple months of flying between Miami and the Caribbean. Then the situation began to deteriorate. Ace would no longer call Miami his home base after he and several of his fellow pilots were reassigned to Flint, Michigan, commonly regarded at that time as the anal pore of the Western World. Here's the kicker to this already bad deal: the flight crews, none of whom were going to permanently move to Flint, would have to commute to work and then pay for food and lodging on their "own nickel." Not only was the salary so despicably low that it was demeaning, but the pilots also had to pay for their hotel rooms. With no per-diem compensation, the copilots and the flight engineers would barely break even. The only pay consisted of a straight hourly rate based on the block time with no monthly guarantee. The link between compensation and hours on the job led to a number of inventive stratagems. The average taxi speed, for example, became a slow creep at three to five miles per hour. During the short flights to Midway Airport in Chicago, Ace flew the aircraft as slowly as possible to make a few more dollars for everyone, including the cabin crew. Occasionally, a passenger would ask a flight attendant, "Why are we flying so slowly?" The canned response placed the finger of blame on air traffic control while the real reason focused on making a few extra bucks for the flight crewmembers.

The Flint assignment, akin to purgatory in "The Black Hole of Calcutta," may well have been penance for all of those previous, pleasant flights to the Caribbean. The owner of Prestige Airways, a very charismatic African-American man who had some political connections in the Caribbean, had initiated 727-scheduled passenger service from Miami to Martinique and Antigua. The approach and landing at Martinique was both beautiful and challenging since there were usually turbulent crosswinds in the touchdown area. The Antigua terminal had a "tropical island" flair—there were no doors or windows, and it was essentially an open-air cabana with the usual ceiling fans and a small bar area crowded with American tourists putting down their last rum drink of the vacation. Ace grudgingly transitioned from this tropical work environment to the new Flint base, where—to make things even worse—he would spend the winter.

Flint's winter was filled with depressing winter days, but spring soon came, and as the snow melted in mid-March, Prestige Airway's house of cards also dissolved. The Prestige owner, Mr. Jackson, had wined and dined the Flint Chamber of Commerce to provide Flint with jet service in exchange for some free advertising and discount operations at the airport. After an extended period of unpaid bills with several agencies in the Flint area, including the fueling vendor, a fuel truck physically blocked a departing passenger flight until payment was received. A few days later, Prestige Airways closed its doors.

Ace then resumed the now long-familiar search for any old 727 to fly for any reasonable amount of compensation. He immediately hooked up with a company called Custom Air Cargo and was projected to be based in Dubai upon completion of training. The first of several ominous signs showed its sardonic smile: rather than staying in hotels, the flight crews would have to live in dormitory-like housing. The second ominous sign produced a similar smile: Their 727-ground-school training was at first administered by a DC-8 mechanic who could barely spell "Boeing," and the man elaborated incessantly on the nuances of the DC-8 aircraft systems. Strong negative feedback from the experienced 727 flight crews, however, soon ensured that he would be speedily replaced. Soon, yet another portentous warning emerged. When simulator training began, the designated check airman, quite inexperienced in the 727, revealed his inadequacies by browbeating and belittling the pilots during the required simulator training. And finally, at roughly the same time, the company CEO gave a major address to the newly hired pilots. Ace's background as a farm boy had instilled in him a very keen sense of smell, and the CEO's "BS" stank worse than the old chicken coops Ace had cleaned during his youth. Ace turned in his manuals and abandoned this extremely dubious operation. The accuracy of his sense of smell was later confirmed when he learned that many of the pilots who went to Dubai had difficulty getting their paychecks.

Ace, *very briefly*, also took part in an extremely amateurish startup company that planned to operate 727-100 aircraft into La Paz, Bolivia. La Paz sits 13,000 feet above sea level and requires special modification to the aircraft's oxygen system. When the management revealed it had no awareness of this requirement as well as no intention to address the problem, Ace *immediately* headed for the exit to search for another job opening. He was soon presented with an offer to live in Kathmandu, Nepal, to fly a 727 aircraft to a variety of destinations in neighboring countries. The day before he was ready to leave, the contract fell through. After he later viewed an aerial photograph of the Kathmandu airport, located on a mountainside high in the Himalayan Mountains, he experienced great relief knowing that he was not going to be flying out of this remote and hazardous location.

Ace was surviving—barely—on his unemployment compensation, and he considered finding a real job and ending this uncertainty of airline roulette. Just as he was near certain that his pilot career had ended, he received an opportunistic phone call from a local-area, ex-pilot colleague alerting him of a new start-up airline. Ace was at first going to ignore this employment possibility, but the siren song of the Boeing 727 once again enticed him. He called the Atlanta number that his colleague had offered and he was courteously and enthusiastically greeted by one of his past cockpit colleagues from Air Atlanta. The warm glow of the pilot camaraderie sent him scurrying off to Atlanta to start his new job with Nation's Air.

The chief pilot, John Graham, was an ex-Air Atlanta pilot, as were several others in the company. The quality of training was exceptionally high and Graham, also a check airman, demanded very high standards in the simulator. Ace's 727 simulator skills had advanced significantly from the initial training days at Braniff. He breezed through the program and was soon out flying "the line"—once again enjoying the good life of an airline pilot, while earning about one third as much as the major airline pilots took home. Except for the paltry salary, all that emerged from the Nation's Air experience symbolized the FAA at its very worst. Ace will share this woeful tale in the upcoming chapter, exposing a portion of the ugly underbelly of that agency. Although the Nation's Air engagement lasted a short while, his golfing buddy and chief pilot, John Graham, would help rescue Ace for the final chapter of his airline career.

As Ace looked for financing to purchase a small condo, he was required to review his income tax records for the previous ten years. The final line of the math revealed that during the "turbulent ten"—1987 through 1997—his average salary amounted to *$35,000 a year.* To make matters worse, during this ten-year period, Ace had been employed as a 727 captain by ten different airlines! The ravaging of pilot employees during this unstable period of the airline environment is difficult for the layman to comprehend. It was not uncommon for Ace to have as second officer at the engineer's panel a pilot who had previously been a captain at a major airline with a salary of $150,000 per year. His salary as a freight dog 727 flight engineer was $35,000 per year. The turmoil and the instability of pilots' careers during this period of time were unprecedented. The shameless exploitation of airline employees often resulted in clinical depression, family upheaval, and even numerous suicides. Ace's unstable and chaotic employment during this time frame greatly contributed to his divorce.

During this ten-year period with ten different aviation employers, Ace also engaged in numerous other income-producing activities, including lawn maintenance, irrigation and landscaping maintenance, and umpiring baseball games. He explored more entrepreneurial avenues as well: several attempts at multilevel marketing, the distribution of gourmet pancake flour, and golf instruction. On the other hand, the very bright side of his employment résumé during this period spoke volumes about Ace's ability to avoid employment with some of the notoriously unsafe and underpaid 727 airline operations. His hunger pangs were at one time so intense that he actually *did apply* for work at a couple of these "bottom feeder" operators. Yet the rejection by these companies was likely precipitated by an awareness that he would refuse to fly their junk airplanes or to acquiesce to unreasonable work conditions.

Some of the anecdotal war stories that have emanated from unethical operators are almost incomprehensible, and one will be enough to bring this chapter to a close. Reportedly, a DC-8 copilot, who had endured an extended period of flying with very little time off, had finally reached his breaking point. It was winter and he had just flown a trip into Miami on one of those perfect, sunny South Florida days. He had been on an extended schedule that took him to cold, desolate airports, and the long winter, combined with the demanding work conditions, apparently took him over the edge. He had no interest in returning to the snow and cold, so he spontaneously picked up his bags, left the aircraft, and headed straight for the beach. When the captain informed his company operations that he no longer had a copilot, he was directed to bring the airplane home anyway, since it was badly needed for more money-making flights. The captain was, of course, reluctant to fly the aircraft without a copilot, but as all businessmen are acutely aware, *everyone has a price.* The captain was made an offer that he couldn't refuse. The burned-out copilot had a great day at the beach, and the aircraft departed Miami with an empty right seat. Unfortunately, we will *never* know how many stories of this nature are available in the vast archives of radical aviation anecdotes.

EXPLOIT THE HUNGRY PILOT—SELL HIM A JOB

Aviation's unstable job market produced a great opening for the ubiquitous con artists. Creative and unscrupulous entrepreneurs fabricated start-up airlines. They preyed on the desperate pilot and the flight attendant alike, requiring a $25 or $50 fee with the flight crew applicant's employment application. These scamming, boiler-room operations were usually alleged to be based out of Florida or out of some other desirable location, and the aviation community's "buzz" about this new, but fictitious airline would attract the enthusiastically naïve. People desperate for a job in the *glamorous* airline profession were bilked out of their money, and many of them never discovered that "Acme Airlines" sole asset consisted of a Post-Office box to receive the ill-gotten gains.

To complement the P.O. Box airlines, there were also *legitimate* airlines that required the flight crews to purchase their pilot's position by paying a very large sum of money up front. It was common for the captain to pay

$50,000 for left-seat employment. The copilot rate usually came to $25,000. That payment also represented a year's salary for the given pilot, who in actual fact paid for his first year's salary. Ace and his buddy, Mike Scala, attended an interview with one of these shyster organizations. Its airport office and a small room filled with travel posters did not entice them to shell out $25,000 to these exploitive scoundrels. The sole success story of these pay-as-you-go airlines, Kiwi Airlines, actually survived for several years, and the company's pilots showed a profit from their investment by receiving more salary than their investment.

CHAPTER TEN

"I'm From The FAA, And I'm Here To Help You"

"Get the gun, Ma, those government people are coming up the driveway." The FAA, arguably a very powerful agency, has had a very favorable effect upon aviation safety in the U.S. However, the agency is far from infallible and does fall victim to many of the shortcomings that are part of any government bureaucracy. The FAA has been horse-collared with dual roles that often collide with each other. The governmental organization is responsible for providing all the necessary oversight of aviation in order to promote the highest possible level of safety. It also has the task to promote commercial aviation. The promotional aspect of its stated mission, however, can often serve as a detriment to its safety-oversight duties.

ARREST THEM CRIMINALS

A dazzling example of the dysfunctional policies of this organization has to do with the imposition of FAR violations on pilots for certain types of extremely nebulous charges. While Ace flew with Nation's Air, the FAA's POI (principle operating inspector), a person responsible for overseeing the safety of the airline doggedly pursued a paperwork snafu until he was able to impose a violation upon Ace. This violation emanated from a training class that Ace had attended and completed, but he did not yet receive credit for the class. Because the person in charge of the training, a flight attendant, most likely had an ax to grind against pilots—her ex-husband was a pilot—and she did not produce the required certificate. The FAA saw an opportunity to impose a violation on a pilot for a trivial paperwork *faux pas*. While, on one hand, the FAA did overlook extreme violations of safety, the aviation authority, on the other hand, expended great effort to punish Ace for a meaningless infraction, resulting in a thirty-day suspension of his pilot's certificate. A few months later, the *same* FAA employee would attempt to sabotage Ace again, when Ace underwent the hiring procedure by TransMeridian Airlines (TMA). Even through TransMeridian management knew about Ace's petty violation, the FAA representative went out of his way to inform TMA that Ace had incurred a recent violation, even suggesting that TMA might want to reconsider his candidacy for the job. The company also knew that Ace had a long track record of both safely and effectively transporting a Boeing 727 from point A to point B. To Ace's good fortune, TransMeridian ultimately ignored this ill-intentioned naysayer. And this represents just one instance of a professional pilot's vulnerability. It also demonstrates the power the FAA holds to shoot down a pilot's career.

In another example of FAA power wrapped around a trivial paperwork deviation, Ace watched one of his captain colleagues get metaphorically kneed in the groin by the FAA—with an assist by a narrow-minded employer—during Ace's previous employment for the Ryan Aviation contract program. The captain in question had experienced difficulty obtaining an appointment for his FAA physical exam because he had to deal with an extremely erratic work schedule. Upon arrival at the sort in Indianapolis, he informed his employer, Ryan Aviation, that he was unable to take the FAA physical that day. The calendar already displayed the thirty-first day of the month, and his physical expired on the thirty-first, so the company immediately grounded him and informed the FAA of the alleged infraction. The vast majority of violations imposed upon pilots are related to *paperwork errors* rather than to actual violations of safety. During the reign of the anti-labor Reagan administration, there was an effort to create a draconian bureaucracy that would actually fine a pilot as much as $10,000 for such petty violations, particularly noteworthy because for many of the underpaid pilots, that sum represented a full six-month salary.

CAPITALISM RUN AMOK

Perhaps surprisingly, underpaid aviation employees played a major role in the ease with which the 9/11 hijackers were able to perpetrate their crimes. A couple of decades earlier, the many people concerned with airline-passenger safety decided to implement a passenger-inspection program before passengers could board a commercial aircraft, certainly at first a sound idea, yet sabotaged in due time by extremely poor implementation—notably by the FAA's willingness to allow the commercial airlines themselves to control the process of inspection. The airline management, primarily concerned, of course, with profitability, hired private companies for this petty detail, and the lowest bidder usually received the contract. To reach even deeper into the depths of poor management, the lowest bidder, likewise concerned about the profitability motive, enhanced its return by paying minimum wage, resulting in the employment of people with very marginal skills. Investigations have revealed that many of these employees received no training regarding duties that were supposed to prevent the hijacking or the sabotaging of airplanes—a clear case of capitalism run amok, since the only objective centered on the short-term bottom line—*at the expense of providing a smooth path for aircraft hijackers.*

Prior to 9/11 far too many people performed incompetently at the airport checkpoints. Some of these low-wage employees consisted of illegal immigrants, whose documents had not been inspected by their employer. As a flight crewmember who passed through these checkpoints as many as fifty or sixty times a month, Ace got a firsthand view of the folly of the FAA/airline airport-security agreements. Even after 9/11, *the incompetence and the overreaction of these marginally functional security people stood out for the whole world to see!* Ace had numerous encounters with these "security" folks as they became fanatically fervent in flaunting their overwhelming power.

While going through airport security on one particular occasion in his airline uniform at the Minneapolis Airport, he personally encountered a situation that would require intervention by the local police. When the male "pat-down" person became extremely overzealous, Ace halted the process and immediately called for a supervisor. The supervisor then called for local law enforcement. When a police officer arrived, Ace reached out with his hands and wrists clamped together and said, "Cuff me if you have to, officer, but I am not going to endure the humiliation of public molestation." The officer very coolly intervened and told the security person simply to use his electronic wand. The inspection concluded, bringing an end to that particular story. Unfortunately, numerous flight crewmembers shared similar experiences. One airline pilot, for instance, lost his job when he remarked on the senselessness to confiscate his fingernail clippers, considering the fact that his aircraft cockpit was equipped with a large, sharp crash-axe.

One of the direct consequences of 9/11, this country's Homeland Security Act, provided for the hiring of infinitely more qualified and competent security people. Nonetheless, there still are far too many instances of the unnecessary, overzealous responses at security checkpoints, resulting in embarrassment and heightened stress for traveling airline passengers. Numerous exposés have revealed that most of the activity at airport security checkpoints is unnecessary and even counterproductive. While the checkpoints are clearly a necessity, much of the time, effort, and money could be more wisely spent in other aspects of airline security. On the brighter side of this controversial issue, there appears to be a growing learning curve, bringing about somewhat more user-friendly airport security checkpoints. Some of the procedures employed come as an irrational over-response to one isolated situation. A little more than three months following 9/11, Richard Reid, now serving three consecutive life sentences, attempted to ignite explosive devices hidden in his shoes during American Airlines Flight 63. Thanks to Richard (noted with a contemptuous tone of voice), today's airline passengers must still remove their shoes during the screening process. Homeland Security should reconsider some of these unnecessary and burdensome policies.

Unfortunately, the nature of bureaucracies, particularly those of the U.S. government, has been to respond *reactively* rather than *proactively* in order to prevent problems from occurring. The FAA, in particular, has exhibited this behavior on a very large scale. Consider FAA's reaction after the high-profile crash of ValuJet Flight 592, into the Florida Everglades on May 11, 1996. The crash snuffed out the lives of 105 passengers, three flight attendants, and two pilots. No one survived. Prior to the accident, the inspector general of the Department of Transportation, Mary Schiavo, had initiated a great effort to have the FAA engage in a much stricter oversight of this rapidly growing discount airline. However, high-level politics got in the way because ValuJet operated as a Wall-Street phenomenon with rapidly increasing stock value. Prior to and following the crash, there were efforts by the airline's management, with assistance from government officials, to head off any interference that might negatively affect the company's profitability, and in turn, the wealth of the stockholders. Mary Schiavo outlines the details of this situation very clearly in a brilliant exposé: *Flying Blind, Flying Safe.*

EVEN STEVE CANYON NEEDS SLEEP

One of the policies that needs more oversight and rule change has a whole lot to do with flight-crew fatigue. Evaluation of aircraft accidents often reveals that the cockpit crew had been away from a restful bed for well in excess of fourteen hours. The major airlines, as a result of intelligent and safety-oriented intervention (with significant impetus from the unions), have created their own duty-and-flight-time limits, which are often more restrictive than the FAA mandates. However, many airlines do operate without union protection, and their flight crews maintain such lengthy duty times that they often enter a state of fatigue that is far beyond normal functionality. Recent research of the FAR 121 flight-time-and-duty-time limitations (under Flag Carrier International Operations) indicates that the only restriction for the cockpit crew of a Boeing 727 aircraft (two pilots and flight engineer) is not to exceed twelve hours flight time in a twenty-four hour period, or twenty hours flight time in a forty-eight-hour period. Amazingly, there is no stated *minimum* rest period. This loophole would allow a flight crew to remain in the cockpit of an aircraft for forty-eight hours as long as they did not exceed twenty hours of flight time. The only conceivable reason for this senseless regulation is to accommodate airline management in its effort to reduce flight-crew cost for the sake of increased profitability.

Equally outrageous was the FAA's failure to impose flight-and-duty-time limits on flight attendants in the cabin. In more recent years, however, the FAA finally did put restrictions on flight and duty times for cabin attendants. Twenty-five years ago, numerous reports circulated about chartered airline flight attendants who had experienced consecutive Europe turnarounds with no rest, amounting to a minimum of forty consecutive hours of duty. Ace recalls a social gathering of pilots and flight attendants who had spent years in the big-airplane, non-sked charter business. The flight attendants engaged in a game of one-upmanship as they sheepishly bragged about their longest-ever duty period. The "winner" of this event stated that she had been on duty for forty-seven hours. The FAR flight-and-duty-time limitations can often undergo nebulous interpretation in such a fashion that the airline flight-operations department is able to manipulate the actual intent of the regulation in order to continue a flight or a series of flights. Ace noticed that this particular procedure was much more commonly used with a recently upgraded captain or with an inexperienced flight crew rather than with employees more secure in their positions. If a flight crew refuses to fly a trip because of fatigue, and if the crew subsequently encounters any type of coercion or reprimand from superiors, the action should justify criminal prosecution of the superiors.

If we now venture over to take a look at the FAR Part 91 regulations that apply to both private pilots and corporate aviation, we note that there are no flight-or-duty-time limitations for the pilots. Therefore, if "Mr. Big" wants to take his jet wherever and whenever he pleases, he can do so with no concern for the pilot's recent rest or degree of fatigue. While most corporate pilots and the people that ride in these private aircraft will use good judgment regarding this issue, extreme deviations do frequently happen. This is evidenced by an NTSB web site that lists all of the accidents in the past five decades involving private aircraft carrying passengers who were musicians, actors, sports stars, and politicians—celebrities who elected to put their lives into the hands of people whom they did not know and who often worked for unscrupulous entrepreneurs. Consider the highly publicized Learjet crash that took the life of famous golfer Payne Stewart.

The total level of Learjet flight experience as well as the background of the two pilots flying this aircraft were so minimal that a seasoned pilot informed of the crew's inexperience would have refused even to ride along as passenger on that aircraft. It is possible, however, that the nature of the malfunction would have handcuffed even an experienced Learjet flight crew, but it is extremely unlikely that very inexperienced pilots would have been able to cope with what appears to have been a problem of rapid depressurization. Many of the airlines have now implemented scheduling procedures that prevent the possibility of two pilots with minimal flight time in a specific aircraft to be assigned to the same flight.

This commonsense policy was probably implemented as a result of both flight crew and union intervention. ALPA and other unions representing pilots have played a significant role in the exceptionally high-quality safety of U.S. air-carrier operations. The ALPA representation of United Airlines put forth a major contribution to airline safety by implementing a program referred to as CRM (cockpit resource management), a simple change yet a giant step forward for the safety of all aircraft flown by more than one pilot. Numerous fatal accidents could have been averted had the captain elected to pay closer attention to input from his fellow crewmembers, the main idea promoted by CRM. The attitude that the captain is always correct and infallible represents a throwback to the modus operandi of military aviation, often resulting in an egotistical disconnect from either a copilot's or a flight engineer's input. Inevitably, the captain arrogantly continued to perpetrate an unsafe activity observed objectively by his cockpit colleagues as potentially dangerous. In many instances, some vigorous intervention by a captain's fellow crewmembers could have prevented an accident.

Once United Airlines had implemented the CRM program, all other airline management teams concerned with safety rapidly adopted the concept. The significant question to ask is, "Why did the FAA, prior to this period, not address the issue." In the modern era of aviation, the absurd concept of the captain as an omniscient, omnipotent, unquestionable "Kahuna" is very rare. Because of this simple but very important improved perspective, aviation safety has significantly improved. Cockpit voice recording tapes indicate that utilization of a CRM policy could possibly have prevented the carnage at Tenerife in the Canary Islands on March 27, 1977. Considered by many sources "the deadliest accident" in the history of aviation, two Boeing 747 planes collided on the runway, killing a total of 583 people. Incredibly, sixty-one people survived.

According to one of many online reports of the Tenerife collision, Robert Bragg, the only surviving cockpit member of both planes, calls the carnage "a perfect storm of catastrophe." He also says that this aviation calamity "remains the benchmark for all that can go wrong in an airplane."

EXPERIENCE IS NOT IMPORTANT: WE'RE FILLING QUOTAS

On the other end of the spectrum, with very little acceptance by the veteran pilots, the EEOC eventually mandated a program of quota-minority hiring. This concept diminished the quality of newly hired pilots and wreaked havoc with airline training departments. Rumors then began to spin out of the United Airline Training Center that some of these recently hired minority pilots were given unlimited training until they could meet the minimum standards. Previously, new hire pilots would receive a standard curriculum of training, and, if they were not "up to speed," their brief career with UAL would come to an end and they would be back on the street seeking employment. EEOC's policy of quota-minority hiring became quite acceptable in most realms of non-aviation employment, where less experienced or less qualified people would have only a minimal effect on the success or the failure of the business. In the commercial airline business, however, in which a small mistake can kill hundreds of people and result in hundreds of millions of dollars of damage, it is certainly more prudent to have the most qualified and the most experienced people available at the controls.

This misguided government policy was complemented by a *lack* of government policy regarding flight crew proficiency. In 1995, to set an example, a heavily loaded United Airlines 747 departed runway 28 at San Francisco in nighttime-IMC (low visibility) meteorological conditions. Shortly after the aircraft became airborne an engine failure occurred. The pilot then engaged in improper control input, which reduced the already diminished rate of climb. He also failed to make the appropriate turn away from the rapidly rising terrain west of the airport. According to reports, the aircraft flew over San Bruno just above treetop level. This aircraft was a hair's breadth away from creating what probably would have resulted in the *second* worst aviation disaster in history—perhaps even surpassing Tenerife's deadly day. The plane's voice recorders indicated that the initial pilot evaluation of the malfunction was improperly diagnosed as a blown tire since the malfunction was accompanied by a loud noise. Reports also asserted that the pilot flying the aircraft had been an EEOC minority hire. The UAL public-relations department did an excellent job of preventing the major news media sources from reporting this near catastrophe.

The FAA, however, as a result of mandatory-malfunction-reporting procedures, would soon respond in its all-too-often-reactive manner. Unbeknownst to the lay public, the pilots who fly large airplanes long distances make very few takeoffs and landings, and all but a few minutes of the flight are conducted by the autopilot and by the onboard computer navigation. It is not at all uncommon for pilots to have only two or three takeoffs and landings per month. The FAA wisely felt a need to respond to this situation of reduced pilot practice and proficiency, implementing a more frequent simulator-training program that required more hands-on, stick-and-rudder flying. Had the fully loaded 747 splattered on the hillside south of San Francisco, those airline-management people, along with the FAA folks who failed to address this problem of reduced pilot proficiency, would quite likely experience extreme difficulty looking at themselves in their mirror.

AGENDA-DRIVEN ACCIDENT INVESTIGATIONS

The FAA's primary method of supervision involves checking and crosschecking the mandated masses of paperwork required to validate the numerous airline-operation elements that relate to safety. The vast majority of pilot violations reveal themselves as results of paperwork *faux pas* rather than as transgressions that may have threatened flight safety. Far less effort is required to find paperwork malfeasance than engagement in aggressive, proactive monitoring of the actual flight operations. Despite this bureaucratic shortcoming, FAA examiners and hands-on overseers have helped create an airline safety record that is quite commendable. Until the crash of the Continental commuter aircraft on approach to Buffalo on February 12, 2009, there had not been a fatal airline crash in the United States in two years. TV's PBS recently produced a one-hour investigative documentary of this accident and the airline that operated the aircraft, Colgan Air. Called *Flying Cheap*, the program transports the viewer directly to the root cause that undermines airline safety—underpaid, overworked, and fatigued flight crews. It reveals the harsh living conditions of the commuter pilots in their "crash pads." It also points out that low pay leads to situations that jeopardize flight safety as it did in the Continental/Colgan Air Flight 3407: everyone onboard lost their lives, and one person on the ground died.

An inexperienced captain piloted the airplane. The crash took place late in the evening, and pilot fatigue was listed as a contributing factor by the National Transportation Safety Board (NTSB) accident-investigation board. The two pilots had very little rest in the previous twenty-four hours, and the cockpit tapes of their conversations indicated that they were very tired. IMC and icing conditions prevailed, and the pilot relied on the autopilot to reduce the cockpit workload. Nearly all aviation accidents result from a chain of events that leads to the final, uncontrollable impact with the terrain. The experienced pilot will have more potential not only to recognize, but also to deal with this "snowballing of negatives," and the experienced pilot will then take appropriate action. The recent popular book by Malcolm Gladwell, *The Outliers: The Story of Success*, expounds upon this premise and other interesting postulations regarding airplane safety.

The ugly aftermath of aircraft accidents is left in the hands of the NTSB. Extremely meticulous and knowledgeable experts sift through the debris to make intelligent, evaluated decisions about the most plausible contributing cause or causes. The extensive accident-investigation results are then made available for all to view in a very user-friendly format on the NTSB website. The NTSB report of the Payne Stewart Learjet crash is highly detailed and points out that this aircraft had a history of pressurization problems. The NTSB has also made several operational recommendations for dealing with pressurization anomalies in this particular model of Learjet, an excellent example of one more job well done by aviation professionals who really *do* have a "dirty rotten job."

Occasionally, the NTSB professionals will be overridden by other government agencies or by other commercial considerations. Consider the accident investigation of an Arrow Air DC-8 aircraft that crashed after takeoff from the Gander airport in Newfoundland in 1985. This airplane crash had significant political ramifications in that the aircraft had been used for U.S. government purposes during the ongoing Iran/Contra affair. A brilliant exposé of the severely flawed and politically motivated investigation was written by a member of the Canadian Air Safety Board responsible for determining the cause of the crash. The author's name is Les Filotas, and his book is titled *Improbable Cause.* As a member of the accident-investigation team, he gained a high level of insight into the actual cause: a bomb aboard the aircraft rather than the icing problem falsely cited as the cause of the accident. It would have been extremely embarrassing and politically damaging to the U.S. government—particularly to the Central Intelligence Agency (CIA)—had the truth been told regarding this accident. *Improbable Cause* in the hands of a good screenwriter would unquestionably provide a great resource for a docudrama film of international intrigue—comparable, say, to a 007 James Bond adventure story.

One particular accident investigation that carries much political relevance involves the death of Paul Wellstone, a progressive and dynamic Democratic senator from Minnesota. Just prior to the 2002 mid-term elections for a Senate seat in Minnesota, the Republican Party had invested a considerable amount of time and effort into unseating the incumbent Paul Wellstone. Both the White House and the Republican Party viewed Wellstone as a thorn in their side, and the *one additional vote* of a new Republican Senator from Minnesota would tip the scale in favor of a Republican majority in the Senate.

Late in the campaign, Wellstone appeared to be pulling ahead of his opponent. Polls revealed that Minnesota voters preferred Senator Wellstone to challenger Norm Coleman by an increasing gap. On October 25, 2002, the chartered airplane in which Senator Wellstone and his family and staff were traveling crashed on approach to Eveleth, Minnesota. *All six occupants were killed.* Immediate media reports claimed an absence of terrorism, reporting, instead, that icing of the aircraft likely caused the crash. Numerous dubious statements of government-or-media-produced information then gushed forth. The anomalies and the incongruities of this accident investigation would continue until two very curious college professors, Jim Fetzer and Donald Trent Jones, decided to get involved, resulting in the publication of *American Assassination: The Strange Death of Senator Paul Wellstone.* Although the reader can get bogged down in the required technical explanations, *the theme of the book and its implications are profound.*

'RX' FOR SAFETY—PREVENTIVE MEDICINE

The two previously mentioned airplane-accident investigations—the Newfoundland incident in 1985 and Senator Wellstone's death in 2002—exemplify Fourth-of-July-fireworks displays of government agencies sacrificing integrity and scruples in favor of political purpose. Usually, this type of "doctoring the books" goes to the interest of profitability—either for a commercial airliner or for an aircraft manufacturer. No one can refute that the Boeing Company produces incredibly safe aircraft, and the many decades of excellent performance with minimal fatalities is highly commendable. With twenty-two years experience and more than 11,000 hours in the Boeing 727, Ace Abbott strongly attests to the durability of the Boeing aircraft. There are, however, in the archives of FAA documents, discussions of various maintenance problems with Boeing aircraft, potential maintenance discrepancies that should have created more rapid and definitive responses. The very recent and highly publicized mandatory inspections of Boeing 737 aircraft indicate that the FAA is now engaging in more *proactive* oversight.

Ace was assigned to F-4 Phantom fighter squadrons for four years. During that period of time, every F-4 Phantom accident, incident, or major mechanical malfunction would create an extensive report that would be available for every Air Force Phantom pilot in the world to read. The knowledge and the insight gained through the availability of this information made a large contribution towards aircraft safety. This procedure has never been evidenced in the civilian-aviation structure. Considering today's much more advanced state of electronic communications capability, a similar policy has to be implemented immediately. All aircraft maintenance anomalies, accidents, or incidents must necessarily create a written report forwarded straightaway to the aircraft manufacturer, to the FAA, and to all airlines that make use of the aircraft involved in the problematic situations. Easy accessibility to this information will prove invaluable to all who are concerned with aviation safety.

The most recent revelation regarding government intervention in aircraft safety appeared in the media on April 8, 2009. The much-publicized US Airways A320 landing on the Hudson River, caused by birds sucked into the engines, stimulated the juices of an investigative reporter. The results were as follows: several years ago a government agency, namely the National Aeronautics and Space Administration, known worldwide as NASA, received an $11 million grant to do an extensive research project regarding all aspects of bird activity in the vicinity of airports, especially to look at bird activity in relationship to aviation safety. The results of this information are not available, and the government spokesman who responded to this withholding of information stated, "It was not in the best interest of commercial aviation." The obvious assumption here is that awareness of birds at a given airport might result in people not taking flights from that particular airport, which in turn, would result in reduced profits. Here again comes the sardonic statement, "I'm from the government and I'm here to help you," now elevated to a higher level.

CHAPTER ELEVEN
The Last Five

A HALF DECADE WITH TRANSMERIDIAN

Many of Nation's Air pilots would soon find themselves in a new-hire class for TransMeridian Airlines (TMA), another Atlanta-based startup airline. However, the newly developing company did appear to have a bit more substance than most of the underfunded, "fly-by-night" operations. Ace finished his IOE and FAA line check and settled into his assigned crew base at Pittsburgh, a comfortable commute from South Florida. Combined with an easy schedule and relatively relaxed flights to Montego Bay and other Caribbean vacation spots, this job seemed too good to be true. Since those things that seem "too good to be true" are usually not true, Ace, along with many of his new-hire classmates, received their furlough notices within a short span of time. And while spring waited just around the corner to unfold, hope did not spring eternal. Ace, now headed to the golf course, had just experienced two employers in a nine-month period. Then, through a bit of fate stemming most likely from the fact that Ace was at home, rather than at the golf course, bad luck turned into good fortune when he received a phone call from TransMeridian.

EUROPEAN HONEYMOON ON THE FREIGHT RUN

TransMeridan's management folks had a relationship with a European company that would hire American pilots on a contract basis. Ace initially rejected this flying opportunity, since he now convinced himself that his aviation career had nose dived into oblivion, and focused instead on heading to the links to embark on a new career. He called Marylee, who had done a short stint in Europe for Carnival Airlines, to inform her of this offer. Evidently not wanting to waste one single breath, she countered with her ever-so-persuasive enthusiastic voice "Don't let this fabulous opportunity get away! Do it!" Not one to go against Marylee's usual sound advice, Ace got in touch with TMA. The company needed one more captain. He had deposited his name into the hat just in time.

Ace and fourteen furloughed TMA pilot colleagues gathered at JFK Airport from various parts of the country and experienced a joyous reunification at the SAS (Scandinavian Airlines) departure gate. The fifteen furloughed pilots would no longer have to beg, borrow, or steal as they settled into their first-class seats bound for Copenhagen, Denmark, often referred to as "the city of love." This aviation adventure would encompass a nine-month contract to fly freight for the worldwide freight operator, TNT. A Danish airline, Sterling International Airlines, provided the appropriate European operating certificate, along with maintenance and training for the new American pilots. The Danish pilot-training staff exhibited a definitive respect for the American pilots, but a minor cultural chasm did reveal itself during the training. The Americans considered the Danish operating style *anal.* The Danish, on the other side, considered the American pilots *cowboys.* Many of the American pilots had already flown the 727 for at least a decade and showed no interest in "dotting the (i)s and crossing the (t)s." The American pilots simply wanted to *kick the tires and light the fires.*

Happily, both sides managed to bridge the cultural gap with only minor difficulties. The American pilots then headed down to Liège, Belgium, where they would live for the next several months. Their quite comfortable four-star hotel soon became a melting pot for numerous TNT pilots from the United States, South Africa, Britain, and Scandinavia as well as from several other countries. Since the Americans dominated the scene, the elegant hotel that normally catered primarily to refined businessmen took on the ambience of a college fraternity house. Most of the flying took place at night, with a departure from the Liège Airport at about four a.m. local time. The trips usually lasted less than two hours of flight time, and the arrival at Edinburgh, Scotland, for instance, would occur just in time for breakfast at the four-star hotel that the Sterling (TNT) pilots demanded. Unlike the U.S., where the flight crew would often wait forty-five minutes for the crew van, a Mercedes-Benz sedan waited punctually at the airport to take the Sterling's pilots to their hotel. After the usual

European-bountiful breakfast buffet, the pilots rested and recuperated for the evening return flight to Liège. Layovers of 12 to 14 hours duration provided enough time for crews (and their wives or girlfriends) to take local tours wherever they landed.

Flying in the European air-traffic-control environment did bring out some challenges for the American pilots as a result of the varying departure and arrival procedures. The Americans would soon adapt, acquainting themselves, for instance, more comfortably with the varying accents of air traffic controllers and other nuances of the system. The European flight-time and duty-time regulations for airline flight crews were much more stringent than those of the U.S. FARs. The significantly more restrictive time limitations and rest requirements resulted in a considerable amount of time-off for the TNT pilots. Many of the layovers were in classic European vacation spots, and the American pilots exalted in this all-inclusive, expense-free vacation, while also receiving a favorable salary.

Ace and his girlfriend, Bebe, had long discussed the possibility of marriage, and Ace had a vision of a spectacular honeymoon. He called Bebe, and she graciously accepted his proposal. During a scheduled week off, Ace flew back to Florida and married the lovely lady. As they entered the aircraft for the return flight to Brussels, Ace briefly engaged the senior flight attendant with his best PR song-and-dance regarding his pilot status in Belgium and, of course, his new bride. Just prior to push back, Ace and Bebe were invited to enjoy the flight in the first-class section. This effectively initiated the start of an extended, first-class honeymoon.

TNT freight had a very liberal jump-seat policy that allowed wives, girlfriends, and others to ride on the cockpit jump seat with their piloting sponsor. Actually, four seats sat there available because the two forward-bulkhead flight-attendant jump seats also functioned as passenger transport. Many of the American pilots had their families join them from the U.S. for this fabulous experience; as a result, the four free seats in the old 727 freighters were well utilized. Following the return from the U.S. to Liège, Ace's next trip took him to Vienna, Austria. Bebe joined him on this trip for a weekend layover, and the all-expense paid European honeymoon hit fourth gear in full swing, later followed by indescribably stunning weekends in Edinburgh Scotland, along with layovers in Portugal, Spain, the UK, and Italy.

During his previous flying from Malta to the UK, Ace regularly flew over Lake Geneva, and was enthralled by its natural beauty. He had a few days off, so he borrowed his pilot friend's marginally functional sub-compact car. He and Bebe then headed along the Autobahn to Lake Geneva. After a day and a half of hard travel in this non-air-conditioned "roller-skate," Ace and Bebe settled into their quaint little hotel on the south shore of Lake Geneva, just a few miles from Evian, France. As they sat on the patio watching the twilight embrace the lake and its spectacular surroundings, Ace offered the following comment: "It sure is beautiful here, but that drive was a bitch. Next time we come, let's just take the jet." He had heard the phrase, "take the jet," many times during the days of flying the very wealthy folks in their private jets. Less than one month later, back at the Bedford Hotel in Liège, Ace checked the weekend flying schedule and noticed that a new destination had been added. It was Geneva, Switzerland, and the captain assigned to fly the trip was Ace. He rushed back to the hotel room to exclaim to Bebe, " *We're taking the jet to Lake Geneva!* " The hour-and-thirty-minute flight to this garden spot was followed by a weekend of traveling through the French Alps, taking in some of the most spectacular scenery in the world. As the old saying goes, "It's a dirty rotten job, but somebody's got to do it."

To *take the jet* for Ace and Bebe also meant trips to Finland, Norway, and various destinations in Sweden. The good life of jet setting about Europe was punctuated by interesting road trips to Holland, Germany, France, and the Normandy Beach area of northern France. Ace befriended his favorite copilot, a Frenchman named Yann, who provided wonderful hospitality and tour-guide service. Yann, a political-science aficionado, possessed a vast amount of knowledge about the U.S. Constitution, U.S. history, and worldwide geopolitical situations. Perhaps the most interesting revelation of the multi-cultural pilot interaction lies with the fact that Europeans and Scandinavians possessed *far more* knowledge about American history and politics than most Americans. Ace felt very fortunate to have established a kinship with this incredibly adventuresome, intelligent and worldly "Renaissance Man."

At one point, Yann seemed to have vanished off the face of the planet for nearly two weeks. When he reappeared, he confided to Ace that he and his nautically oriented colleague had sailed a catamaran sailboat from the Brittany Coast of France to Martinique in the Caribbean. Following another extended period of absence, he reported he had gone "hiking in the Himalayas." Yann has also traveled extensively throughout Africa, where he met his wife, a nurse doing volunteer work in the middle of a war zone. The common misperception held by too many Americans that Frenchmen are wimps is totally invalid. Ace and Yann established an instant rapport and shared many good times not only side-by-side in the cockpit but also together on the golf course. Ace introduced Yann to golf, and he became so obsessed with hitting the tantalizing, little-dimpled spheroid that he resorted to the same obscene four-letter word so commonly heard on golf courses in America.

Creeping out of the dark side of the Belgian vacation experience, northern European weather patterns often resulted in dark days for extended periods of time. Low ceiling and reduced visibility forced many early-morning CAT II ILS approaches down to the one-hundred-foot minimums. After several days of looking out the hotel window at fog and drizzle during the autumn of 1998, Ace yearned for the blue skies and the bright sunshine of South Florida. He also had grown hungry for the more user-friendly ATC system in the United States. After departure from Bergamo, Italy (just north of Milan), the traffic controllers seriously dropped the bocce ball.

The TNT airfreight 727 that Ace was flying was caught from behind by a DHL 757 that had a much higher climb-performance capability. The FO looked out the right window and, to his horror, saw another aircraft dangerously close, even though Ace's TNT 727 was flying in low-visibility IMC conditions, and he had no report of other traffic from ATC. The copilot, attempting to keep his calm declared, "An aircraft is passing underneath us from right to left." About three seconds later, Ace looked out the left window and was nearly able to see "the whites of their eyes" as the 757 passed below at a distance of less than 200 feet. Ace instantaneously questioned the Milan ATC facility about this intruding aircraft and why it had flown so close to the TNT 727. When ATC failed to respond, Ace surmised that the Italian controllers were probably engaging in cappuccino and biscotti rather than monitoring their radarscopes. The airways in Europe are very congested, always requiring intense vigilance, because they are just as busy as the crowded "northeast corridor" of the United States.

COMPUTER CRASH

The European experience for Ace and for all of his American colleagues turned into a fantastic opportunity to experience an extensive European vacation while getting paid well at the same time. However, by mid-November of 1998, just about everyone came down with a severe case of "get-home-itis." Upon arrival back in the U.S., the vagabond 727 pilots soon discovered that the TransMeridian 727 operation had terminated. As luck would have it, the returning pilots then gathered for the opportunity to transition to the Airbus A320 aircraft. Most of the pilots greeted this opportunity with great enthusiasm. Ace, however, could not stop the flashbacks to the earlier days of his company indoctrination at TransMeridian when the instructor informed the class of a recent TMA A320 computer malfunction resulting in an emergency landing in the middle of the night at a remote airport in Mexico. This eerie tale of mysterious electronic-signal gremlins was complemented with a film that showed an Airbus A320 aircraft crash at an air show in France. Apparently, the very experienced test pilot had pulled some circuit breakers in an attempt to trick one of the many airborne computers. When he attempted a go-around from a low-level fly-by, the engines would not accelerate, and the airplane flew uncontrollably into the trees at the end of the runway. The large ball of fire created by the crash did not exactly endear Ace to the Airbus A320 aircraft.

Nonetheless, Ace accepted the invitation to go to Minneapolis, where he and his fellow prospective TransMeridian A320 pilots commenced their training at the Northwest Airlines training facility. Circulating throughout the training center were reports that many of the Northwest pilots preferred to stay in their old noisy and nearly antiquated DC-9 aircraft to avoid the slings and arrows of the Airbus training. Ace had been a nearly devout Luddite (to save the reader from heading to the glossary, a 21st century slang term for people who have an aversion to modern gadgetry), and the mere mention of a computer would accelerate his pulse rate and cause a spike in his blood pressure. Despite this disdain for computers, he trudged through ground training with a reasonable measure of success.

The continuation of training shifted to the United Training Center at Denver since simulator time was not available at the Northwest Training Facility. The prelude to the actual simulator flying consisted of the CPT (cockpit procedural trainer), and during this phase Ace could feel himself slipping behind the eight ball. Much of his previous thirty-three years of flying experience currently held no value, for now Ace would necessarily have to rely on the advanced capabilities of the computer—actually, of several computers— to fly the aircraft. Ace struggled with all these new and alien concepts of piloting an aircraft. When he reported for simulator session number one, he did so with great trepidation. After nearly twenty years of intimate familiarity with the 727, Ace found the profound differences between *that* craft and every aspect of *this* A320 overwhelming. Besides his uncertainty and lack of confidence, Ace would be subjected to his first "screamer" instructor, whose overbearing and intimidating nature came across as demeaning and disrespectful. The transition from the "steam gauges" of his beloved Boeing to the glass cockpit of the Airbus left Ace trapped in the "cone of confusion." Without further fanfare he ended his Airbus training voluntarily.

A few hours later, he met with Chief Pilot John Graham to inform him that he was not up to the task of this newfangled Airbus air machine. Ace turned in his manuals and headed for home. Apart from the puzzling new airplane, Ace had too much professional pride to allow himself ever again to be browbeaten by an overbearing instructor pilot. After a few days of decompressing, he wrote TMA's director of operations a letter of apology, explaining that he felt it was in the best interest of both TMA and Ace to discontinue the Airbus training. He also requested to receive no pay for this period of training, waiving his per diem pay for the training period as well.

Should TMA once again operate 727 aircraft, Ace added, he would certainly appreciate recall consideration. While this final addition sounded like an absurd request, it was Ace's last-ditch effort to continue a career in aviation.

Once again Ace gravitated to the golf course and soon discovered that riding around in a golf cart in the warm Florida sun was infinitely more enjoyable than riding in an Airbus simulator with a hard-ass instructor. On the downside, the golf-course income represented less than twenty percent of a TMA Airbus captain's salary. Free golf and free lunches still left him well short of the sufficient resources needed to survive on moderate subsistence. Ace prepared to dive into his new career as a golf teacher when, disbelievingly, he received a call from the assistant to TMA's director of operations, asking if he would like to return to TMA to fly 727s. Based on the circumstances of his sudden departure only a few months earlier, this recall represented a rare and perhaps unprecedented airline-employment rehiring. Ace graciously accepted the job offer and traveled to Atlanta for recurrent training. He reconnected with Chief Pilot John Graham for the simulator and line-check training. However, whipped cream and cherry dangled on top of this dessert: an offer for Ace to become a check airman (training captain). Ace readily accepted this position since the benefits were numerous, and the *additional pay would allow him to commence his retirement-fund investment—at age 57!*

BACK TO THE BELOVED BOEING

The next two-and-one-half years prior to the mandatory retirement age of sixty zipped by very fast, keeping Ace busy administering IOE training for new hires and upgrading pilots. Even though the check-airman override pay totaled up to quite a generous amount, the training environment produced unique challenges. In several instances, Ace was assigned to administer IOE to a flight engineer who intended to move to the right seat with a very minimal amount of total time. Some of these upgrading pilots had far fewer than 1,000 hours total flight time and no jet-aircraft experience other than the flight engineer's panel of the 727. As a consequence, IOE training required great patience, and it would also frequently require Ace's intervention at the flight controls to salvage a rapidly deteriorating situation. But as the new Chief Pilot Billy Smith would often say, "That's why we pay you the big bucks."

All but a very few of the FAA examiners with whom Ace had worked over the years were very high-quality people who performed their duties in an exemplary fashion. TMI was lucky enough to be assigned a POI (Principal Operating Inspector) from the Atlanta FAA regional office who was an absolute prince to work with. He exhibited great respect for the flight crews and a very common-sense approach to his critiques and evaluation, but he still demanded the maximum possible level of safety. His friendly and polite demeanor created a very pleasant cockpit environment whenever he rode in the jump seat administering line checks for the new pilots.

The TMA core group of highly experienced pilots consisted of many ex-major airline pilots whose experience and professionalism contributed to a relatively high-quality product for a non-sked airline. They were also instrumental in creating an in-house union, referred to as the TMA Pilot Association. Non-sked flight operations can become extremely arduous, with ridiculously long duty hours coupled with fleabag hotels and lack of access to decent food. The TMA Pilot Association negotiated with management in order to provide a better quality of work life for the pilots while also enhancing safety. Despite these efforts, the nature of the non-sked (charter) modus operandi would often create situations that diminished the quality of crewmember comfort. On several occasions, Ace was required to inform crew scheduling that he and his crew were too tired to safely fly that additionally requested flight. At many non-sked airlines, this response would not have been tolerated; the captain would be immediately fired. But never once did Ace receive a reprimand for his decision to "shut it down" because of flight-crew fatigue, despite the fact that the company might lose tens of thousands of dollars in revenue.

The occasional long-duty days were offset with layovers in Cancun and in other warm and friendly vacation sites. TMA brought together a contract with a tour company to provide transportation for college students during their spring break. The drunken decadence that Ace observed during this duty is too appalling to describe. Although he himself would "party hardy" during his younger days, his advice to parents still stands, "Mama, don't let your daughters go on spring break!" The youthful revelers would often show up for their flight already in a state of severe intoxication. On several occasions, prior to takeoff, Ace had to leave his seat to go to the cabin to help establish some semblance of order. There are far too many instances of flight-attendant horror stories about the wreaking of havoc in the cabin by intoxicated passengers. On numerous occasions throughout his 727 career, Ace denied boarding of the aircraft if a passenger was severely intoxicated.

He was equally intolerant of cockpit crewmembers that would push the edge of the envelope regarding alcohol consumption for an early-morning departure. It is common in the aviation charter business for flight crews to be on the road for an extended period of time. This would often result in the cockpit crews and the cabin crews establishing a camaraderie enhanced by partaking of the juices that are referred to as "the lubricants of social intercourse." Ace made it very clear to pilots flying with him that to show up for work in any state other than perfectly sober would result in not being allowed on the flight deck and would probably result in him being "called on the carpet." The slow-but-sure ageing process resulted in Ace's transition from a youthful *bon vivant* to the "two-beer Ace."

On the other hand, Ace often pretended to be a ganja-smoking Rastafarian Reggae Rock star on flights to Jamaica. Just prior to descent into Montego Bay, he would often pick up the PA microphone and, after informing passengers of the current weather and arrival time, he would expose his total inability to carry a tune by singing a few lines of a Bob Marley song. The passengers would be happy to hear the words (from a Marley favorite), "Don't worry 'bout a thing, 'cause every little thing's gonna be OK." This would provide a bit of lighthearted comic relief for the passengers, while providing Ace a sense of reconnecting with his inner-Rastafarian alter ego. During thirty years and approximately one-hundred-and-fifty flights to Montego Bay, Ace never once had the opportunity to leave the airport, since all of his flights were "quick-turns" with only one hour on the ground. But the spectacular view from the cockpit during the arrival and the approach into Montego Bay presented an experience that could overshadow a week of rum drinks at poolside.

The TMA job resulted in a tremendous variety of passengers and destinations. The majority of the trips flew as one-day roundtrip flights from Chicago or Boston, frequently to a warm vacation paradise, such as Aruba or Puerta Vallarta. There were also many charters with sports teams, including the Chicago White Sox. During passenger disembarkation, Ace, the hard-core baseball fan, engaged White Sox star Frank Thomas, aka, "The Big Hurt," in conversation. Ace also flew several other major-league baseball teams, along with numerous Division I college football teams. These flights were particularly desirable since they were catered with thousands of dollars of near gourmet food, very little of which was actually consumed by the players. The flight-crew members capitalized on the left-over food, since, as a group, they are world renowned for seeking out the free lunch. On the opposite end of the spectrum, Ace captained flights for the U.S. Marshals Service. This duty involved moving prisoners around the country to different prisons, usually to solve overcrowding problems. During these flights, flight crewmembers were provided with only basic box lunches with cold sandwiches. The worst part of this duty was observing the empty-stare sadness of the shackled prisoners.

COUNTDOWN TO FINAL SHUTDOWN

Although Ace enjoyed his pilot duties out of Boston and flying primarily to Aruba, the prospect of retirement hovered over his shoulders as his sixtieth birthday waited just around the corner. The commercial pilot's mandatory retirement age of sixty has recently been changed to sixty-five, but that severely overdue legislation was enacted long after the FAA had snatched away Ace's ability to ply his trade in the sky. Today, an airline captain is required every six months to have his job fitness evaluated with both a simulator check ride and a very demanding physical examination, perhaps the most bizarre element of this nonsensical discarding of talent and experience. This mandated seal of approval could be effectuated a month before the captain's sixty-fifth birthday, and he would still be unable to fly past age sixty-five. With only about one month to go, Ace had slid into a state of FIGMO (old military term for advanced indifference), so when the Boston Center controller issued a clearance to proceed directly to an intersection named BIGGO, Ace responded spontaneously with the statement, "My wife frequently asks me to take her to the *Big O.*" Ace noted the extended silence on the frequency, as most of the listeners were likely asking themselves something like, "Did he mean what we think he means?"

The day of reckoning approached, and Ace was near exhilaration because he would not have to squander the upcoming winter commuting to Boston. He had spent most of the previous winters based in Chicago and Minneapolis and by now had completely lost interest in snow and ice. At Chicago's O'Hare Airport, the airplane was parked in a remote spot on the ramp, and the flight crew, including the flight attendants, would have no option but to walk several hundred yards across the ice-covered, deicing fluid-contaminated ramp, with a subzero wind chill added to the "ambience." After completing the Chicago O'Hare version of "The Bataan Death March," the flight crew would then board a dark, cold-soaked airplane in their cold or wet shoes and feet. This scenario is just one of the many "back alleys of aviation," and these draconian work conditions were part of the non-glamorous, non-sked world of charter flights on their way to exotic destinations. A small consolation was that the flight crews could witness one of great marvels of modern aviation: the marvelous phenomenon of O'Hare International Airport continuing to function during a heavy snowstorm. Observing the many snow-removal vehicles, fuel trucks, catering trucks, etc., along with the large cumbersome aircraft awkwardly attempting to maneuver to or from their gates in a heavy snowstorm at night can only be described as surreal.

On December 8, 2002, on what would be Ace's *final* commercial flight, a FIGMO-induced complacency resulted in a nearly spectacular finale. After a long duty day, with a bit of fatigue setting in, Ace would pilot the aircraft into Boston's Logan after a long flight from Aruba. The weather was good at the destination, and TransMeridian Flight 608 was cleared for a visual approach to runway 27 at Boston's Logan International Airport. A few unique variables that would increase the landing roll distance now come into play: the TMA aircraft was a modified heavyweight airplane, and the actual aircraft weight was heavier than normal. Runway 27 was the shortest runway at Logan, and Ace had never landed the 727 on runway 27 since the larger aircraft were usually assigned to the longer runways. This massive missile of kinetic energy was such that a slight tailwind component for this landing created an extended landing-roll situation.

Ace got a little lazy and came over the threshold a few knots fast. In his attempt to make his final landing a smooth one, delicately feeling for the runway for the grand finale, silky-smooth grease-job landing, he managed to land a bit long. This minor error was intensified by slightly delayed braking and thrust reverser activation. A few seconds later, Ace observed red runway centerline lights indicating that only 3,000 feet of runway were available, and the airspeed was still well in excess of one hundred knots. As he immediately engaged in maximum braking and thrust reversing, he experienced the brief and the frightening possibility of not getting the aircraft stopped on the runway. After thirty-six years of an unblemished record, without scratching an airplane, or even taxiing one into the mud, there was for a fleeting moment the nightmarish possibility that the final flight of his career would end up in Boston Harbor. This potentially embarrassing ending did not occur when the glorious engineering of the Boeing 727's braking system reliably performed its magic. Ace's final flight, to put it boldly, came nearly to a very spectacular but undesirably majestic climax. He had managed to make his final landing an adrenalin-gushing experience

The *crème de la crème* of grand finales would occur nine days later on December 17, 2002: Ace's sixtieth birthday, which officially ended his aviation career, also coincided with the date of the TransMeridian Christmas party in Atlanta. The company complemented the Christmas party with a retirement party for Captain Ace, unaware of this added celebration. The outpouring of goodwill and expression of gratitude by his many fellow employees, including the TMA management, created a sense of pride that was unequaled in Ace's previous sixty years. The many mementoes, good-luck cards, and letters of thanks and congratulations will always be cherished. This ceremony ensured that Ace's tumultuous aviation career culminated with an expression of appreciation that would more than offset all of those ventures through "the back alleys of aviation." Ace will forever be indebted to TransMeridian Airlines for this very gracious recognition of his services.

"The chocks are in. Let's call the hotel van and bring this 'long ride on the wild side' to a full stop. I'll see you at the golf course."

ACE AND FLIGHT ATTENDANT FRIENDS AT THE FINALE

CHAPTER TWELVE

Conclusion (Debriefing)

Ace spent thirty-six years chasing airplanes around the world while subjecting himself to a career of uncertainties, social and family disruption, life-threatening situations, and sub-standard pay. In retrospect, when he considers those almost uncountable, incomparable life experiences, the positive side of the career overshadows the negative by an unquantifiable margin.

The exposure and the interaction with numerous unique and fascinating characters that pervade the aviation community will always be well remembered. The many celebrities and icons with whom Ace came into contact include: Jimmy Buffett, Bob Marley, Helen Reddy, Olivia Newton-John, John Glenn, Jack Nicklaus, William Simon (past secretary of the treasury), the White House Press Corps, Evil Knievel, Bobby and Donnie Allison (race car drivers), and more. Ace would, by coincidence, once encounter the legendary maverick aviation entrepreneur Connie Kalitta on a cargo ramp at Wilmington, Ohio. He and his colleagues had enjoyed exchanging Kalitta "war stories" for thirty-five years. For example, it has been reported repeatedly that Connie Kalitta flew a Twin Beech aircraft across the North Atlantic—*solo*—with a cargo load of nitroglycerin. Ace also had the opportunity to work for and to befriend Lloyd Zantop, who was not only a successful aviation entrepreneur but also a World War II ferry pilot certified to fly nearly every airplane in the Air Force inventory.

The lifelong friendships often formed through intense cockpit teamwork in the efforts to accomplish the mission will be cherished forever. When Ace's wife, Bebe, traveled with him in the 727, she commented on the unmistakable, strong bond evident in the cockpit as the three pilots functioned in total harmony. A major contributing factor to this teamwork was the knowledge that their longevity was intractably intertwined with the quality of their performance of their cockpit duties. Unbeknownst to most travelers, the attentive flight engineer in the Boeing 727 has prevented innumerable aircraft crashes.

The aviator camaraderie, combined with the joy of sharing stories, extends from the Cessna 172 pilots to the Boeing 777 captains, since Boeing pilots were likely to have flown a Cessna 172 or a similar, small, propeller-driven airplane during the early phase of their aviation careers. Those similar experiences contribute to the bond that exists throughout the aviation community.

Moreover, Ace's special aviation environment allowed him to share the airplane experience with friends and relatives. His father, his son, his cousin, his wife, and his brother-in-law all had the rare experience of flying in the cockpit of a 727 perched in the cockpit's jump seat. Captain Ace also shared his 727 cockpit during ferry flights (no passengers) by allowing flight attendants and aircraft mechanics to sit in the right seat to get a little "stick time." On some occasions, particularly on cargo flights, Ace would have the FO and SO swap seats. It was always a special treat for the flight engineer to abandon his "wrench" or "greaser" chair to get up and into the *window seat.*

The Learjet experience also resulted in many opportunities to provide friends, relatives, and neighbors with unique aviation and travel experiences. During Learjet training flights, Ace often invited his aviator friends and neighbors to ride in the jump seat. On numerous occasions, he would drop passengers off in the Northeast U.S. and, since the aircraft was going to fly back to Florida with no passengers, he gathered up friends and family to provide them with private jet travel for a Florida vacation. His golf buddy, Bill, was a private pilot, and years earlier, when he gave Ace a ride in his propeller-driven Yankee aircraft, he relinquished the controls to Ace so he could do some small-airplane, high-performance maneuvering. Ace reciprocated a few years later when he took Bill and his family to Florida in a Learjet. He put Bill into the right seat for the approach into PBI and turned the controls over to the very inexperienced novice pilot, who leveled the aircraft at the assigned altitude of 5,000 feet and maintained perfect altitude control. Ace looked around for the smoke and mirrors, which were used for this rare display of skill by a rookie pilot, while he sarcastically accused Bill of engaging the autopilot.

To share one's "wealth," particularly when it is effectively cost free, is a wonderful thing to do, and Ace's opportunities to share his private jet with friends and family carved out an immense niche in his career. Ace's best friend from high school, a fellow named Charlie who lived in California at the time, badly needed to get back East for a family crisis. Unfortunately, he was extremely broke and could not afford airfare. Rick Zantop graciously extended a hand and put Charlie in the Learjet for a flight from San Jose to Detroit. This bit of sharing the wealth made a profound impact on Charlie, who, now thirty-five years later, continues to express gratitude for the helping hand.

ONE LAST VIEW FROM THE COCKPIT

To complement these priceless experiences, many of the stunning panoramic views from the cockpit will remain as enduring memories until the cranial synapses stop snapping. The often-used aviation cliché, "The money was lousy, but I had a great view from the office," struck the bull's eye for Ace's career. The spectacular lightning emanating from the tops of thunderstorms during night flights complemented the panoramic island views during good weather in the Caribbean. The bright lights of the Northeast United States provided Ace with a nearly indescribable view from the cockpit.

On a frigid January night after the cold front had passed through the East Coast, purging the air of any moisture or particulates, Ace departed Boston in a Learjet headed westbound for Detroit. After only a few minutes of climb, the lights of Providence, Rhode Island, Albany, New York, New York City, and most of the other cities in the Northeast came into view. By the time the aircraft reached 45,000 feet, the lights of Montréal, Toronto, and Buffalo, sparkled brightly in view on the right side of the aircraft. From the left side of the aircraft, Philadelphia, Baltimore, Washington D.C., and Richmond easily came into view. While passing over the area of Binghamton, New York, Ace could make out the gleaming lights of his small hometown in the Finger Lakes. By then following the residential lights that outlined the road he had so often traveled by bike and by car as a youth, he was able to zero in on the floodlight at the old farmhouse where he had grown up. This visual transition from the entire East Coast of the U.S. to the old farmhouse and then back to the bright lights of the many East Coast cities was analogous to an out-of-body experience, or perhaps a Google-Earth-like experience long before Google Earth technology. The clarity of this intoxicating scenario remains embedded in the rapidly deteriorating memory bank of the now elderly Ace.

Ace had generated a few million dollars of revenue for aviation's entrepreneurial masters, and now he would fade away into the relative obscurity of old, retired pilots who thrive on rehashing airplane stories. His meager financial status placed him barely beyond penniless, particularly in relationship to the "legacy airline" retired pilots, but his cadre of friends remained intact. The many conversations of aviation-related romantic nostalgia with former pilot friends would carry far more value than a sailboat excursion in Martinique—**they inspired him to write this book!**

Ace, and many of his colleagues who also spent time in the trenches of "the back alleys of aviation," validated the notion that the variety of one's life experiences, along with eternally bonding, quality relationships, will always outshine large portfolios and *meaningless stuff.*

Ace ventured into the retirement phase with no retirement pension program, but the richness of his aviation experiences and relationships will leave him forever wealthy.

THE END

Appendix

ACE'S RÉSUMÉ

U.S. Air Force: F-4 Phantom pilot; November 1965 thru March 1971

World Aviation: Learjet copilot; February 1972 thru March 1973

Zantop Airways: Learjet Captain; June 1973 thru November 1974

Imperial Air: Learjet Captain; November 1974 thru June 1975

BizJet: Learjet Captain; June 1975 thru April 1977

Benson & Benson: Learjet Captain; May 1977 thru October 1977

Graff Jets: Learjet Captain; January 1978 thru June 1979

National Jets (part-time): Learjet Captain; June 1979 thru May 1981

Zantop Airways: Gulfstream G-159 Captain; June 1979 thru January 1980

Orion Air: Gulfstream G-159 Captain; January 1980 thru March 1981

Ryan International Airlines: Boeing 727 Captain; March 1981 thru April 1984

Air Atlanta: Boeing 727 Captain; April 1984 thru February 1987

Sun Coast Airlines: Boeing 727 Captain; June 1987 thru February 1988

Draw Tight (Jim Worden): Learjet Copilot; June, July 1988

Gulf Air: Boeing 727 Captain; August 1988 thru July 1989

Carnival Airlines: Boeing 727 Captain; July 1989 thru August 1990

Broward Yachts (part-time): Cessna Citation Copilot; August 1990 thru November 1990

USPS (Ryan International Airlines): Boeing 727 Captain; January 1991 thru May 1992

Arrow Air: Boeing 727 Captain; January 1993 thru March 1994

Strongfield Aviation: Boeing 727 Captain; May 1994 thru June 1994

Prestige Airways: Boeing 727 Captain; September 1994 thru March 1995

Nation's Air: Boeing 727 Captain; April 1996 thru August 1997

TransMeridian Airlines: Boeing 727 Captain; November 1997 thru March 1998

TNT Freight (Sterling International): Boeing 727 Captain; March 1998 thru November 1998

TransMeridian Airlines (TMA): Boeing 727 Captain; April 1999 thru December 2002

December 17, 2002: (sixtieth birthday; *"Saved by the bell!"*) TMA shutdown two years later

Suggested Reading

A Gift of Wings by Richard Bach, Creative Enterprises, Inc., 1971

Air Travelers Survival Guide: The Plane Truth from 35,000 Feet by I. A. Frank Stewart

Air War—Vietnam with an introduction by Drew Middleton, Arno Press, 1978

American Assassination: The Strange Death of Senator Paul Wellstone by Jim Fetzer and Donald Trent Jones (AKA Four Arrows), United Graphics, March 2 005

Collision Course: The Truth about Airline Safety by Ralph Nader and Wesley J. Smith

Fate Is the Hunter by Ernest K Gann, 1986

Flying Blind, Flying Safe by Mary Schiavo

Flying High with A. Frank Steward by James Wysong, 2008

Improbable Cause by Les Filotas

Jonathan Livingston Seagull by Richard Bach, 1976

Pak Six by G.I. Basel, 1982

Plane Insanity by Elliot Hester, 2003

Safety Last—The Dangers of Commercial Aviation: An Indictment by an Airline Pilot by Brian Powers-Waters

Takeoff: The Story of a Woman Pilot for a Major Airline by Bonnie Tiburzi, 1984

The Great Santini by Pat Conroy, 1987 (also depicted in a film version)

The Real Unfriendly Skies: Saga of Corruption by Rodney Stich, 1990; according to a review by one retired airline captain, the U.S. government "put Rodney in prison because he dared to reveal FAA's little secrets."

The Right Stuff by Thomas Wolfe, 1979

To Be A U.S. Air Force Pilot by Henry Holden, 2004

Glossary

A/C–Aircraft Commander (Captain)

ACM–aerial combat maneuvers ("dog fighting")

ADF–automatic directional finder (antiquated aircraft navigational system)

ADI–attitude directional indicator (artificial horizon–provides a pictorial view of the aircraft's position in relationship to the horizon)

AGL–above ground level (the aircraft distance, usually measured in feet, above the terrain

ALPA–Airline pilots union; the union that represents most of the pilots that work for the major airlines in the U.S, and Canada

ASAP–as soon as possible

ATC–air traffic control

Barber Pole–a point on the airspeed indicator that designates the maximum allowable airspeed

Bone Yard–a storage area for aircraft that are taken out of use; the military bone yard is at Davis–Monthan Air Force Base in Tucson, Arizona, and the civilian bone yard is located at Marana Airpark also in Arizona

Boondoggle–a large group interacting in a dysfunctional fashion

Box Canyon–when the aircraft is below the terrain (in a valley) and is flying towards an area of terrain that is much higher than the aircraft's altitude

CAT II ILS Approach–approach minimums (decision height) is 100 feet AGL; normal ILS decision height is 200 feet AGL

CIA—Central Intelligence Agency—according to Wikipedia online, a U.S. civilian agency that reports to the Director of National Intelligence; responsible for providing national security intelligence assessment and engages in covert activities at the request of the U.S. president

CONUS–Continental United States (excludes Alaska and Hawaii)

DB Cooper Vane–an aerodynamically activated mechanical device on the exterior of the 727 aircraft that is designed to prevent airborne extension of the aft air stair

DME–(distance measuring equipment)–provides distance (in nautical miles) to a give geographic point

DMI–(deferred maintenance item)–an aircraft maintenance discrepancy that can be repaired at a later date

DOD–Department of Defense

DOS–date of separation (the actual day of discharge from the military)

EEOC–Equal Employment Opportunity Commission

FBO–the terminal and tarmac used for servicing private aircraft

FE–flight engineer (the pilot on the flight deck of a large aircraft responsible for monitoring and controlling many of the aircraft systems)

FO–first officer (copilot)

FCF–functional check flight; a mandatory test flight on a military aircraft that has undergone major mechanical repairs

FIGMO—F__ it! I Got My Orders–military slang for a slack attitude as a result of a new job location

FUBAR–Fouled Up Beyond All Recognition

Furloughed–airline jargon for being "laid off" from work.

Goat Rope–confusion and chaos intensified through incompetence

GPS–global positioning satellite (the navigational system used in most modern aircraft)

Grease Job–an exceptionally smooth landing

Grunt–one who does the dirty work; aviation slang term for either the copilot or the flight engineer

HSI–horizontal situation indicator–aircraft navigational instrument that informs the pilot of his position in space relative to his selected navigational aid

Icarus–a Greek mythological character who flew too close to the sun and his wings melted

ILS–instrument landing system–electronic navigation that is used for landing aircraft when there are low ceilings and low visibility conditions

IMC–instrument meteorological conditions (weather conditions dictate that the aircraft be flown with reference to cockpit instruments rather than outside visual references)

INS–inertial navigation system–an aircraft navigational system that indicates position in geographic latitude and longitude coordinates

IOE–initial operating experience; a minimum amount of actual flight time in the aircraft with a designated check airman under FAR 121 (airline regulations) for a pilot new to a specific aircraft prior to being released for "line flying"

IRAN–inspect and repair as necessary

Kimshi–a cabbage-based food staple on South Koreans' diet

L/D–lift over drag; the relationship of lift to the amount of drag that is being created by the aircraft wing

Load Sheets–the information relative to the cargo weight and position that the aircraft cargo loaders provide to the pilots for weight and balance computation

Luddite–a group of 19th century English people who rejected technology; a 21st century slang term for people who have an aversion to modern gadgetry

Mach–a measurement of the airspeed of an aircraft relative to the speed of sound; at, say, 10,000 ft. an aircraft travels at about 735 mph at Mach 1 or at about 675 mph at 30,000 ft.

MIG–a Russian-built fighter jet used by the North Vietnam Air Force and several other Communist-bloc countries

Modus Operandi–method of doing things

NASA—National Aeronautics and Space Administration—describes itself since February of 2006 as a "pioneer" in future space exploration, scientific discovery, and aeronautics research

NTSB—National Transportation Safety Board—an independent federal agency charged by Congress with investigating, among various responsibilities, every civil aviation accident in the U.S.

PACAF–Pacific Area Command of the U.S. Air Force

PCS–permanent change of station; a new duty station for military personnel (also used to designate one's current duty station)

Pitot tube–A probe-like device mounted externally on an aircraft to measure the aircraft airspeed

Pink Slipped–a slang term for being fired from one's job

PIC–the pilot in command of the aircraft (the captain)

POI–principal operating inspector; the FAA employee responsible for overseeing an airline and assuring that the appropriate FAA rules and regulations are followed

PR–public relations

Pull Gear–aviation slang term for functioning as a copilot

Rigging–the adjustment of a mechanical device so that it becomes functional

RTU–replacement training unit; a military designation for a training unit that is designed to train people for a combat assignment

St. Elmo's fire–an accumulation of static electricity in an airborne aircraft that elicits visible areas of electricity in red and yellow and blue colors

SAS–Scandinavian Airlines

SOP–standard operating procedures

Sort–The process at the hub airport of a freight operator designed to redistribute the cargo and to have it loaded on the appropriate outbound aircraft

Stall Warning Vane–A device that indicates the angle of attack or a relationship of the airflow over the wing of the aircraft

TAC–Tactical Air Command–the U.S. Air Force organization that oversees CONUS-based fighter aircraft

Tanker Fuel–to carry additional fuel on a flight that exceeds that amount actually needed for the flight

TDY–a temporary duty assignment to a station away from one's home base

Thunderstorm Anvil–that portion of the thunderstorm that extends from the main thunderstorm cell and creates what is often referred to as "the overhang"

Up Locks–mechanical devices that hold an aircraft component (usually the landing gear) into a specific position

USPS–United States Postal Service

VFR–visual flight rules (flying in good visibility conditions that allow for navigation and aircraft control based on outside-the-cockpit-visual references)

Bibliography

American Assassination: The Strange Death of Senator Paul Wellstone by James Fetzer and Donald "Four Arrows" Jones, United Graphics, 1022 Cortelyou Rd., Brooklyn, NY 11218-5302, March, 2005.

FAR 121 Regulations available at government web site.

Flying Blind, Flying Safe by Mary Schiavo, William Morrow, 1st edition, May 1997.

Outliers: The Story of Success by Malcolm Caldwell, Little, Brown & Company, 237 Park Ave., NY, NY

Even Cowgirls Get the Blues by Tom Robbins.